GIGGSY

GIGGSY

THE BIOGRAPHY OF RYAN GIGGS

FRANK
WORRALL

JOHN BLAKE

Published by John Blake Publishing Ltd,
3 Bramber Court, 2 Bramber Road,
London W14 9PB, England

www.johnblakepublishing.co.uk

www.facebook.com/Johnblakepub facebook
twitter.com/johnblakepub twitter

First published in hardback in 2010
This edition published in 2013

ISBN: 978-1-84358-322-6

British Library Cataloguing-in-Publication Data:

A catalogue record for this book is available from the British Library.

Design by www.envydesign.co.uk

Printed in Great Britain by CPI Group (UK) Ltd

1 3 5 7 9 10 8 6 4 2

Papers used by John Blake Publishing are natural, recyclable products made from
wood grown in sustainable forests. The manufacturing processes conform to the
environmental regulations of the country of origin.

Every attempt has been made to contact the relevant copyright-holders,
but some were unobtainable. We would be grateful if the appropriate people
could contact us.

This book is dedicated to Kit Tomlinson of Unveiled,
Mark Maddock of lastminute.com, and Mike Gould.

CONTENTS

ACKNOWLEDGEMENTS

SPECIAL THANKS: John Blake and Allie Collins, and all at John Blake Publishing, Ben Felsenburg at the *Daily Mail* and Alex Butler at the *Sunday Times*.

THANKS: At the *Sun* – Alan Feltham, Nick Jones, Graham Warwick, Jo Hernon, Gareth Davies, Phil Bryant, Lee Smith, Danny Bottono, Dave Morgan, Jon Moorhead and Darren 'Dazza' O'Driscoll. At the *Mail on Sunday*: Ian Rondeau, Gary Edwards, Colin Forshaw, Tim Smith, Adrian Baker, Ash Hussein, Ben Green and John Powell. Not forgetting: Angela, Frankie, Jude, Nat, Barbara, Frank, Bob and Stephen, Gill, Suzanne, Lucy, Alex, Michael and William, Steven Gordon, Martin Creasy and Pravina Patel, Russell Forgham and Fernando Duarte, and Neil, Stewart, Steve, Alan, Jean, Liz, the two Marions, Pat and all the hard-working staff on the night train.

ACKNOWLEDGEMENTS

'One day they might even say that I was another Ryan Giggs.'

George Best, 1992

'Giggs, Giggs will tear you apart, again.'

Terrace chant from his adoring fans

'I'm more sad about what is going to happen to the team now he [Ronaldo] has gone... but he wasn't my favourite player, and he wasn't a United legend, so it's nothing like it's going to be for me when Ryan Giggs retires... then I will probably need some serious counselling to get over my loss.'

United fan Daisy, June 2009

CHAPTER 1

LAND OF HIS FATHER

He would become the most decorated, successful and, many would contend, the best player ever to pull on the proud red shirt of Manchester United. But the road to legend and riches wasn't presented on the proverbial plate for Ryan Giggs. When he finally established himself in the first team at Old Trafford, he would talk about how important the history and the traditions of the club were to him – because he was a local lad. Yet while it is true that he was picked out from obscurity while living just a few miles from Old Trafford, he had been born and bred in an altogether different environment. In a different country, in fact; in a country in which he had known hardship and had had to contend with learning and developing within the confines of a fractured and fractious family.

Yes, he was a local lad (in Manchester) from the age of six, but before that Wales was his home, or more precisely, a tough district of Cardiff. He would never forget his Welsh upbringing, how it moulded and formed him and, in later life, would talk of his pride in being Welsh and how he never considered himself English, even when he captained the England schoolboys' team.

What we are trying to establish early on is this: Ryan Giggs is undoubtedly a phenomenon in world football, but he is not the stereotyped straightforward, straitlaced, somewhat boring 'Mr Manchester United' some pundits would have you believe. Of course, he is an honourable, respectable man – one of the nicest guys in football, for sure – but he is also an intense thinker and a complex character prone to deep introspection and self-analysis, and is at heart a very private being.

It is these very contradictions that help make Ryan the man – and the footballer – he is. Even some of his friends would tell you he can be stubborn, defensive in attitude and dismissive of fools. On the other hand, he is warm, generous, compassionate, and has time for anyone.

It is perhaps surprising that he could ever have been dismissed as one-dimensional, given the contradictions and vagaries of his upbringing. He had to battle his way to the very top of world football after being born into a poor, broken home, with no father by his side for his formative years. But he would overcome all the obstacles to reach the very top of his profession and always remain a truly nice guy. All in all, no mean achievement.

Ryan Giggs is a winner – always was, from the very first day he kicked a football – and a man who gets what he wants. He is driven by a desire for perfection and the goal of being the best. So where do all these complexities of character and ambition come from? It's easy to guess – it was down to his childhood in Wales, the love-hate relationship he 'enjoyed' with his rugby playing, womanising, boozing father over the years and the move to Manchester. It was also due to the bond he has always shared with his mother and subsequently Sir Alex Ferguson, manager of Manchester United and a surrogate father figure during the early days of their relationship and of Giggs's footballing career.

Giggs weighed 7lb when he was born Ryan Joseph Wilson in Cardiff on 29 November 1973, to labourer and rugby-playing father, Danny Wilson, and children's nurse and cook mother, Lynne Ceri Giggs. The couple met when they were still at school and by the time Ryan arrived on the scene, they were both still only seventeen.

Lynne was Welsh and hailed from the more tranquil Pentrebane in west Cardiff; Danny was born to a Welsh mother and a father from Sierra Leone, and would become a promising halfback with Cardiff Rugby Union Club. His mother Winnie – a hospital cleaner – and Danny senior – a merchant seaman – hailed from the then rough dockland area known as Tiger Bay.

Ryan's first home would be with his mum and his dad on the Ely council estate. The surname on his birth certificate was registered as Giggs, and his mother gave her parents' address in Pentrebane. The space where his father's name should have been entered was left blank.

3

The relationship between Lynne and Danny hardly augured well from the start. Inevitably, there were arguments as money was tight and they were very young to be coping with a baby. And they wanted different things. Lynne was a reserved girl who wanted stability; Danny was more rough and ready – he was handsome and would become known for his eye for the girls. She had no time for clubs and discos; he loved nothing more than a night on the town.

It was a potentially explosive mix – looking at it, even on paper you would say they were hardly suited from the start. And so it would prove. They would never marry and life was tough: at times, Lynne worked two jobs, and had to rely on her parents to look after Ryan.

That was the one solid base the youngster had throughout his life – the love, care and reliability of his maternal grandparents, Dennis and Margaret. In reality, he would alternate his time as he grew up between staying with his parents in Cardiff and with Dennis and Margaret in Pentrebane. He would become a regular sight in the district as he played with a football and a rugby ball for hours on end outside his grandparents' home.

Staying with them provided him with the stability he needed and which he was often denied when his dad was home. The rows between Danny and Lynne would worsen as the years rolled by and their relationship was in no way cemented when another son, Rhodri, was born three years after Ryan. Indeed, Ryan admitted that the arguments took on a more unpleasant aspect – not just shouting and crying – but 'physical'. Visits from the local constabulary weren't uncommon. In fact, after Rhodri was born, Danny would be arrested after 'one particularly bad fight' and told to get out by Lynne.

Ryan admitted that as he grew up and came to realise the way his father treated his mother, he found he liked him less and less. He was a self-confessed 'mummy's boy' and drifted apart from Danny, rarely talking to him as he grew from boy to man.

In his 2005 autobiography, Ryan described his relationship with his father in these terms: 'I have to admit that at one time I did look up to my dad... It wasn't until we moved to Manchester that I realised the full extent of the rotten life my dad gave her [Lynne]. He was a real rogue, and a ladies man.' He also revealed that his father 'didn't exactly set the right sort of example.'

The growing rift would lead to Ryan eventually changing his name from Wilson to Giggs when he was sixteen. He would take the decision then, two years after his parents' separation, so 'the world would know he was his mother's son'. The rift would also, inevitably maybe, lead to him becoming a more inward-looking, insular boy. On the plus side, it also made him more determined not to be like his father (whom he considered a failure for wasting his talent) and set him on a path to find perfection in his own career. Ryan would also admit, 'I didn't set out purposely to be different to my dad, but it influenced me subconsciously. He had a great talent and that was wasted. People tell me he was the greatest player they've seen.'

With his troubled early background, it was little wonder Ryan Giggs would suffer something of an identity crisis and strive to find himself in later years. Manchester United and Sir Alex Ferguson would play a vital role in helping him come to terms with his life and himself. Like a surrogate father and family, Sir Alex and the cosseted world of United provided him with the background he had in some ways been denied as a boy.

Ryan went to Hwyel Dda infant school in Ely and remembers his time there not for playing football – he never played for the school team – but for learning the Welsh national anthem 'Mae Hen Wlad Fy Nhadau' ('Land Of My Fathers').

One day in 1979 he came home from school and found his mother and father deep in conversation. Danny had been offered the chance to switch rugby codes – to swap from union to league – by Swinton, a team in Salford, a few miles north of Manchester. It would be the turning point of his life, a move for the better, although both Ryan and his mother Lynne were against it at the time. It would mean moving away from her mother and father, his beloved granddad Dennis and grandmother Margaret.

There were tears, but Danny insisted they had to go. He talked of it being a new start for them all; the money was good and he could make it in the big time.

The family moved into a house owned by the club and Danny was welcomed as a conquering hero. He settled quickly at Swinton RL club, on the then princely salary of £10,000 a year and the red-brick semi thrown in. Even now, he is fondly remembered as a 'great' for his exploits on the field for Swinton by the club's fans. As one fan writing recently on the Swinton Lions website said: 'Surely Manchester United FC should contribute to our stadium fund! After all, if the club hadn't signed the great Danny Wilson way back in 1979 then in all likelihood Ryan Giggs would have been lost to football and Manchester United and would probably have pursued a career in Rugby Union.'

Ryan and brother Rhodri didn't settle as easily as their father. Growing up in multiracial Cardiff, they had never thought about the colour of their skin. In north Manchester, they had to learn how to cope with being called 'nigger' and being laughed at and abused. Ryan would later admit it was a shock to hear the abuse when he attended Grosvenor Road School in Swinton, but that he dealt with it by dismissing it with contempt – unlike Rhodri, who would regularly get into fights with his abusers.

Giggsy would elucidate more about his struggles in an interview with the *Daily Mirror* in 2008, saying: 'My dad was quite a famous rugby player where we were growing up. Everyone knew that, and I used to get quite a bit of stick at school because of the colour of his skin. It's obviously not nice, and I wouldn't wish it on anyone. My way of coping was to keep it to myself. I was a quiet, shy boy and what I should have done is tell the teachers.' But he didn't even tell his parents. 'It made me feel that I was different, because I felt that I should be fitting in with all these other kids at the school and I couldn't. It was especially difficult at my school. There just weren't that many pupils from different backgrounds. We didn't have many Chinese, Indian or black kids. If there had been six or seven kids in the class who were black or mixed race that would have helped.'

Ryan found another way of deflecting the abuse and getting his schoolmates to see him in a different light – through his sporting prowess. He excelled at rugby and football. His progress in rugby surprised everyone – apart from his father – as he was such a sprightly, wiry figure. Yet he stuck with the game all the way through comprehensive school from the age of ten to fourteen, and turned out for local side Langworthy and Salford Boys. He did well at stand-off and out on the wing – and was also good enough to represent Lancashire, playing one game for the county.

It was a busy time, but somehow he had enough energy in his tank to keep his hand in at football, playing up front for Sunday League outfit Deans FC and representing Salford Boys at football as well as rugby.

It was at Deans that he would make an impact – even though his first game for them ended in a crushing 9-0 loss – and at Deans that he would meet the man who would put him on the first rung of the professional ladder. The team was coached by milkman Dennis Schofield and he would certainly come to deliver on the promise he made to Giggs to help him make the big time.

Schofield knew a quality player and a star in the making when he saw one – and at the age of thirteen, he secured Ryan a trial at Manchester City. Even then our boy was a Red through and through – he used to watch Manchester United from the Stretford End when he wasn't playing rugby or football – and he hardly endeared himself to the City youth team bosses by wearing a red United top for training!

Nevertheless, his talent shone through and did the talking for him, so he played one game for City youth when he was thirteen. But for Ryan, it was one game too many – his heart lay across the city, at Old Trafford, and he still dreamed of the chance of making it at United. His dream became reality, thanks to another man who had his interests at heart – a newsagent by the name of Harry Wood.

Wood was a steward at Old Trafford and he persuaded Alex

Ferguson to take a look at the boy. Ryan headed to Old Trafford for a week-long trial. But Ferguson caught a glimpse of his genius before the trial and is said to have made up his mind that he would sign him right there and then. Giggs was playing in a match for Salford Boys against a United under-15s side at The Cliff, United's then training ground, and he scored a hat trick. As he played, Ryan spotted the United boss watching with interest from his office window.

Ryan believed he had done enough already, but still attended the trial. And on his 14th birthday, his dream became reality. Returning home from school, he saw a gold Mercedes parked outside the house. He hurried anxiously inside and saw Sir Alex Ferguson sitting in an armchair, sipping a cup of tea out of some of the best china Lynne could find. Ferguson didn't beat about the bush, quickly offering his protégé a two-year deal as an associate schoolboy with Manchester United.

Ryan was fourteen, captain of England Schoolboys, and he had signed for Manchester United. The boy with the tough start in life now had the world at his feet... literally. He was about to embark on the most glittering career ever in British football: a legend was in the making.

CHAPTER 2
RED ALERT

'I shall always remember my first sight of him, floating over the pitch at The Cliff so effortlessly that you would have sworn his feet weren't touching the ground.'

Sir Alex Ferguson, *Managing My Life*

'When Ryan ran, he ran like the wind. You couldn't hear him, he was that light on his feet. No disrespect to Beckham and Scholesy, but he's the only one who was always going to be a superstar.'

Former United skipper, Steve Bruce

Ryan officially joined Manchester United FC on 9 July 1990, when he was sixteen – and he turned professional on 29 November 1990, his 17th birthday. Alex Ferguson knew he had a special talent on his hands, but resisted the heavy temptation to throw the wonderboy into the first team at once. Instead, he decided on a softly-softly approach with the lad who would become a United legend – and in doing so, formulated a programme of development that he would employ with countless other young stars during the next 20 years of his reign.

He wrapped Ryan in cotton wool, using him sparingly and keeping him well away from the wolves of the media, whom he did not trust back then (and for the most part still doesn't now). Ferguson would tell the pack to back off; that, no, Ryan was not available for a chat after a particularly inspiring showing, and, no, he would not be doing columns, adverts or promotions until Ferguson, the manager, decided the time was right for him to do so.

Fourteen years later Ferguson would sum up the methodology he used in his treatment of Ryan and other so-called 'fledglings' over the years when he spoke about how new boy Wayne Rooney would be handled. He said, 'We won't ask the lad to climb a mountain tomorrow. The important thing is that he is a major player in five years' time. We have a job to do to make sure he fulfils his potential. We have a reputation for looking after young players here. He will get the same protection the others have had.'

Of course, United were more wary than other clubs may have been with Giggs – little wonder, given they'd had the original whiz kid, George Best, under their wings. After Best's death, many fans believe that United, as a club, still felt some guilt that they had not done enough to help him, and to get help for him. It hadn't been the done thing in the Matt Busby era: you didn't talk through problems, you just fronted it out.

Busby was hardly a therapist or a psychologist, and he never wanted to be. Ferguson was from the same down-to-earth Scottish upbringing – the idea that 'we're all big boys who don't cry' – but, to his credit, he was aware that Ryan Giggs would need his attention and his protection. He knew there would be comparisons with Best and that some pundits would sniff out Ryan's background, find out that he was from a broken home and suggest he could easily go the way of the late, great Georgie Boy and so he determined, from day one, that it would not happen: that Ryan would not be George Best, Mark 2. He would be Ryan Giggs, Mark 1.

Paul Parker, the former United full back who played in the United team of Ryan's early career, summed up Ferguson's influence: 'The boss brought Ryan through from a troubled childhood and always saw him as one of his own. Ryan [also] got very close to Paul Ince, and Incey took him under his wing. Ryan would also socialise quite a lot with Lee Sharpe. But he was always his own man and made his own decisions.

'He didn't go out looking for publicity. Apart from doing a few promotional things for his boot company, he was content to be known as Giggs the footballer.'

Fergie's protectiveness helps explain why it was only in August 1993 – three years after he joined United and a good two years after his debut – that Ryan was allowed to have an agent to find him marketing deals. The lure of the boy was apparent when the agent quickly did a £500,000 deal for Ryan with a boot manufacturer. That same year the press got their bite of the cherry when he did his first major interview with the men's magazine *FHM*.

Giggs made his league debut at the tender age of seventeen in the old Division One against Everton at Old Trafford on 2 March 1991, as a substitute for Denis Irwin. I was fortunate to be at the match, along with *Sunday Times* sports editor Alex Butler. Alex had told me on the way up to Manchester that there had been talk among the men who covered United for the nationals of a young lad who was going to leave everyone stunned when he finally made it into United's first team. Name of Giggs, he had been nurtured through the club's academy and was expected to bypass the traditional route of years in the reserves. Butler had been given the nod that Ferguson might blood the kid against Everton, and so it was that we headed up north, hopefully to be a part of history in the making.

I recall it being a bitterly cold March day as we arrived at Old Trafford – and the match was not particularly memorable. United were already trailing 2-0 when Denis Irwin fell awkwardly and was taken off. I half-expected Ferguson to bring on Lee Sharpe, or maybe even Russell Beardsmore. But then Butler nudged me and said, 'This is it, he'll bring on the lad Giggs.' The big man of Fleet Street wasn't wrong – a gawky, skinny boy with dark hair took off his tracksuit and headed towards the touchline.

At that moment a chill wind blew in from the nearby Ship Canal and I feared it might blow the boy over. Yes, he was that lightweight and featherlike; wafer thin and looking like he needed a good meal (or two).

Fergie patted him on the back and whispered in his ear: it was that sort of moment, history defining, epoch making. 'Good luck Ryan,' I am told the boss said affectionately. 'And give 'em hell!'

It took the new boy a few minutes to get into the game but his first touch confirmed that everything I had been told about him was spot on. He had a deft control, a talent for beating a man with trickery and pace. And he roared off like a greyhound down that left wing for the first time; he would come to call the territory his own, but back then he was like a kid with a new toy. Then came the real surprise: we had been warned that he would be good, even brilliant, but we never expected him to have the strength and determination that he exuded when a desperate Toffees defender tried to upend him. He shoulder-charged him back and stood his ground. How had he managed that when he looked like a slight wind would blow him over?

It would later emerge that Fergie hadn't just been wrapping Ryan in cotton wool and protecting him from the press; he had been encouraging him to build up his strength and physique and had told his backroom staff to work on that side of the boy's development. The work had clearly paid off.

As Ryan trooped off, Fergie threw a protective arm around him and senior players, including Gary Pallister, Steve Bruce and Paul Parker, spoke words of encouragement to the boy wonder. The era of Ryan Giggs as a public face had begun in earnest. Parker would one day famously make the comment that while everyone likened Giggs to George Best, Ryan was, 'so much quicker than Best.'

Welsh goalkeeping legend Neville Southall was between the sticks for the Toffees that day and he told BBC Sport in 2009: 'I'd heard the hype beforehand and when he came on I thought what a scrawny, thin kid with dodgy hair! But he had incredible blistering pace, dribbling ability, superb balance and great vision for a teenager – and you could immediately see the comparisons with George Best.'

Former Welsh skipper Kevin Ratcliffe was the man with the task of being the first to mark Ryan on his debut in 1991. He said he could see the massive potential in the boy, and that he was pleased he was Welsh born and bred – as it meant that he would not have to face him at international level!

He hadn't scored or been able to turn the game around for the Reds, but he had shown glimpses of just why Manchester United FC were so excited by one boy's emergence.

If his sub's role had whetted the appetite, Ryan's full debut would leave few doubting that here was a real talent, someone who could light up the Premier League for years to come. His first full start for the club would come at Old Trafford almost exactly two months later and would also never be forgotten, coming as it did against local archrivals Manchester City. He would mark the occasion by scoring his first goal – although even diehard United fans would concede that it did take a major deflection off Blues defender Colin Hendry and could have been credited to the big Scot. No matter, it was a goal, and it was the only goal as United chalked up a 1-0 win in the match that mattered most for local pride and bragging rights.

And it was Ryan who had pulled off the fairytale to send United fans out into the city streets celebrating that night. He became an overnight sensation, a hero in the making, because it was he who had won the derby match. Fergie then pulled the protective cloak over his wunderkind and shielded him from an inquisitive media and public. He took him back out of the limelight, knowing his time would come (and it would not be long) and that he also had the not inconsiderable talents of Lee Sharpe and Andrei Kanchelskis to keep the wings warm until Giggs was finally ready to step permanently into the first team.

Indeed, it would be Sharpe to whom the manager would turn just 11 days after the win in the Manchester derby. Fergie would not even include Giggs in the squad of 16 who defeated Barcelona in the European Cup Winners' Cup final in

Rotterdam on 15 May 1991. Danny Wallace was on the bench as Sharpe's deputy – ironically, Lee had been Danny's stand-in until he took the older man's place at the start of that season.

Without Ryan, United would beat Barcelona 2-1 to celebrate the re-admission of English clubs to Europe after a 5-year absence in the wake of the Heysel disaster.

The next season, 1991/92, Ryan would become much more involved in the first team, turning out regularly and really starting to make a name for himself. To an extent, Fergie was still treating him with kid gloves and he left him out of the starting line-up for the first match of the season: the league encounter with Notts County at Old Trafford. But he was brought on in the second half to replace Fergie's son, Darren, and when Lee Sharpe suffered a series of injuries, young Ryan was retained in the first 11. The era of Giggs had definitely begun.

He scored his first 'proper' goal (one that did not need a deflection to take it into the net) for the club on 7 September 1991, in the league clash against Norwich City at Old Trafford, which United won 3-0. That season, he would go on to score another five league goals.

Two months later, Ryan savoured his first taste of senior glory as United beat Red Star Belgrade 1-0 in the European Super Cup final. The match took place at Old Trafford and Ryan, wearing the No. 16 shirt, came on for left-back Lee Martin after 71 minutes. Brian McClair grabbed the winner for the Red Devils, who were playing in the game because they had won the 1991 European Cup Winners' Cup (Red Star had lifted the European Cup). It was supposed to have been a two-legged affair but the troubles in Belgrade led UEFA to play it over one leg, in Manchester.

It would not be long before Giggs was taking home more silverware. Just 5 months after the win over Red Star, he was again in the first team and helped United to a 1-0 win over Nottingham Forest in the League Cup final (then known as the Rumbelows Cup). He had played a major role in getting the Red Devils to Wembley, scoring the winner in the two-legged semi-final against Middlesbrough.

But it was Scottish ace McClair who grabbed the decisive goal in the final, as Ryan lapped up his first taste of success at Wembley on 12 April 1992. It was all the more special as it was United's first League Cup win – as well as Giggs's first major domestic honour in the pro game.

Giggs lined up on the left with his best mate Paul Ince playing alongside him in central midfield. Mike Phelan, now assistant manager at Old Trafford, was alongside Ince, with Kanchelskis on the right wing. Mark Hughes, who would of course go on to manage Manchester City, led the attack with McClair. Ryan was a constant threat down the left wing and he completed a fine performance by setting up McClair for his winner after just 14 minutes. He was still only eighteen years old.

His joy was complete when he went on to win the PFA Young Player of the Year award for 1992 – and played in the final of the Youth Cup, skippering the side to a 6-3 triumph over Crystal Palace (he played in the second leg, which United won 3-2). It was the first time the club had won the trophy since 1964, when they beat Swindon 5-2. The triumphant team of '92 included some other youngsters who would go on to join Ryan in the United senior side at the very top of the game – namely David Beckham, Gary Neville, Paul Scholes and Nicky Butt.

Despite the accolades coming Ryan's way, some assessed the season as a failure – because United exited at an early stage from both the Cup Winners' Cup and FA Cup and, more crucially, did not win the league title when it had appeared to be theirs for the taking. The Red Devils lost out to Leeds United after leading the race for much of the season: the collapse that cost them so dearly began at Easter 1992, with three defeats in their final four games ending the dream. It led to major inquests in the Press and in the pubs around Old Trafford – and even Fergie conceded 'many in the media felt that [his] mistakes had contributed to the misery.'

He admitted his side needed an 'extra dimension' if they were to go one step further the following season and end 26 years of darkness by lifting the crown.

The boss had tried to sign Mick Harford from Luton Town to bring that spark, and said he believed United would have won the title with the big striker in tow. We'll never know whether Harford would have inspired United to greatness, but the man who would finally arrive at Old Trafford the following November certainly did: yes, Eric Cantona appeared with his collar turned up and nothing would ever be the same again at the Theatre of Dreams. Certainly, Ryan Giggs was entranced by his spell – admitting Cantona was his favourite player ever and that his own game improved as he tried to match 'The King's' rigorous standards in training and on the pitch.

If Paul Ince was his best mate, Eric Cantona was Ryan Giggs's role model. And the Frenchman took time out to help him reach his potential. He taught him that you can take nothing for granted – that you need to search all the time for perfection, find it and tap into your potential to become a great player, not just a damned good one. Cantona was world-class – and Ryan would join him, much to his satisfaction: he said he felt Giggs was the best young player that he had ever come across and that he had all the raw ingredients to become the finest footballer in the world.

Ryan would go some way to showing his potential – and the fact that he would work hard to exploit it – in the 1992/93 season, his third as a professional at United. He was still only eighteen, but raring to go and to help United hopefully break the title jinx that continued to cast a long, dark shadow over Old Trafford. Over the campaign, he would contribute with 11 goals in all.

But by the beginning of November, United were lagging behind in the newly-formed Premier League table. Ryan had scored in the 1-1 draw at Spurs in the middle of September and was playing his part with some fine performances down the left wing as United desperately tried to step up a gear to title-winning form. But a disappointing European exit – 4-3 on penalties to Torpedo Moscow in the UEFA Cup first round – and inconsistent form by his team in the league, with 1-0 losses at home to Wimbledon and away at Aston Villa, led Ferguson to plunge into the transfer market.

On 26 November 1992, he bought the catalyst, the man who would make the league title dream come true, finally ending that 26-year nightmare. The great Eric Cantona arrived from Leeds United for a fee of just over £1 million. It was like buying a Picasso for a fiver; Fergie had picked up a genuine masterpiece on the cheap. Cantona would prove the final missing piece of the jigsaw: he was to take United to a new level through his skill, genius and incomparable self-confidence.

During the first part of the campaign, Mark Hughes and Brian McClair had been struggling as a partnership – even with Ryan winging in inch-perfect crosses – but that would all change as the French talisman made his presence felt. Cantona quickly settled into the team, not only scoring goals but also creating chances for others. Ryan would later admit that he had looked on in some awe as the Frenchman strutted his stuff, but also said that he was grateful to have had him at his side as nerves threatened to overwhelm United's push for glory.

'The King', as United fans quickly came to call him, gave the whole team the belief that they could be champions. Cantona formed a strong partnership with Mark Hughes and fired the club to the top of the table.

He made his debut in the derby match against Manchester City on 6 December 1992, at Old Trafford, and his 9 goals in 22 league games helped bring the inaugural Premier League title to the club by the following May. His first United goal came in the 1-1 draw against Chelsea at Stamford Bridge on 19 December 1992. Controversy was, of course, his second name and on his return to Elland Road, on 8 February 1993, he was in trouble after spitting at one of the Leeds fans who tried to make his return visit to Yorkshire as inhospitable as possible: he was subsequently fined £1,000 by the FA.

Two months later, Cantona would have the last laugh by leading United to their first Premier League crown – a feat in itself as he became the first player to win the top-flight crown with different teams in successive seasons. And United had not taken the title with a whimper – no, they had done it with a roar, finishing a massive 10 points clear of runners-up Aston Villa.

A spin-off of the success was that Ferguson was voted Manager of the Year, while Giggs was rewarded for his excellent showings with another Young Player of the Year award. He would also claim a little bit of history as the first player to be given the accolade in successive seasons.

Ryan had certainly played his part in the run-in, setting up goals from that leftwing and grabbing the opener himself in the 3-1 win over Blackburn on 3 May 1993. He had played in a total of 46 matches with a decent return of 11 goals. But no way was the Welsh wing wizard happy to sit back and bask in complacency after that pivotal title win; like the team and manager he played for, he wanted more: much more – and quickly. The title albatross may have been removed from Old Trafford and Ryan was delighted to have been part of the history-making team that finally lifted the weight, but now he was aiming even higher – he wanted to win the double of the Premier League and FA Cup, and then steal glory in Europe.

And he wouldn't have to wait long to achieve the first part of his new target – less than 12 months, in fact.

CHAPTER 3
MINE'S A DOUBLE

'Ryan could play football in a phone box and find the door, no matter how many players were in there with him.'
Carlos Queiroz, former Manchester United assistant manager

Ryan Giggs knew he had a lot to live up to as the 1993/94 campaign dawned. During the summer, he had enjoyed a good rest and a holiday with his mates in Crete, but realised everything had changed when he returned to Old Trafford for pre-season training in July 1993. No longer was he a minor character at Manchester United – already he was being compared to George Best and hailed a matchwinner. His feats of the previous season had ensured things would never be the same again – but, typically of the boy whose feet were firmly on the ground, he did not let it bother him.

OK, there was much more attention, more autograph hunters and more press men pushing microphones in his face – as was exemplified during United's tour of South Africa a few weeks earlier when he was literally mobbed by fans and well-wishers – but for him, life went on much as usual. Even on that pre-season tour he preferred to avoid the crowds and the adulation, often staying in the team's Johannesburg hotel listening to his favourite music on his personal CD player, or having a laugh with his room-mate. Typical of the boss, Ferguson even had a say in who roomed with the boy Giggs on the tour – and who better to keep an eye on him than his son, Darren?

No, there was little chance that young Ryan would stray. His mother Lynne and manager Ferguson helped him stay on course by vetting his lifestyle and keeping him away from too much temptation. Giggs was still living at home with Lynne and his stepfather Richard Johnson, a chef whom she had married four years earlier. Their three-bedroom house was located on the main Worsley Road in Swinton (which led to Manchester and Old Trafford) and Ryan enjoyed their company and that of his eighteen-month-old half-sister, Bethany.

The only sign of ostentation was the sight of his red Golf GTI parked outside on double-yellow lines when he had to nip back for something he had forgotten on the way to training. Otherwise, he was living the life of a typical nineteen-year-old – going out with his friends for a game of snooker or a pint and seeing his girlfriend when time permitted. He may have been a shy lad, but he was a winner with the girls – including a model, Dawn Thomas, who he had briefly dated. And by the start of the new campaign in August 1993 he was going steady with Suzanne Rothwell, a nineteen-year-old building society worker, who lived nearby and had attended the same secondary school.

It was the kind of lifestyle that Fergie advocated. He didn't want Ryan going the same way as players like Lee Sharpe, who preferred to walk on the wild side. No, the boss knew Giggsy had huge potential and so he continued his policy of ensuring that he did not do too much, too young. He encouraged him to continue to live at home, to lark about with his long-time friends and to stay the course with one girl. Some would call Ferguson a control freak for pulling the strings with Giggs, but Ryan was privately grateful for the boss's time and concern.

He knew all about George Best and didn't want anything to derail him from his prime objective – becoming one of the finest footballers in the world at one of the best football clubs in the world. Anyway, he was never bedevilled by the same addictions and distractions that had cost the Northern Ireland genius so dearly.

So Ryan agreed when Ferguson suggested it might be a good idea if he stayed at home with Lynne and Richard until he was at least twenty-one. And he was happy to fall in with the boss's suggestion that he learn how to cook, with the help of United's chef, in preparation for when he did leave home– after all, Ferguson told him, you can't live on cereal and toast for ever!

'Alex Ferguson has got permission from his mother to look after him,' the then United chief executive Martin Edwards told *Today* journalist David Jones in August 1993. 'He is extremely protective of Ryan. He has seen what has happened to other young boys with agents, and so on. Ryan has a particular talent and the last thing he wants is for the boy to go astray. It is for the boy's – and the club's – own good.'

Fergie was pleased with the way his young signing was

developing and felt that he would step up another level during the imminent campaign – and he would not be wrong on that score. Ryan was to turn twenty in the November of 1993 and his performances throughout the campaign would parallel his growing maturity. This would be his best season goals-wise at the club – he would score a total of 17.

To add to the team's strength, Ferguson had pulled off another masterstroke in the transfer market a month before the new season opened – bringing in Roy Keane from Nottingham Forest for a then British record fee of £3.75 million. The Irishman would go on to captain the club and be the boss's eyes and ears on the pitch, leading United to an unprecedented era of glory during the 1990s.

The Reds were beginning to look unbeatable – with a rock-solid defence containing the massive goalkeeping presence of Peter Schmeichel and centre-backs Steve Bruce and Gary Pallister, and a midfield that would revolve around Keane and Giggs on the wing. Plus, there was a whole host of other youngsters – the so-called 'Fergie Fledglings' – knocking on the first-team door.

With Giggs in splendid form, United would win the league again in May 1994 – notching a second consecutive title for the first time since 1957, before winning the FA Cup to complete the first 'Double' in the club's history.

Ryan got off to a flyer at the start of the campaign, grabbing United's first goal in the 2-0 win at Norwich on 15 August 1993. It was a goal that would highlight his poaching skills in the 6-yard box. Keeper Bryan Gunn could only deflect an effort from Mark Hughes and Giggs was on hand to tap the ball home in the 26th minute.

The match marked Keane's league debut for United, and the midfield maestro set up Ryan for his opener with a splendid cross that Giggs duly converted. If Keane was a rookie for United that day – and Giggs was still relatively wet behind the ears – there was another man learning his trade and heading for the big time in the press box.

Colin Forshaw would later go on to make his name on the *Mail on Sunday*, but on Roy Keane's debut he was honing his craft on the sports desk of the *Eastern Daily Press* in Norwich. Forshaw saw enough in Keane's performance to convince him that he had seen the heartbeat future of Manchester United but he was also bedazzled by the skills and ingenuity of the boy on the leftwing. He said: 'There was a bit of a buzz in the press box that day – what with Keane making his debut and being the most expensive player in British football. The United boys had told us he had been buzzing in training and that they reckoned he would take over from Bryan Robson as the key man in the side sooner rather than later. Sure enough, he wasn't in the least afraid of letting Robbo or Paul Ince know if he felt they had messed up, or not gone in hard enough.'

He remembered Keane as being the one who came out on top – the one who dictated the play rather than Ince: 'Keane set up the goal for Giggs and helped United keep their shape when Norwich occasionally threatened. There was no disgrace for City losing to United that day – in Keane they had found a gem of a player, but Giggs was also amazing. Keane stole the headline because it was his debut and he was the most expensive player in Britain, but for me, Giggs was just as good, if not better. He ran Norwich ragged and had so much confidence and ability for a young lad. He was still wiry and skinny, but he was developing, you could see that. He was so fast, virtually unstoppable, and the Norwich defenders would be having nightmares about him for months after that showing.'

Forshaw was not at all surprised that Giggs went on to become one of United's best players: 'Even back in 1993 it was clear that he was going to be a world-class footballer. It was just a shame that my hometown team had to be the ones who suffered as he started to really make his name!'

Just 6 days later Ryan was on the scoresheet again – this time in front of his own adoring fans at Old Trafford. Giggs delivered from a marvellous free kick that spun beyond the despairing reach of Newcastle keeper Pavel Srnicek in a 1-1 Premier League draw.

With Cantona at his side, there was no stopping the boy wonder that history-making season. His season's haul of 17 goals in the campaign would make him the team's third-highest scorer after Mark Hughes and Eric Cantona as United lost only 6 out of 62 games.

The only disappointment came at Wembley in March 1994, when Giggs and co. lost 3-1 to Aston Villa in the League Cup final. They had been so close to lifting an unprecedented domestic treble. There was also dismay as United's much-heralded return to the European Cup ended in tears in November as they crashed out on the away-goals rule to Galatasaray. The first leg in Manchester ended 3-3 and United could only draw 0-0 in Istanbul on the return.

But another plus for Ryan came in October 1993 – a month before his 20th birthday – when he signed a new 5-year deal that would tie him to Old Trafford until at least 1998. The fans and Fergie breathed a collective sigh of relief – and Giggs started to work out exactly how he would spend the readies as his salary increased to £350,000 a year (around £7,000 a week).

Shortly afterwards, United won 3-2 at neighbours Manchester City and the excellent league results continued for the next four months. From 30 October 1993 until 5 March 1994 Giggs and his team-mates lost only once in 18 matches. Certainly, it was title-winning form, which included some fine highlights from Giggs.

He grabbed a brace in the 5-2 win at Oldham's Boundary Park just after Christmas 1993, and scored United's second in the cracker of a match that led to a 3-3 draw with Liverpool at Anfield on 4 January 1994. Ryan was also on target in the first leg of the League Cup semi-final against Sheffield Wednesday at Old Trafford on 13 February 1994. The goal sealed a 1-0 win for the Reds and put them in confident mood for the return at Hillsborough, which they duly won at a canter, 4-1.

Disappointment would come in the final against Villa, a month later. Goals from Dalian Atkinson and Dean Saunders (2) killed off United, who had only Mark Hughes's consolation strike to show for their trip to London. Ryan would feel low as he clutched his runners-up medal on the coach trip back to Manchester, but he knew greater glories were within reach.

United were roaring towards the retention of their league crown and reached the FA Cup final with a commendable win over neighbours Oldham Athletic. Again, Giggs was instrumental in the triumph. The first match ended in a 1-1 draw after extra time, but United made no mistake in the replay, winning 4-1. Giggs lashed home the first goal to send

United on their way, with Denis Irwin (against his old club), Andrei Kanchelskis and Bryan Robson putting the contest beyond doubt.

United wrapped up their second successive title win by winning 4 of their final 6 league matches after the FA Cup victory over Oldham. Surprisingly, they would lose 1-0 away at Wimbledon three days after beating the Latics, but went on to beat Manchester City, Leeds, Ipswich and Southampton before parading the trophy around Old Trafford after an anti-climatic 0-0 draw with Coventry in their final league encounter of the season.

Again, Ryan chipped in by scoring the opener in the 2-0 win at Leeds and the winner in the 2-1 victory at Ipswich. United were champions again – finishing 8 points clear of runners-up Blackburn.

Six days after wrapping up another title, Giggs and his team-mates headed back to Wembley on 14 May in an attempt to lift the FA Cup and their first double. Chelsea stood between them and their moment of history – but only for an hour.

While United were going all out to become only the fourth 20th-century team to complete the Double, Chelsea finally emerged from a period of gloom. This would be their first major final since 1971, but they were ranked underdogs, having finished 13 places behind the Reds in the league.

Bryan Robson, the man who had lifted the trophy three times as captain of United, was famously dropped from the squad for Brian McClair while Chelsea player-manager Glenn Hoddle left himself out of the starting line-up. Yet it would be the Blues who took charge of the match, proving to be the better side in a rain-soaked first half at the national stadium. But it was a different United after the interval and they crushed Chelsea with a demoralising 30-minute display of football from the hour onward.

Again, it was Giggs who was instrumental in setting United on their way. He and Kanchelskis were becoming more and more influential as Chelsea tired early and the damp surface made tackling a lottery. Giggs set up Irwin for a run into the box, where the Irishman was fouled by a desperate Frank Sinclair. Eric Cantona made no mistake from the penalty spot. Six minutes later 'the King' made it 2-0 with another penalty after Kanchelskis was upended in the box by Eddie Newton. Goals by Mark Hughes and Brian McClair – proving Fergie was right to choose him instead of Robbo on this occasion – killed off the match. Four-nil and Giggs and the boys had won the double.

Ryan celebrated into the night with his team-mates and United fans everywhere were convinced this was the start of an era in which the Reds would be invincible for many years at home – and hopefully they would begin to make inroads in the European Cup too. But the phrase 'counting your chickens before they had hatched' came to mind as Giggs joined United for pre-season training in the summer of 1994 after an enjoyable holiday with team-mate Paul Ince. Ferguson brought in David May from Blackburn to add strength to his squad and would sign goal-machine Andy Cole from Newcastle in the January of the campaign, but United were to falter dramatically and end the season empty-handed.

It was a situation Giggs described as 'horrible' and 'a nightmare', one that he was determined he would never have to suffer again. He did not want to go through the heartache of having the league and the FA Cup both within his grasp – another double – and seeing them snatched away at the last moment.

Of course, there were mitigating circumstances that season – none more so than Eric Cantona's 8-month ban after his 'kung-fu' attack on a fan at Crystal Palace at the end of January 1995. But United should still have had enough to complete the job with the available players. It's often said that they simply cracked up after Cantona's exit, but the statistics directly after the incident do not back this up. They won 8 of their next 10 matches – including the 9-0 rout over Ipswich, the 3-0 win at Manchester City in the league and the 3-1 win over Leeds in the FA Cup.

No, it is a tad too simple to say they collapsed just because Eric was absent – and the boss was to agree with that when it came to putting things right during the next summer break. A certain complacency had set in with some of the big players perhaps thinking they were the cream of the crop, that they just had to turn up to win.

But Ryan Giggs was not among their number. If anything, one might argue that his absence during the season at key times due to injury – he was restricted to 29 Premier League games and one goal because of fitness problems – cost United as dearly as Eric Cantona's absence.

His only goal in the league came in the 3-0 win over Wimbledon at Old Trafford in the opening month of the season, although he also scored another in the 5-2 home win over Wrexham in the FA Cup at the end of January, 1995, plus two more in the 4-2 European Cup first round first-leg victory over Gothenburg at Old Trafford in September 1994.

Yes, it was undoubtedly a poor return for a player at the top of his game and a player of such majestic talent; but, as we have said, it was also down to a series of injury setbacks. That season Ryan suffered the first major injury of his career in the 3-2 loss at Ipswich in September 1994. He hobbled off with a calf problem and then suffered ankle, Achilles tendon and hamstring setbacks as the campaign progressed. At one stage, he would admit that he had played in some games when he was not fully fit, so keen was he to continue his glory run at United, but this obviously didn't help the injuries – indeed, it explains why one setback seemed to merge into another. He never had the chance to get fit and fully recover.

By the end of the campaign Giggs was still only twenty-one and was part of what Ferguson saw as a new golden future. He would survive the ensuing summer cull and would be joined by fellow kids from the youth team as Fergie blew away the cobwebs of dismay that engulfed the club.

The new era was effectively launched when United collapsed in their final two games of the season. Their failure to win at West Ham on 14 May 1995 (they drew 1-1) allowed Blackburn to sneak in and claim their Premier League crown. Six days later there was another shock at Wembley as United went down 1-0 to Everton in the FA Cup final. The win was totally unexpected – Everton had experienced a topsy-turvy season and the bookies were convinced Giggs and co. would wipe the floor with them.

But new boss Joe Royle inspired them to turn around their season and beat the drop – and to also win the Cup. Paul Rideout scored the goal that sent Everton fans into raptures and had United's army of supporters crying into their beer.

The goal meant the Toffees had won a trophy for the first time in 8 years – while United were left potless for the first time since 1989. Giggs admitted he had only been half-fit and the boss kept him on the bench until half time, when he came on for Steve Bruce. Lee Sharpe started on the left, but found it difficult to break through the Toffees' famed 'Dogs of War' – defenders and midfielders who tackled as if their lives depended on it and would use any means, fair or foul, to stop someone breaking past them. Ryan had been suffering from the hamstring problem that had irritated him throughout the season and was unsure whether he should even take part. He had to be persuaded by the boss that he could play half the match.

Afterwards Ferguson would show how much he had come to rely on Giggs when he admitted the outcome of the lost double might have been different, had his boy wonder been playing. 'It is arguable that he could have won us the league at the death. He nearly turned the Cup Final around for us when we brought him on as a substitute,' he conceded.

Giggs admitted he did enjoy the after-match party – which had been organised to take place whether United won or lost. The boss told him and the rest of the lads to go out and enjoy themselves, that it had been a long tough season, and to come back refreshed and more determined than ever. And so they did just that, drowning their sorrows at the swanky Royal Lancaster Hotel in London.

But Fergie himself didn't bother with the after-match party: already he was thinking up plans to put things right. And he gave a hint that, yes, he did think complacency may have set in among certain players when he observed, 'It's five years since we won nothing. Sometimes our players forget what defeat is like – they know now.'

The course of action that the boss eventually decided on would initially have the fans questioning his sanity, but it was to work beyond his wildest dreams – bringing the greatest haul of trophies and glory that the club had ever known. Indeed, Ryan Giggs would often remark that he was thankful to have been parachuted into Old Trafford at a time when Ferguson was boss. The outcome of the following season would go a long way towards explaining just why he admired and respected his mentor so much.

CHAPTER 4

KIDS DO WIN TITLES

'You'll never win anything with kids.'
Alan Hansen, BBC *Match of the Day*, 19 August 1995

'Ryan Giggs was a hero to the younger lads, like me.'
David Beckham

It would turn out to be one of the biggest clangers dropped on national TV since Michael Fish's infamous 'there's no hurricane on the way' assertion the night before severe storms and gales battered Britain in 1987. And, in much the same way as the hapless Fish would be remembered for his wide-of-the-mark comment, so too would Alan Hansen's words of wisdom come back to haunt him for the rest of his television career.

Hansen was a pundit on the BBC show *Match of the Day* and following Manchester United's 3–1 defeat at Aston Villa on the opening day of the 1995/96 Premier League season, he uttered those famous words: 'You'll never win anything with kids.' Alex Ferguson laughed it off but many of the United faithful found themselves nodding in agreement that night, even though Hansen was renowned as a Liverpool fanatic after starring for the Anfield club for the most part of a glittering playing career.

Some Reds felt they had no choice but to concur with the man so closely linked to their most hated rivals. After all, United had sold off major names from their squad during the summer of 1995 – and the boss had said that he was not planning to splash out to replace them. No, he was going to give gilded youth its big chance at Old Trafford.

Three big stars had paid the price for the barren campaign of 1994/95 when the club ended up trophy-less after falling at the last hurdles in both the league and the FA cups. Paul Ince, the self-styled 'guv'nor', was shown the door after Ferguson felt he had grown too big for his boots. Legend has it that the writing was firmly on the wall for Ince after one particular episode involving him and Ferguson in 1995.

The two men had jumped out of their cars – Incey's boasting the registration GUV 8 – after parking up outside Old Trafford, and both were heading for the entrance to the ground at the same time. As they arrived, the guard at the door nodded his head in respect and said, 'Afternoon, guv.' Ferguson said 'Hello' back, but the doorman and Ince shared a sly wink as the player followed his boss through the door. No prizes for guessing the sting in the tail – the guard had been acknowledging Incey, not Fergie!

Giggs was upset at Paul Ince's departure. He had become firm friends with the midfielder, who was to decamp to Italy and Inter Milan. They had gone away on holiday together and enjoyed nights and meals out. Ince had been somebody Ryan could talk to and confide in about any problems or dilemmas that he had. Plus, there was the not inconsiderable fact that Paul would look out for Ryan on the pitch and dive in with crunching tackles if anybody was giving him a hard time.

The other two stars shown the door were Mark Hughes, who would head to London and Chelsea, and Andrei Kanchelskis, who was to turn up just 35 miles up the East Lancs Road at Everton.

There were protests outside Old Trafford as United fans vented their feelings but Ferguson had shown an iron grip in his disposal of the three big men and sent out a warning to any of his other players who might think they could sit on their laurels after the success they had enjoyed during the double season. That interim season of failure had forced the boss into the most drastic reshaping of his squad throughout his entire career and sent out a clear message: we only want players hungry for success in this team.

In their place, he would showcase the most exciting, talented batch of youngsters that the club had possessed since the glory and heartache of the 'Busby Babes'.

But it was not as if Ferguson had just come up with the idea from nowhere. In fact, he had been secretly planning the revolution for some time. Youth team coach Eric Harrison told him that he had unearthed the most exciting set of kids that he had ever known and the boss had witnessed the proof with his own eyes.

Several players from that much-vaunted youth team – including Paul Scholes, David Beckham, Nicky Butt and Gary Neville – were now given their chance to emulate the progress Giggs had already made in the first team. Ferguson also believed that Roy Keane was a better player than Ince and that he could do well without Kanchelsksis and Hughes. Plus, he knew that by October he would have the return of the inspirational Cantona once his 8-month ban came to an end. And he reckoned the Frenchman would be fired up to lead the kids forward, that he would be their talisman.

And the boss was right in all his calls.

The new boys would let no one down – by the end of the season the kids who Hansen had infamously claimed would win nothing had won the double. Or, as United fans dubbed it, 'the double double' – as it was the second time they had now achieved the feat after the 1993/94 glory campaign.

Ryan Giggs played a vital role in the achievement. He put the injuries that had dogged his previous campaign behind him and enjoyed a brilliant season, emerging as one of United's best players along, inevitably, with Cantona. At only twenty-one, he also played his part in helping the youngsters merge into the first team; he was there to help them and offer encouragement. Nicky Butt, in particular, would say how much he appreciated Giggs's contributions that season.

The United team for that opening-game defeat at Villa Park on 19 August read: Schmeichel, Parker, Irwin, Neville, Pallister (O'Kane, 59), Sharpe, Butt, Keane, McClair, Scholes, P. Neville (Beckham, 45). Sub not used: Davies.

The phrase 'Fergie's Fledglings' was born as the kids started to make their mark in the first team. It shows how far they would go in their first season when you compare the line-up at Villa with the one that ended the campaign at Wembley in the FA Cup final against Liverpool: Schmeichel, Irwin, Neville, May, Pallister, Keane, Cantona,

Butt, Cole (Scholes, 65), Beckham (P. Neville, 89), Giggs. Sub not used: Sharpe.

Gary Neville had taken over from Paul Parker at right-back, Butt cemented his place as Ince's replacement in central midfield, Beckham was making good progress in his bid to become Kanchelskis's replacement, Phil Neville was proving what a top-class all-rounder he was, and of course, Ryan Giggs was back in the side, reclaiming his No. 11 shirt. Plus, of course, there was the little matter of the King's return – but more of Cantona later.

In the opening-day fixture against Villa, Beckham would come on at the interval for Phil Neville and mark his appearance by scoring 8 minutes from time. His reward was to be a starting slot in the next match – the Premier League home encounter against West Ham – which United won 2-1, thanks to a Scholes goal.

Giggs was still working his way back from his hamstring woes and his reintroduction to the team of new boys was gentle. He came on as a 72nd-minute substitute for Andy Cole in the third match of the campaign, a 3-1 win over Wimbledon, again at home and again in the league.

Giggs was sub once more in the next game: the 2-1 Premier League win at Blackburn, this time coming on after 75 minutes for Scholes. He was feeling his way back and starting to build up his strength again, but Ferguson resisted the temptation to thrown him back in – keeping him on the bench for the big 3-2 win at Everton (again, in the league), in the first week of September.

Once again, he came on as a sub for Scholes, this time on 66 minutes, scoring a cracker of a goal. Word was around Old

Trafford that Ryan had been getting slightly peeved at not being back in the thrust of the action, but the boss told him that he would have to be patient; that he knew best, and that he did not want to rush it and risk losing his player to injury again.

But after Giggs's winner in the match at Everton on 9 September, Fergie knew he could not hold the boy back much longer. Not after he had scored a goal that was already a contender for Goal of the Season (eventually only beaten at the end of the campaign by another wonder goal by Manchester City's Georgi Kinkladze).

The Goodison match was an early-season opportunity for United to gain revenge on the team who pipped them to the FA Cup at Wembley just over three months previously. It was also a chance for Everton fans to finally witness the debut of Kanchelskis, who had signed for £5 million. But it was the boys who still had a future at Old Trafford who sealed the win for United. Everton went behind to a Lee Sharpe strike after only 3 minutes, and on 15 minutes Toffees fans would realise it was not going to be their day when Kanchelskis left the field in agony with a shoulder injury. Anders Limpar made it 1-1 on 27 minutes, but Sharpe put United back in front just after the interval. Everton equalised again with a Paul Rideout tap-in on 55 minutes, but Giggs killed off the contest with his acclaimed goal, just before Everton suffered a final misery when David Unsworth was sent off for a second bookable offence.

The Giggs goal had come after good work by David Beckham. The latter passed to Ryan and he waltzed to the edge of the penalty area before lashing the ball home past Neville Southall.

Pure genius and pure class.

United were now scrapping for top spot in the Premier League, separated from Newcastle only on goal difference. Giggs was hitting form and they still had the bonus of Eric Cantona's imminent return from his 8-month suspension.

A week earlier, Ryan started for the first time in the league that season – and was on target again. The Red Devils cruised to a 3-0 win over Bolton at home, with Scholes grabbing the other two goals. Ryan scored the second goal on 33 minutes; he was getting better and better as he started to put his injury woes behind him. United were starting to look awesome.

Now they had won five Premier League matches on the trot and the pundits were starting to talk about Giggs and the team in awed terms once again. Then, inexplicably, they lost form in three key matches. They exited the League Cup after a disastrous night saw them lose 3-0 at home to minnows York City and draw 0-0 at Hillsborough in a league match against Sheffield Wednesday. Then followed the most disappointing result of their season – a 2-2 draw at home to the Russians of Rotor Volgograd in the UEFA Cup first round. United had drawn 0-0 in Russia – when Giggs had given a daring wing display – and were now out on the away-goals ruling.

True, there had been mitigating circumstances. United were in the middle of a defensive injury crisis that meant youngsters Phil Neville and John O'Kane had to fill in as full-backs, but Ryan would later say that for him, this was the most disappointing moment of the campaign.

United were two down inside 30 minutes and could not manage a winner despite goals from Scholes and Schmeichel (the big Danish keeper famously headed the Reds level with 1 minute to go but sadly, it was not enough). United had 18 shots on target, but the players were disconsolate. 'We lost the game in the first 20 minutes,' said Ferguson. 'You go 2-0 down and you have a mountain to climb in Europe. They were bad goals to lose because the last thing we said before the match was that a clean sheet would win it for us – we knew we would make enough chances.'

Despite the loss, Giggs had once again been United's star man, having a hand in both goals and sending the Russian defenders dizzy with his constant running and dribbling. He played a part in the opener by setting up Andy Cole for a shot. When that shot was half-cleared, Scholes had been on hand to score. And the second United goal of the night – from Big Peter's head – was a result of the inch-perfect cross Ryan floated in for the keeper.

Heads were low as the players left Old Trafford that disappointing night at the end of September 1995. But the boss knew he didn't need to give any major morale-boosting exercises; he was convinced things would be OK and that the team would soon be back in business because the return of the King was nigh.

Yes, after a suspension lasting eight months – but seeming immeasurably longer to United fans – Eric Cantona was ready to make his comeback for the only club he ever truly cared about during his wonderful, controversial career.

Cantona returned in the red shirt on 1 October 1995, and the match couldn't have been any bigger or more heated – against their biggest, most-hated rivals, Liverpool, at home. Ryan had been one of the first to greet Cantona when he returned to first-team training a couple of weeks earlier and made a point of talking with the great man as they warmed up on the Old Trafford pitch before kick-off.

He had already freely admitted Cantona was his footballing hero and that he had learned more from him than any other player. Eric's approach to training, practising free kicks and the general search for perfection greatly impressed the young Giggs, who had taken many of the lessons he'd learned to improve his own game. He would say this of Cantona in the book *Ryan Giggs: Chasing Perfection*: 'I used to watch the way Eric trained and rested, how he lived his life. He would give me advice and I would learn from it. I would be out with Eric and someone would offer him a drink and he would turn it down, because he never drank for four days or so before a game. I took that on board. I don't have role models, but Eric's as close to one as I've had.'

And in his first autobiography, *My Story*, published in 1994, he said: 'And we signed Eric Cantona from Leeds. That was the missing piece of the jigsaw. Eric is such an incredible character; his presence alone was enough to lift us, but he was a brilliant player, too, the best in Britain and pretty close to being the best in the world. With Eric on board we believed in ourselves completely.'

The King's return against the Kop idols ended in a 2-2 draw and, typically, he would score for United – a 71-minute equaliser from the penalty spot when the Red Devils looked to be heading for a 2-1 defeat after Robbie Fowler bagged a brace. Cantona set up Nicky Butt for the opener after just a couple of minutes, but Fowler seemed set to hog the headlines with two fine goals – the first a blast past Schmeichel, the second a lob that had the keeper reeling backward in agony as it landed in the net.

But it was Cantona who would have the last laugh,

hugging a goalpost after his dramatic saving goal – a penalty brought about after Jamie Redknapp hauled Ryan to the ground in the box.

The Eric and Ryan show was back on the road and would soon wow audiences across the nation as the duo picked up the telepathic understanding they had developed before the Frenchman's ban. Ryan seemed to have an unerring ability to know where Eric was and when he should release the ball to him. Similarly, Eric would float balls to Ryan that left the opposing defenders perplexed. It was a two-man show with no equal at that time in British football.

Giggs grabbed United's third goal in the 4-1 win at Chelsea just three weeks after Cantona's return and by November the pair were back at the top of their game as individuals and a partnership of unrivalled wizardry and skill. On 18 November, Ryan put in one of his best performances of the season, destroying Southampton with a two-goal blast in the first 3 minutes at Old Trafford. United would finish 4-1 winners (the other goals coming from Scholes and Cole), but it would be Giggs who would earn all the plaudits.

The first goal was the third-quickest in Premier League history (and the fastest ever for United) and it was Eric who set him up. Scholes got Cantona moving with a pass into the opposing end of the field and Eric instinctively set up Ryan with the goal at his mercy. With just 15 seconds on the clock, the ball was in the back of the net.

Four days later Giggs was causing mayhem again, this time setting United up for a 4-0 league win at Coventry. His link with Cantona was causing rival teams problems they simply could not deal with.

But then United suffered a dip in form. December 1995 would see them fluff their lines in four of six key Premier League matches. Some pundits put it down to overconfidence, but Ferguson dished out the legendary 'hairdryer treatment' to his men after the 1-1 and 2-2 draws at home to Chelsea and Sheffield Wednesday respectively, and the 2-0 loss at Liverpool which was followed by the equally depressing 3-1 defeat at Leeds. Surely it was no coincidence that Ryan had missed three of the matches through injury, playing only at Liverpool?

But this United team were made of stern stuff: they would fight for each other and for their right to be champions again. None of them, Ryan especially, wanted to face the heartache suffered the previous season. At one time they were 13 points behind runaway leaders Newcastle, but a combination of sheer guts from the players and mind games by Fergie on nervy Toon boss Kevin Keegan meant they turned around a massive deficit to win the title.

Fergie decided to try and destabilise the man known in his playing days as 'Mighty Mouse'. Newcastle had just beaten Leeds 1-0 and Keegan famously claimed Ferguson had implied that Leeds would roll over against Newcastle – a catalyst for his rant on Sky TV: 'Things which have been said over the last few days have been almost slanderous. I think you will have to send a tape of the game to Alex Ferguson, don't you? Isn't that what he wants? You just don't say what he said about Leeds. I would love it if we could beat them. Love it. He's gone down in my estimation. Manchester United haven't won this yet; I'd love it if we beat them.'

Keegan's loss of composure certainly seemed to filter through to his team. From a position of major strength, they were eventually overwhelmed by a rampant Manchester United. The Red Devils won their final 9 league games of the season to take the title.

Giggs had again played a big part, scoring the winner in the vital match at Maine Road as United finally overpowered neighbours Manchester City 3-2. He also scored in the 5-0 win over Nottingham Forest in the penultimate league match of the season – and had the honour of grabbing United's final league goal of the season (and making sure the title was theirs) as they stole glory from Newcastle with a 3-0 home win over Middlesbrough. 'It was a great feeling to get such an important goal for the club,' he said. 'Definitely one of my best goals ever.'

'Ryan Giggs completed another day of triumph for Ferguson with another memorable goal,' trumpeted the *Guardian*.

It had been a magnificent campaign for Giggs and his partner-in-crime Cantona, and it was not over yet. There was the little matter of the FA Cup final at Wembley to come – against United's bitterest rivals, Liverpool. After the win over Boro, Ryan and the boys headed off for a celebration at the Four Seasons Hotel, near Manchester airport. The morning afterwards, they all had sore heads but knew they still had almost a week to recover before the Cup final. By the day of the game, they were all fit and raring to go.

If the pre-match entertainment and laughs were provided by Liverpool in their white suits ('John Travolta suits' as Ryan would have it), the match itself belonged to United.

For the second time in two years, Ryan Giggs would win a Cup winner's medal – but now he was to become one of the rare few who could call themselves winners of the 'double

double' – the first club to do so and the first to win the FA Cup nine times. It was a magnificent achievement, both for the club and for Ryan Giggs, a man-boy who was still only twenty-two.

This was United's third FA Cup final in as many seasons and Giggs and co. had been determined to wipe away the bad memory of the defeat by Everton the previous May. The match itself was a bit of a damp squib until 5 minutes from time when Cantona finally set it alight as he slotted the ball home after David James punched it straight to him from a corner.

Cantona, the newly crowned Footballer of the Year, was swamped by his grateful team-mates. Once again he had produced a miracle for United – his legend was now assured at the Theatre of Dreams. As was Giggs's: the two had been in fine form that season, but both wanted more. In particular, they wanted to win the European Cup. That would prove a step too far for Cantona, but for Giggs the dream would begin to take shape the following season as United finally started to make an impact in the competition for the first time since 1968.

CHAPTER 5

EURO STAR

'Giggs does things for his team that nobody else in the game can match.'

George Best, 1996

'I want to win the European Cup with United.'

Ryan Giggs, 1996

In May 1996 Ryan Giggs attended the European Champions League final as a spectator. He enjoyed the football served up by Juventus and Ajax, as well as the drama as the match ended 1-1 and went to penalties. When Juve finally triumphed 4-2 in the last-gasp shoot-out in Rome, he was on the edge of his seat but while he would never forget the night as an observer, it also had the effect of lighting a flame of fierce ambition within him.

In short, the spectacle made him want to play his own part in the ultimate club competition. Already, he had won every domestic honour with United at the age of twenty-two and now he set his sights on a new horizon: Europe and the

Champions League. After the match, he admitted, 'Seeing the atmosphere here and how big a game it is, I'd love to be involved in it next year.' His wish was not to be granted, but he was only three years away from realising the new dream.

The 1996/97 season was a pivotal one for Giggs and United in that the manager, the club, the players and the fans now set their sights on glory in the big one: the European Cup. It was as if a light had been switched on that said: 'Let's all focus on Europe now' – as if United as a club said: 'We've won the league three times after all those years of heartache, now let's set about putting that other jinx to bed.'

And it showed in the boss's transfer dealings for the new season in the summer of 1996. He brought in players that he believed possessed the necessary craft and skill to bring European Cup glory. In came five new stars, and all five were from the Continent. Karel Poborsky, a leading light for the Czech Republic in Euro '96, which was held in England, was the biggest name. Ferguson had great hopes for the winger who cost £3.5 million, but his career would ultimately fizzle out after an initial sparkling start.

Also brought in was the great Dutch maestro Johan Cruyff's son Jordi, a midfielder of promise, plus striker Ole Gunnar Solskjaer, the Norwegian who would go on to become a United legend, defender Ronny Johnsen (another Norwegian) and Dutch goalkeeper Raimond van der Gouw.

With the benefit of hindsight, only Solskjaer and Johnsen might be called long-term successes. Over the next few seasons, the two would play key roles in United's European campaigns, culminating, of course, with their contributions in the 1999 Champions League final win over Bayern Munich in

Barcelona. Solskjaer was one of Ferguson's greatest buys ever at just £1.5 million from FC Molde – he would go on to amass a pile of honours at Old Trafford.

Johnsen was less exulted among the United faithful but still played his part in taking them to the very summit of club football in his 6-year spell at the club. The centre-back was another bargain buy at just £1.2 million from Turkish outfit Besiktas.

With these new signings it was clear that Ferguson was now trying to bend and mould United into a veritable force in Europe. He was aiming to bring in players who could add a deftness and more thoughtful approach; players who would slow the game down and help United avoid the pitfalls of playing at their traditional gung-ho pace – a pace that often left them exposed at the back as everyone dashed up field to try and be hero.

This tactic would not prove an overnight success, but United certainly took giant strides towards becoming more competitive in Europe that season. For the first time since 1969, they would reach the semi-finals of the European Cup, losing out at that stage to eventual winners, Borussia Dortmund.

Giggs was distraught after the defeat by the Germans, but consoled himself with the thought that genuine progress had been made on this all-important new front. And his performances along the way brought him personal accolades from writers among the foreign press that conjured up those bestowed on George Best in the mid-1960s.

United had drawn the short straw in their opening salvos in the competition – defending champions Juventus were up against them in Group C. On the plus side, they had also come out of the hat with two less-fancied teams – Fenerbahce of Turkey and Rapid Vienna from Austria.

The Reds' form in the group is best described as topsy-turvy: they lost both matches to Juve and managed to lose at home to the Turks. Yet they also won in Turkey and Vienna, and beat Rapid at home to qualify for the quarter-finals on 9 points – 2 ahead of Fenerbahce and 7 behind runaway group winners, Juve.

The 1-0 loss at Old Trafford to the Italian champions marked United's second home defeat in Europe for 40 years (the first had come a few weeks earlier against Fenerbahce). But the defeat had its upside – namely a fabulous second-half showing from Giggs, who tormented the visiting defence with his dazzling runs and deft skills. He sent over several fine crosses that the strike force of Cantona and Solskjaer would normally be expected to bury. It also made up for his poor showing in the first match against the Italians, two months earlier. He had been so ineffective that the boss had withdrawn him at half time and sent on Brian McClair. Ryan was angry about the decision, but at least it had the effect of firing him up for the home return. Yet even he could not dismantle the mighty Juve alone. As it was, a penalty converted by Alessandro del Piero killed off United at Old Trafford.

Though wounded at their double defeat by the champions, the Reds were not in despair. The boss told them they still had a great chance of winning the competition. Ryan and his team-mates determined to put all their efforts into trying to do so, even though it meant they would relinquish their hold on the FA Cup. Something had to give as United began to push for the European Cup.

Giggs showed his confidence had not been affected by the Juve defeat as the Reds travelled to Austria for their final group match against Rapid on 4 December 1996. It was a must-win game if they were to progress beyond the group stage for the first time – and they did just that. On a cold night by the Danube, Ryan was the star man as he and Cantona led the Austrians a merry dance. He opened the scoring on 24 minutes and Eric sealed the win at 19 minutes from the end.

The Giggs goal was a classic as both he and the King passed the ball around from the halfway line before Ryan finished off the move with a precision shot. At the same time, Fenerbahce went down 2-0 in Turin to Juve, confirming United's progress to the last eight.

In the quarter-finals they were paired with Porto, and for the first time since Wembley 1968 Manchester United truly looked like candidates to lift the European Cup. They simply steamrolled the Portuguese challenge and once again Giggs was the man who sparkled most. As in Vienna, he and Cantona were simply unstoppable and tormented the poor Portuguese backline with their non-stop flicks, tricks, killer passes plus a goal apiece in the 4-0 first-leg triumph at Old Trafford on 5 March 1997.

Afterwards the *Daily Telegraph* said of the Ryan and Eric show: 'United they attacked. Ryan Giggs and Eric Cantona conjuring pass after precision pass to embarrass the pride of Portugal.' At the time Giggs would say that it was 'probably the best game I've ever had for United.'

The return leg in Portugal would be something of an anti-climax after the thrills and spills at Old Trafford but for United the 0-0 draw meant mission accomplished. Giggs told friends it was one of the best moments of his short, but already glittering career and that he couldn't wait to 'get among' the Germans of Borussia in the two-legged semi that now loomed.

I have spoken to United insiders and staff from that period and there is a general acceptance that some in the Red camp tended to underestimate their opponents; there was a belief that somehow the hard work had now been done and the only real threat would come if, and when, they made the final against Juventus. I am also told that Giggs and Ferguson were certainly not among those who allowed a bit of complacency to creep in.

No, both men knew that the Germans were not the team to just sit back and accept defeat. They would work their socks off and battle for the right to be in the final themselves. And so it proved.

Ryan would later admit this to be one of the most disappointing moments of his career when United lost at the semi-final hurdles of the tournament that season. And the taste of defeat was all the more bitter as they managed to lose both legs, by a single goal on each occasion. In the first leg in Dortmund, on 9 April 1997, Raimond van der Gouw was beaten by a long-range speculative effort from René Tretschok. But United left the Westfalenstadion still confident they could overturn the 1-0 deficit.

However, they got off to the worst possible start at Old Trafford a fortnight later when a seventh-minute goal from Lars Ricken put them 2-0 behind and chasing the game. Given United's traditional renowned resilience and ability to rally even in the last minutes of matches, you would still not have written them off. Yet, amazingly, the usually reliable Cantona and Andy Cole missed a series of half-chances and United were out of the competition, humbled by a team most pundits would never have picked to make the final.

It would be scant consolation to Giggs that Dortmund would go on to cause an even bigger upset in the final by beating Juve 3-1 in Munich. That was one Champions League final the Welsh wonder certainly had little appetite to observe, let alone savour.

Ferguson felt United had exited in the worst manner in that they had not made a proper fight of it against the Germans. They appeared limp and out-of-sorts and he admitted to being frustrated as well as disappointed with his players' work over the two legs but at least his United were making progress in the Champions League at long last – and the rest of the season had been a relative success for them.

It began with a 4-0 trouncing of Newcastle in the predecessor to the Community Shield, the Charity Shield at Wembley. United had a new captain in Cantona, who had taken the armband from Birmingham-bound Steve Bruce. In David Beckham, they had a new star to match Giggs and he announced his arrival on the world stage with a stunning goal against Wimbledon in the opening-day league fixture at Selhurst Park, when he lobbed the ball over goalkeeper Neil Sullivan's head from the halfway line. At the end of the season Beckham was to earn further acclaim when he was voted PFA Young Player of the Year – just as Ryan Giggs had been voted at the start of his pro career.

Meanwhile, Ryan was trying to shake off a lingering injury when the season began and would not make his first league start until the end of August: in the 2-2 draw with Blackburn at Old Trafford. United suffered an unusual rocky spell at the end of October 1996, with shock 5-0 losses away at Newcastle and 6-3 at Southampton. They also lost their next league match, at home to Chelsea, 2-1. Giggs missed all three setbacks through injury but his return in the following game, against Arsenal at home, coincided with United's own return to form. Was this coincidence or indeed, proof of the Welsh magician's ability to turn a game for the Reds?

United beat Arsenal 1-0, thanks to an own-goal from Nigel Winterburn, and stormed off on a brilliant 16-game unbeaten league run. It would last from the match against the Gunners (16 November 1996) to 8 March 1997 and would turn the season around for them, helping to secure their fourth title in five seasons. United would finish 7 points clear of Newcastle, Arsenal and Liverpool, who all achieved 68 points.

Giggs excelled during January 1997, scoring a couple of fine goals in the midst of United's unbeaten run. He lashed home the opener in his team's 2-0 win at Highfield Road and 11 days later came to United's rescue at Old Trafford against Wimbledon. The Reds had been losing 1-0 to a Chris Perry goal on the hour, but 11 minutes later Ryan settled nerves with the equaliser and Andy Cole won the match with his goal, 7 minutes from time. By the end of the campaign, Giggs's trophy cupboard was already beginning to sag beneath the weight of his honours: he had won four Premier League titles, two FA Cups, a League Cup, the European Super Cup, four Charity Shields and two PFA Young Player of the Year awards. And he was still only twenty-three!

Nevertheless, the next 12 months would prove to be a real

anti-climax for him. The bad news would begin shortly after the season ended with the shock revelation that his mentor and hero, the great Cantona, was quitting United and football. Eric was only thirty years old and Ryan was stunned by the retirement, telling friends he couldn't believe it.

On 11 May 1997 Cantona, as United captain, lifted the Premiership trophy aloft at Old Trafford after a 2-0 win over West Ham and then walked out of Old Trafford for the last time. He had made 191 appearances and scored 88 goals for United. In a prepared statement, he explained that he wanted to do other things outside of football, including acting, something he was particularly attracted to (and at which he would prove more than adept, especially in the wonderful 2009 movie *Looking For Eric*).

He said, 'I have played professional football for 13 years, which is a long time. I now wish to do other things. I have always planned to retire when I was at the top and at Manchester United I have reached the pinnacle of my career. In the last four and a half years I have enjoyed my best football and had a wonderful time. I have had a marvellous relationship with the manager, coach, staff, players and not least the fans. I wish Manchester United even more success in the future.'

At the time, inside sources at the club also told me that Cantona had become disillusioned with the finances of the game – that he did not like the idea of being a 'cash cow' for United in terms of how many shirts or souvenirs bearing his name and the number 7 were sold.

His decision to leave most definitely took the club by surprise. The bombshell was announced by chairman Martin

Edwards at a hastily convened news conference. Ferguson was also present, but the King had already returned to France. Edwards said, 'Eric Cantona has indicated his wish to retire from the game. He is away on holiday with his family at the moment. Eric has been a marvellous servant for United. He came to see me on Thursday and told me of his intentions.'

'It's a sad day for United,' said a clearly shell-shocked Ferguson. 'He has been a fantastic player for the club and we have won six trophies in his time with us. Eric has had a huge impact on the development of our younger players. He has been a model professional in the way he conducted himself and has been a joy to manage. Whenever fans discuss United's greatest-ever side, you can be sure that for many Eric's name will be very high up on the list.

'He leaves with our best wishes and will always be welcome at Old Trafford.'

Six years later (in 2003), Eric Cantona was in London to accept the award for being voted the Overseas Player of the Decade (covering the first 10 years of the Premiership). He admitted he may have exited United and the game too early: 'When you quit football it is not easy, your life becomes difficult. I should know because sometimes I feel I quit too young. I loved the game, but I no longer had the passion to go to bed early, not to go out with my friends, not to drink, and not to do a lot of other things – the things I like in life.'

The view that Cantona had quit too young was one shared by many at United, but after he had gone, it opened a door for other players to shine and take on his mantle as United's leader. Roy Keane became the new skipper, followed by Gary Neville – and Ryan Giggs would eventually become Neville's deputy. Giggs had already been putting in plenty of effort to help nurture the production line of youngsters from the youth team into the first team. Now he would step up his work and become respected as one of United's senior pros – at the tender age of twenty-three.

Six years after Cantona's retirement, he would also be named in that Premiership Team of the Decade although, amazingly, Roy Keane would not go on to do so (controversially, the Irish lionheart lost out to Patrick Vieira). The team read: Peter Schmeichel, Gary Neville, Tony Adams, Marcel Desailly, Denis Irwin, David Beckham, Paul Scholes, Patrick Vieira, Ryan Giggs, Alan Shearer, Eric Cantona.

The new 1997/98 season began with hope but more than a little trepidation for Giggsy and his team-mates. They were aiming to keep their title and hopefully go one step further in Europe – by reaching the final of the Champions League – but there was the small factor of Cantona's retirement and whether they could cope without his inspiration and leadership.

The answer, a resounding 'no', came within two months of the opening of the campaign but it would not just be down to the massive hole left by Eric's departure – Keane himself would also miss the season after sustaining a terrible injury at Elland Road on 27 September. Leeds triumphed with a goal from big defender David Wetherall, 10 minutes before the interval, but the big talking point came when Keane suffered a cruciate ligament injury in a clash with Alf-Inge Haaland. Some claim that he deliberately tripped the Norwegian and fell from the alleged foul. But it was Keane – and United – who would suffer most with the injury that was to wreck his season. It was also an incident that would have an acrimonious ending, years later: Keane would never forget how Haaland stood over him, shouting that he was not injured and that he was a cheat who was pretending. He would controversially tackle him in a derby match against Manchester City (whom Haaland had since joined) in 2001.

Meanwhile, Keane was written off for the whole of the 1997/98 season. Without the influential skipper and the wondrous Cantona, it was simply asking too much of United's kids to steer the ship home. The campaign would prove a write-off for Ryan. It would be only the second season since he turned pro in 1991/92 that he would not win a major honour (the other being in that barren campaign of 1994/95). His only double would be a Charity Shield winner's medal and the in-house award at United of the Sir Matt Busby Player of the Year trophy (voted for by the fans).

In the Charity Shield, United beat Chelsea 4-2 on penalties at Wembley after the match ended 1-1. Even then, Ryan's joy was muted – he was withdrawn to make way for David Beckham, 18 minutes from time.

And he was devastated when United surrendered their league crown that season. He had played as well as anyone in the absence of Keane and did his level best to keep United firing on all cylinders but United finished runners-up, 1 point behind their then bitterest rivals, Arsenal. This was despite some quality performances without Keane at the heart of the team – they certainly didn't lack goal power, finishing with 73 scored, 5 more than the Gunners. Once again, Ferguson had bought well in the summer, bringing in the class footballing brain and scoring boots of Teddy Sheringham as Cantona's direct replacement. The £3 million bargain buy from Spurs proved an effective, subtle foil for the more abrasive, direct work of Cole and Solskjaer.

In October and November 1997, United crushed the finest South Yorkshire had to offer in two consecutive weeks: they beat Barnsley 7-0 at home on 25 October and followed this up with the 6-1 demolition of Sheffield Wednesday on 1 November. Giggs helped himself to a brace against the Tykes. United led the league for most of the season, but this success and the flurry of goals was not enough as the Gunners sneaked in to take the crown.

The rush of goals was also a staple in United's FA Cup campaign – they won 5-3 at Chelsea in the third round and lashed Walsall 5-1 in the next. But they would disappointingly – and unexpectedly – exit in the fifth round to Barnsley. Giggs was rested from the team that lost the replay 3-2 at Oakwell on 22 February 1998, after the first match ended 1-1 at Old Trafford.

There would also be gloom in Europe as the Reds went out a stage earlier than in the previous season, losing to French outfit Monaco in the quarter-finals. Hopes had been high that United might just be good enough to progress to the final when, four days after Keane was carried off at Elland Road, they overcame the might of Juventus in the group stages at Old Trafford. On 1 October, Ryan played one of his greatest games for the club – and scored one of his greatest goals – as United won 3-2. Giggsy stole in for what would prove to be the winner, 1 minute from time. His goal made it 3-1 after Alessandro del Piero put Juve in front after just 13 seconds. Sheringham and Scholes then put United 2-1 ahead and gave them control of the match before Giggsy's strike. But the great

Zinedine Zidane grabbed the Turin giants' second goal a minute after Ryan's effort, ensuring a nerve-racking finale.

United would lose the return 1-0 in Turin, but still topped the group with 15 points, 3 ahead of Juve.

After all the optimism and clamour for success that had built up during the winter break for their chances in the competition, they blew it at the next stage, losing a quarter-final encounter against Monaco that they were expected to have won comfortably. Ryan missed both legs as United lost on the away-goals rule after drawing 0-0 in France and 1-1 at Old Trafford, a fortnight later. It was a blow for the winger and the club: their European dream cancelled out for yet another year. Again, it could hardly have been mere coincidence that Giggs was missing for five crucial matches with a hamstring injury, from 4 to 18 March. In two of them, against Monaco, they would exit the Champions League, and in the other three they would suffer major damage to their chances of retaining their Premier League crown. Without Ryan, United lost 2-0 at Sheffield Wednesday and drew 1-1 at West Ham – and, most damagingly, lost the vital battle against Arsenal 1-0 at Old Trafford on 14 March. The loss, courtesy of a Marc Overmars goal on 79 minutes, would be a real blow to morale.

What if Giggs had been involved in those key games? Maybe I would have been writing now about how United concluded a remarkable double of the Premier League and Champions League in 1998, without the influence of their injured skipper. But it was not to be, and it would be Real Madrid who would go on to claim their seventh European Cup win as they beat Juventus 1-0.

Naturally, Ryan was downhearted, wondering if he and United would ever break the jinx that had haunted the club since 1968. But, as the darkness of a miserable season settled, little did he know that the next campaign was to be the greatest of his life – and the greatest in the wonderful heritage of Manchester United FC as they stormed to an incredible Treble triumph.

CHAPTER 6

TREBLES ALL ROUND

'I got twisted blood trying to mark him in training.'
Former United centre-half Gary Pallister, 2003

One year on from the heartache of winning nothing, Ryan Giggs was to celebrate lifting the most amazing set of trophies ever in British football. By the end of the next campaign, the 1998/99 season, he would take home medals for United's triumphs in the FA Cup, the Premier League and of course, most important of all, the Champions League as the club finally ended the hoodoo that had haunted Old Trafford for all of 31 unforgiving years.

In fact, as wondrous glory followed wondrous glory, the only question at the end of that season was this: Why, given the quality of his performances and his contribution to the magical Treble, was Ryan Giggs not named Footballer of the

Year? Not that he himself would complain. He was too much of a gent to do that, but privately he must have wondered what it would take for him to win the award if a Treble and the goal of the season against Arsenal in the FA Cup wasn't enough. Eventually, his patience was to be rewarded, but not for another 10 years!

Finally he had got the misery of the previous campaign's ultimate collapse out of his system as he joined United on their pre-season tour to Scandinavia and he worked his way back to fitness in the two matches there and with regular pre-season training. He was delighted to learn that the boss had brought in two top-quality reinforcements in Jaap Stam, signed for £10.8 million from PSV Eindhoven and thought to be one of the world's best defenders, and the attacking strength of Dwight Yorke, a £12 million purchase from Aston Villa.

Both signings added to the sense of purpose around the place as Old Trafford buzzed with pre-season anticipation. Stam would surely add a rock-solid presence at the heart of the backline – he was renowned as 'a one-man defence' back in Holland and Ryan labelled him 'a beast of a man' – and Yorke, with his bubbly personality and cheery demeanour, might be just the man to bring out the best in the introspective Andy Cole. Cole had struck up a good partnership with Sheringham, but the pair had never got on, off the pitch. Yorke was to become the ideal partner up front for him.

Jesper Blomqvist, a tricky winger from Parma, was also brought in. Unlike his fellow Scandinavian, Jesper Olsen – a real star at United in the 1980s – he never set the club alight. Having said that, Blomqvist would ultimately land a place in United's history books as he played his part in the Treble campaign, particularly in the European Champions League final, when he was called upon because of the suspensions ruling out Scholes and Keane.

The season began with a surprise as Ryan failed to pick up his now-customary Charity Shield winner's medal. This time United were overpowered 3-0 by Arsenal and some fans wondered if this might be a bad omen. With 20 minutes still to go, Giggs – along with Andy Cole – was subbed by an impatient Ferguson.

But the boss was not in the mood to take chances – he had a bigger clash on his mind than the charity bash against the Gunners. Just three days afterwards, United were in action for the first of two August games that would define their season – the home clash in the European Cup second qualifying round against Lodz of Poland. Naturally, Ferguson didn't want his key players such as Giggs and Cole missing because of what was, essentially, a pre-season friendly.

It was good thinking and produced the right result – Giggs scored the first goal as United beat Lodz 2-0 at Old Trafford, with Cole notching the second. It is striking how many vital goals Ryan has come up with during his career; how many led United on to much greater things. And this was just another one, and it would end with them becoming the first team who had to qualify for the actual competition to lift the Champions League. Another first brought about by another Giggsy first as United held out comfortably for a 0-0 draw in Lodz, a fortnight later.

Their league campaign began three days after the home match with the Poles and United looked tired. Yes, even though the season had just begun. Giggs played the full 90 against Leicester, but at times found the going tough in a game the Reds were always chasing. They managed a 2-2 draw but had to come back from 2-0 down, with just 11 minutes remaining. A week later they drew their next league match 0-0 at West Ham and the fans began to question aloud whether this was going to be, after all, another dud season like the last one, even with Keane back in business.

But they needn't have worried for the team would now go on a run that would see them unbeaten in 19 out of 20 matches – with Ryan impressing down that left wing and firing in crosses the strikers hungrily fed upon. And the results in the league and Europe were commendable: in the Champions League group stages, they drew 3-3 twice against the might of Barcelona, drew 2-2 at Bayern Munich and thrashed Brondby 6-2 away. Typically, it was Giggs who opened the scoring in the first clash with Barca, at Old Trafford on 16 September 1998. And it was a rarity – a Ryan Giggs' header! Afterwards, he admitted that he had 'really enjoyed the match' and 'Neither team deserved to lose, but that doesn't mean we're happy with a point, especially after leading for so long.' He would miss the return at the Camp Nou at the end of November where United led 3-2 until Rivaldo equalised.

In the league they beat Liverpool 2-0 at home and Everton 4-1 away, the double-mugging of their Mersey rivals proving particularly sweet to United fans. And a 1-1 draw with Bayern in the final match of Group D meant United successfully qualified for the next Champions League stage as runners-up to the Germans.

By Christmas, Aston Villa were unexpected league leaders,

but they would come down along with the lights on the tree as the festive season turned into the New Year. Then it became a three-horse race for the title between United, Arsenal and Chelsea. By the turn of the year, Giggs and co. were set up for what looked like an exciting push to the finishing line in three competitions – the FA Cup, the Premier League and the Champions League.

On 3 January, they walloped Middlesbrough 3-1 in the third round of the FA Cup, with Ryan grabbing the second Reds goal. And the amazing landmark fact of that encounter is this: the Boro match was the first of 31 ties in the Cup, the league and the Champions League that United would play from January 1999 to the end of the season in May 1999 – and they would go unbeaten in *all* of them!

It was a remarkable achievement, given the stress that Ryan and the rest of the boys must have been under as they battled to stay in contention for the Treble by achieving back-to-back results in all three competitions. As the pressure mounted, Giggs and Keane were the key men: Giggs for his calmness and composure, Keane for his never-say-die attitude and belief. They needed to be in the run-in, with Arsenal still breathing down their necks in the league and tough challenges in the Champions League and the FA Cup.

In the league, it would all come down to the final game of the season – the home clash with Spurs. This was the first of three matches in a 10-day period that would decide the Treble: Spurs on 16 May, Newcastle in the FA Cup final on 22 May and the big one, Bayern Munich in the Champions League final on 26 May. Coincidentally, 26 May would have been Sir Matt Busby's 90th birthday.

The Reds knew they had to beat Spurs to win the league – even a draw could see Arsenal overtake them. In a tense encounter, they kept their nerve, eventually coming through 2-1 after falling behind to a Les Ferdinand goal on 24 minutes. With Ryan's flowing passes and dribbling, they eventually broke down the Spurs' rearguard with goals from Beckham and Cole to lift the title by a single point from Arsenal (79 points to the Gunners' 78), with Chelsea third on 75.

It was Ryan Giggs's fifth league title and he celebrated quietly with the rest of his squad, knowing full well that the job was only a third done. He knew there would be plenty of time for a proper drink and a party if they managed to clear the subsequent two hurdles.

Next up was the FA Cup final against the Toon at Wembley. It was Giggs who had done more than anyone to get the boys to the final, with that goal against Arsenal in the semi-replay at Villa Park. He described it as, 'My best goal ever, and the one I'd like to be remembered by.' Suffice it to say, it is a goal that will be up there among the greatest ever scored by a United man, and the real beauty was that it instilled in the team a new hope and inspiration that they could win the Treble at a time when their chances seemed to be ebbing away. United had been at a disadvantage after Keane was sent off and heads were dropping. Ryan stormed in to blow away the cobwebs of gloom and lashed United forward to their dream date with destiny.

It is also worth remembering that Schmeichel had had to save a last-minute penalty from Dennis Bergkamp in the semi, and that along the way United also saw off the challenges of Liverpool and Chelsea. As they staggered on to those final three games of the campaign, the Reds had hardly had an easy ride.

After the tension and drama of the semi, the final against Newcastle was a much more low-key affair, almost an anti-climax. On 22 May 1999, the two Uniteds clashed at the old Wembley Stadium in what would turn out to be a one-sided affair. Newcastle were hardly distinguished rivals – they had finished the league campaign in 13th position and it was 30 years exactly since they won a major trophy: the Inter-Cities Fairs Cup, one of the predecessors to the UEFA Cup. They last lifted the FA Cup in 1955 and the top-flight championship in 1927.

Yet they were managed by brilliant former AC Milan and Holland international Ruud Gullit and so hopes were high on Tyneside this might be their year: the night before the big game I talked with him at the Kensington Hotel, where the Toon were based for the final. Gullit told me he was confident his team could end the long wait for major trophy glory. He was in a bubbly mood, as was key man Alan Shearer – the player Giggs told me United feared most at Wembley.

Gullit gave me two VIP tickets for the final – as a sports writer on the *Sun*, I was going to escort a deserving Newcastle fan, who had won a competition set up by the club in tandem with the paper.

I must say that the antics of the guests we were sitting among in the Newcastle VIP section were far more entertaining than the match itself. TV presenters Ant and Dec were enjoying several crafty fags, much to the annoyance of nearby pop star Sting. And another rock legend, Bryan Ferry of Roxy Music fame, tried to look cool in the heat in a suit and tie. Everyone else was in short sleeves, but Bryan insisted on striking his pose, even though the cool customer act was ruined when he consistently drew a hanky out of his pocket to mop his brow.

Their hometown team was just as much off the pace (and out of place) on the field. Newcastle never posed much of a threat to the newly crowned league champions: they were a disappointment, a real let-down to the loyal army who followed them, week in, week out, and who had been looking for an escape, however temporary, from the bread-and-butter football their team served up over the season. For sure, it was a day out for the Geordie hordes, but a miserable one at that. Even their constant chants of 'You can stick yer fuckin' Treble up yer arse' ultimately faded as they realised the only glory team on the pitch was the one in red.

Afterwards, I was told that Ryan and his team-mates were surprised at how little threat the Toon had posed and how they had expected them to at least provide a stern test. Instead, they simply didn't turn up as United sauntered to a record tenth FA Cup win – and another double. United won 2-0, with goals from Scholes and Sheringham.

Giggs came into his own during the second half as Newcastle started to tire. He sent over a wonderful cross that Andy Cole should have converted and went so close to making it 3-0 with a fine volley. With minutes remaining, he then set up Sheringham from close range, but Teddy could only angle the ball onto the crossbar when it would have been easier to claim his second goal of the match.

Afterwards Ferguson said he was delighted with the result. 'That's fantastic – three doubles in five years. The boys were marvellous. This has been a tremendous season and once again, the players produced when it mattered,' he purred, adding that the three key men had been Sheringham, Beckham and Giggs. He knew they were strong players who would last the course of the match (Sheringham had come on after just 8 minutes as a sub for the injured Keane) – and that their stamina and trickery would ultimately be too much for the Toon to cope with.

And so it would prove.

At the end of the match Giggs was also dancing a jig of joy but like the rest of the United squad, he would refrain from wild partying for the moment. Instead, the boys went from Wembley to Bisham Abbey for a day's preparation for the big one. They watched videos of Bayern Munich and worked on tactics. It was a case of two down, one to go – and the one left was the big one, the one that mattered most. Just four days after beating the Toon, United would attempt to bring the European Cup home.

This was no time for gambling: Giggs knew that he and his team-mates had to stay calm, cool and composed for one more battle, one more success: then, and only then, could they pop open the champagne bottles with abandon. He told friends: 'We haven't completed the job – we're two-thirds there, but the hardest bit is to come on Wednesday. We will need to turn up and be at our best, if we are to be the winners. But we are confident. Roll on, Wednesday!'

Before we analyse the biggest night in Ryan Giggs's life – that firecracker of a final at the Nou Camp – let's first backtrack a little to fill in the gaps of United's European campaign from the New Year of 1999. After successfully negotiating the group stages, the Reds were paired with Inter Milan in the last eight. On 3 March 1999, they beat the Italians 2-0 at Old Trafford, thanks to a brace from Dwight Yorke, and drew the return 1-1, a fortnight later.

That set up a tough showdown in the semis – with another trip to Italy against Juventus. Giggs skinned Inter full back Francesco Colonnese over the two legs in the previous match and was now full of confidence that he could repeat his feats against Juve – although he would be up against a much tougher and resilient character in the Serb Zoran Mirkovic. United would draw the first leg 1-1 at Old Trafford. The Italians took the lead on 25 minutes when Edgar Davids set up Antonio Conte – with the midfielder hammering the ball past Peter Schmeichel. Juve held on to their lead until the last minute of normal time, when Giggs saved United from despair as he fired home from 5 yards after Juve failed to clear their lines. Ryan was jubilant, running across to salute the relieved home fans and earning a warm embrace from his manager as he left the field. But he urged caution when asked how he felt: yes, he had saved the day, but the toughest test was still to come as he and his team-mates now had to somehow grind out a result in Turin a fortnight later or forget their Treble dream.

The return would be the watershed between the glory of Wembley in '68 and the barren European years up to the night of 21 April 1999. Manchester United would at last overcome the fear, nerves and disappointment that marred those 31 years as they returned to the biggest stage in world club football with a tremendous win in Turin. It was arguably their greatest result ever away from home in Europe because so much rested upon it and because they recorded it only after overcoming the greatest adversity.

More than that, they had to do so without Giggs. The boy was gutted to miss out on the Turin return, thanks to the ankle strain he had suffered in the famous FA Cup semi-final against Arsenal the week before. United had lost their key man of the season, the man whose inspirational goals had taken them to the FA Cup final and given them hope that all was not lost as they travelled to Italy for the second leg of this semi-final.

Juve were over-confident when they learned Giggs would be missing. On the night, they walked out, heads high with just a swagger of arrogance, for what they anticipated would be a comfortable win that would propel them to their fourth consecutive European Cup final.

It appeared their assessment was spot on as they went 2-0 up within 11 minutes, thanks to a double from Filippo Inzaghi. United heads started to drop – they had a mountain to climb – and they would have to go onwards and upwards without Giggs. Meanwhile, his replacement, Jesper Blomqvist, was proving a wholly inadequate stand-in.

But cometh the hour, cometh the man, as Keane – urged on by 6,000 United fans in the Stade Delle Alpi – turned in a true captain's performance. By the end of the night those loyalists would be celebrating, silencing the fireworks and taunts of the Old Lady's Ultra fanatics.

From a David Beckham corner on 25 minutes, Keane rose superbly to head home, the precision and power of his effort giving keeper Peruzzi no chance. Then calamity struck: Keane received a yellow card 8 minutes later for catching Zidane with a tackle. It would rule him out of the final, should United get there. But this was no Paul 'Gazza' Gascoigne. Ironically enough, it had been at the same stadium that Gazza suffered an emotional breakdown when booked, 9 years earlier. Playing for England against Germany in the World Cup semi final, he burst into tears when it dawned upon him that the indiscretion would rule him out of the final, should England make it.

But Keane was made of sterner stuff; he was club captain and would die for United. Now he proved it as he regained his cool and led the team to the Promised Land against all odds. More annoyed than self-pitiful for putting himself in a similar position to Gascoigne, he would only wallow in his own loss after the match ended and rebuke himself for losing out on what should have been the greatest night of his footballing life because of a silly tackle. Two minutes after his booking, United showed they could never be written off as Yorke put them level on the night, but ahead on the away-goals' rule. He had failed to find the net in seven games, but now made amends with a diving header in the same corner as Keane's opener.

Then, 6 minutes from time, the miracle comeback was complete as Andy Cole fired the ball home to take the Red Devils into the final. They would meet Bayern Munich, with whom they had twice drawn in the group stages.

Giggs admitted that he owed his first-ever European Cup Final appearance to the starring performance of his skipper, Roy Keane. 'He's world-class, a true great,' he would rave. And Juve legend Roberto Bettega would compliment Giggs, Keane and all the United men on their achievements over the two legs, saying simply, 'Congratulations gentlemen – you outclassed us.'

Now it was on to stage three of the so-called impossible dream: the final in Barcelona. United flew to Barcelona on Concorde and then set up HQ at their hotel in the nearby coastal resort of Sitges. Giggs had returned to fitness and starred in the FA Cup final win. The day after that Wembley waltz over Newcastle he knew he was fit and ready for the big one. No way was he going to miss out!

Ferguson admitted he had rested two of his big players at Wembley – Jaap Stam and Dwight Yorke – but said both would definitely be fit to play in Barcelona. Of course, Keane and Scholes were out with suspensions (although Roy would have missed the match anyway through the injury he picked up at Wembley), which meant the roles and performances of two other red heroes were vital. In the absence of Keane and Scholes, Beckham would be required to pick up the pieces in central midfield while Giggs would be asked to contribute in a different role.

The left-winger would start on the right as Ferguson brought in Jesper Blomqvist in Giggs's usual role on the left wing. Again, it was part of the boss's plan to consolidate the midfield. Nicky Butt was to complete the midfield line-up, being asked to play the Keane role alongside Beckham's adaptation of Scholes's duties. Not all would pan out as well as United hoped, however: if you assess the final in purely unemotional terms, from a neutral perspective the Reds were outplayed by the Germans for most of the match and were chasing the game for the majority of the normal 90 minutes.

They were fortunate, maybe even charmed, to have won

with those two late wonder strikes from Sheringham and Solskjaer after Mario Basler put Bayern ahead after just 6 minutes. Bayern's skipper Lothar Matthaus, who captained West Germany to World Cup victory in 1990, went on record to say that United were very lucky to have won: 'To lose a final is always hard, especially this way. Tonight it was not the best team that won, but the luckiest. But we must not blame anyone, especially in normal time. It's bitter, sad and unbelievable. We're all disappointed. You can't blame the team – we had the match in control for 90 minutes, we had bad luck, hitting the post and the crossbar. What happened afterwards is simply inexplicable.'

Naturally, Fergie disagreed, saying United had deservedly triumphed. 'This is the best moment of my life,' he said. 'I'm really proud of my players, proud of my heritage and my family for what they have given me. I simply don't know where to begin, but you can't deny people with this spirit we have and that's why we have won this trophy. Football is such a funny game – it's a fairytale, really.'

He would also pay tribute to Giggs for his role in the win, saying, 'The strain Ryan put on the opposition was one of the factors that steadily drained them in the second half.'

But was it any surprise that United struggled over the 90 minutes, given the tricky re-working of the team and the fact that they couldn't rely on the tactics and formation that the players had grown accustomed to over a formidable season? Without Keane and Scholes any team might have struggled. Ryan did well in his adaptive role, setting up attacks and spraying the ball about as he went right, left and ventured into central midfield. And let's not forget that it was he who set up the United equaliser: after meeting a Beckham corner, he let fly from the edge of the box with his right foot only to see Sheringham latch onto it and turn the ball home at the edge of the 6-yard box.

But Beckham and Blomqvist were not so impressive. For months, Beckham had been pleading to be given a chance to show that he could be the creative fulcrum of the team, but when the chance came he was found lacking – just as he would, when tried for England. Up against a powerful Bayern midfield, he was unable to dictate play. The simple fact was that he was an unequalled ball-crosser and taker of free kicks, but he was no Scholes in central midfield.

Giggs would add that another contributing factor was that United simply froze on the night and that the occasion got to them so they were too inhibited to play their normal game. Yet they followed up the Miracle of Turin in the semi-final with the Miracle of Barca in the final itself. In his 2005 autobiography, Ryan described the feeling at the final whistle in this way: 'I've never known anything like the emotion that spilled out in that moment, and I never will again.'

The triumph meant United had become only the fourth side in history to win both their domestic league and cup competitions as well as Europe's premier club tournament in the same season. Only Celtic in 1967, Ajax Amsterdam in 1972 and PSV Eindhoven in 1988 previously managed the same feat.

Of a total of 62 competitive games in the Treble season, United had won 36, drew 22 and lost just 4 – three matches in the league and one in the Carling Cup when Ferguson fielded the reserves. They had scored a total of 128 goals, conceded 60 and remained unbeaten in all 13 European matches, winning 6 and drawing 7.

The stoppage-time goals from Sheringham and Solskjaer would gloss over the failings of the side put out by Ferguson that night in Barcelona, but Ryan Giggs was not be fooled. United had been fortunate to come back from 1-0 down, and even though Keane and Scholes would return, the fear was that the success would go to some of the other players' heads. Little wonder, as much of the talk after the final centred on whether United were now the best club side ever.

Fans of the Beautiful Game were not convinced – most agreed that United had been lucky and that they had been outplayed. One such fan, Darren Jalland, summed up the general feeling, saying, 'I don't see how a team who were lucky to get two goals in injury time in the European Cup final when they didn't look like scoring for the other 90 minutes can be called the best side around now, let alone ever! Let's not forget that if it wasn't for similar luck earlier on in the season against Liverpool, they wouldn't have won the FA Cup. Sure, they are a very good team, but if anyone thinks that they are the best ever, then they need a reality check!'

Another footie fan, Craig Bloomfield, also spoke for many (including several United followers) when he remarked, 'Escaping from the hype for a moment, let's analyse what actually happened in Barcelona. United were outplayed and outclassed for the entire match and then scrambled two goals to clinch what was, from a neutral perspective, an undeserved victory. It has been a memorable season for United, but they have to go down as one of the most unconvincing sides to ever win the European Cup. Bayern must be kicking themselves because they will surely never play such poor opposition in a major final.'

Certainly, Roy Keane did not believe that he and United had 'made it'. He was worried that complacency could set in and I am told Ryan had similar misgivings in private. There was a dreaded feeling that if United now sat on their laurels, the only way would be down after that balmy, wonderful night in Barca. After all, the great Peter Schmeichel had played his final match for the club that night and the team would need fine-tuning in other key areas, if success was to be maintained.

It wasn't something that Giggs and the rest of the team particularly wanted to contemplate as they headed back out on the pitch for a lap of honour in front of their 40,000 band of delirious fans, or as they let their hair down with one drink too many at the after-party. But those thoughts would become a talking point once the celebrations died down – the only way they could prove that they weren't on the mark would be to keep the trophies coming the next season. Giggs and Keane knew they were hungry enough to demand more success – but what about their team-mates?

CHAPTER 7

MILLENNIUM MAN

'He's a splendid man. What we're seeing is Ryan's maturing as a person and a player.'

Alex Ferguson, 2001

After winning the Treble, Ryan Giggs rightly indulged himself. He partied with his team-mates and had a great summer holidaying with his family. It was only when he packed his bag for pre-season training that he would once again be haunted by the thoughts that had troubled both him and Roy Keane. Were his team-mates still up for more glory – did they still have the hunger?

If he could have glimpsed the future 10 months on, he might have found the answers – and, overall, he would have been pleased and relieved. The first post-Treble season was bound to be something of an anti-climax, unless they won the Treble once again.

In the 1999/2000 campaign United decided, foolishly or wisely depending on your view, to opt out of the FA Cup. Instead, they would take part in the FIFA World Club Championship, which was formerly known as the Toyota Cup, and would eventually become known as the FIFA Club World Cup.

By 2000 the competition had been extended to become a mini-tournament. United won the Toyota with a Roy Keane goal after a man-of-the-match performance from Ryan, but would go on to fare poorly in the newly named event in Brazil.

That season the Reds would also surrender their European crown, but the squad of players – which was essentially the same as the one that won the Treble apart from goalkeeping changes – proved that they were still hungry and ambitious for more silverware by winning the league title for the sixth time in 8 years. And they did it in real style – lifting the crown with a record haul of 91 points, a massive 12 more than the previous season. At the same time, United would score 97 goals, as opposed to 80 the previous season, and would lose only 3 games, the same number as in 1998/99.

But while they finished 1998/99 on 79 points, just one ahead of Arsenal, now they would finish 18 points clear of the Gunners, who once again were the runners-up. Clearly, these were not statistics to suggest a team that had gone off the boil, or one that was taking it easy, or indeed a team that was living off its reputation. No, Keane and Giggs would be able to breathe a lot more easily by the end of the campaign; United were as ambitious and hungry for success as ever. They were still winners despite the glory they had gobbled up the previous season.

United still meant business, which was essential to Giggs and his future with the Reds, as the likes of Inter Milan still circled like vultures – eager to grab his signature at the first sign of him becoming restless or discontent.

As the season got underway, the main difference in the team that Ryan and the fans had to come to terms with was United's goalkeeping position. Peter Schmeichel was now retired and Ferguson had come up with what he believed to be the remedy to the problem of how to replace such a hero: he brought in Aston Villa's Aussie international Mark Bosnich on a Bosman free transfer. On paper, it looked a fair bet – Bosnich would be returning to the club with whom he began his career in the UK (he played just three games from 1989 to 1992) and had already stated that he wanted to play for United and win trophies. But Fergie was not impressed by his attitude as the season progressed and brought in another keeper in November 1999, Massimo Taibi. Clearly, the Italian would not be warming the bench when he had cost £4.5 million.

But Taibi would also prove unreliable and only when Ferguson bought French World Cup winner Fabien Barthez the following summer did United's goalkeeping nightmare finally calm down. It simply proved just how magnificent and formidable a No. 1 Schmeichel had been – and how virtually irreplaceable he was to the United cause.

Despite the goalkeeping jitters, the Reds did extraordinarily well in the league – they were unbeaten for the first nine games of the season and the last 14. Ryan missed the first two games of the campaign with a niggling injury – the 2-1 loss to Arsenal in the Charity Shield and the 1-1 draw at Everton in the Premier League. But he was back in business by the time of the 4-0 win over Sheffield Wednesday on 11 August 1999, playing a part in the first three goals before Ferguson withdrew him just before the hour mark.

He scored his first goal of the season on 30 August – the final one in the 5-1 drubbing of Newcastle at Old Trafford. Ryan played well as United cruised through to January 2000, but seemed to step up a gear after the dawn of the new millennium. His performances drew gasps of admiration as he led United to yet another Premier League title up to May 2000, contributing vital goals in the 4-3 win at Middlesbrough and the 3-2 victory at Watford in April – as well as setting up countless others for United's grateful strikers.

In the Champions League, however, he was not so lucky. He opened the scoring as the competition started up again after its winter break as United beat Bordeaux 2-0 at Old Trafford in Group B, and was part of the disciplined showing that allowed the Reds to walk away from the Bernabeu with a 0-0 draw in the first leg of the quarter-final against Real Madrid. But he was as helpless as his team-mates to defy Real – and more specifically the brilliant Spaniard Raúl González – in the return at Old Trafford on 19 April. In the first half, Giggs gave the visiting defence a real runaround as he lashed in cross after cross, but it would be one of those nights when Cole and Yorke were in a profligate mood.

By the end of the 90 minutes, Real ran out 3-2 winners, with Raúl grabbing a brace. Giggs was low, his Champions League dream had ended so cruelly; it was not as if United had been outclassed – they just didn't show on the night. And that, in Giggsy's book, was the worst way to exit any competition. Still, there was at least the consolation of having won the

Toyota Cup and the Premiership. He was also praised by skipper Keane for his influence on the team – and for helping the Irishman win both the PFA Players' Player of the Year and the Football Writers' Association Footballer of the Year awards at the end of the season.

The next campaign – the 2000/01 season – would have a special place in Ryan's heart, and not just because he would clinch his seventh Premier League winner's medal by May 2001. No, it was more sentimental than that – on 29 November 2000, Giggs, now twenty-seven, celebrated the tenth anniversary of his signing pro forms at United. And on 2 March 2001, he recalled the tenth anniversary of his first-team debut, when he came on as a sub against Everton at the tender age of seventeen. A month later, he signed a new five-year contract with United.

Arsenal would once again be United's closest rivals – and they closed the gap at the top, finishing 10 points behind in the runners-up slot. The Reds had won the title by mid-April, with five matches still to play – yet lost three of those five as they struggled to hit form after the crushing blow of being knocked out of the Champions League in the match that took place before those final five. The league triumph meant Ferguson had become the first manager to win the league three times on the trot.

Ryan opened his goal-scoring account in the competition on 16 September 2000, scoring United's second in their 3-1 win at Everton. But, once again, there were setbacks for him. United were knocked out of the FA Cup when they lost 1-0 at home to West Ham, and while the team may have won the league without too much fuss, they seemed as far away as ever from dominating in Europe. This time, they would exit the Champions League in the last eight (the same as the previous season) to Bayern Munich, losing 3-1 on aggregate. Some critics cruelly claimed it was karmic retribution: that the German outfit was 'owed' after United's lucky win over them in the final in 1999.

Giggs did not smile at comments like that; he was down in the dumps at his team's failure to build on that win in 1999. Like Ferguson, he believed United should be able to dominate the event, year after year – in the same way as the likes of Real Madrid and AC Milan had done in previous decades. Also, like his manager, he was frustrated by their inability to do so: it was the one area of his club football career that he wished he could change.

He at least had the distinction of grabbing the goal for United in the loss to Bayern but that was not much consolation, he would admit. United lost the first leg 1-0 at Old Trafford and then went down 2-1 in Munich, Ryan's goal coming four minutes after the break.

Once again, he had the consolation of the league win and knowing that he had played a major part in keeping the two national Player of the Year awards at Old Trafford. Like Keane the previous season, Teddy Sheringham now won both the Football Writers' and the PFA honours – and also like the skipper, he was quick to praise his team-mate. He said Ryan had helped to make it possible more than most by setting him up to become United's top scorer that season (with 29) with his constant stream of excellent crosses and assists. 'I owe him, he's a true great,' Teddy would say.

The plaudits were nice, but they didn't stop Ryan worrying

about whether United would ever make it back to the very top; whether they would ever win the Champions League again. His fears were compounded in May 2001, when the boss revealed that he planned to retire in just 12 months. 'I will be leaving Manchester United at the end of the season and that is it,' Ferguson said.

It was a bombshell – and left Giggsy feeling insecure and uncertain about his future, just as it would have done any player who had worked with only one manager for the whole of his 10-year career. Ryan walked away from Old Trafford for his summer break in 2001 with a heavy heart and a worried frown on his face.

As it transpired, he was right to be fearful – in the next season he and the team would end up trophyless, the first time that had happened since 1998. They were to finish up third in the table, the lowest they had ever finished since the conception of the Premiership. And both Giggs and Ferguson would be despondent as United also failed to make the manager's dream of playing a Champions League final in his hometown of Glasgow come true. They exited the competition in the semis on the away-goals ruling to Bayer Leverkusen, a German outfit they should have beaten.

But amid all the doom and gloom, there was some light and cheer for Giggsy. For a start, United had showed that they still meant business by splashing a combined £47 million on striker Ruud van Nistelrooy and midfielder Juan Sebastián Veron, the latter becoming the club's then record purchase at £28.1 million. Giggs was delighted at their arrival – it suggested United were going all out to win the Champions League again, which remained his major ambition.

The next piece of good news came on 5 February 2002. Ryan breathed a huge sigh of relief when it was announced that Ferguson had done a massive U-turn by deciding to stay on at Old Trafford after all. The move immediately boosted the club's share value by 2 per cent, but it boosted Giggs even more. Inevitably, his game had seemed to suffer (although he would deny it) as the countdown continued to Ferguson's retirement date of May 2002. Now, he could put his fears aside in the knowledge that he and his mentor would be continuing side by side. United put out a statement confirming that it had been Ferguson who had come to them asking to reverse his decision: 'The board of Manchester United PLC confirms that it was recently approached by Sir Alex Ferguson on Sir Alex remaining as manager of the club beyond this season. The board has entered into discussions with Sir Alex and his advisors on a new contract. These discussions are continuing and a further announcement will be made in due course.'

Ferguson would stay on and be rewarded for his U-turn with a salary increase from £2 million to £2.5 million a year; not bad going when you consider that he had only upped it the previous summer, from £1.7 million to £2 million for what was envisaged as his final season.

Giggs was the first senior player at the club to publicly applaud Ferguson when news leaked out that the manager was considering an about-face. He said: 'There's no doubt it would be great for the team, the club and the fans if he changed his mind about retirement. He's as passionate and committed now as I remember when I first joined the club. His appetite for football is phenomenal.' He went on to compare him with the success Bobby Robson was enjoying at

Newcastle: 'It proves that age is absolutely no barrier to managerial success. It all depends on your passion and hunger, and they've both got plenty left in the tank. There has been so much speculation about the new manager, or lack of one, that it's difficult to know what to believe but it would be great if he was still the boss next season. I just can't see any negatives if that is what happened.'

So why did the boss change his mind? Some pundits still contend it was to thwart Sven-Goran Eriksson – then England boss – from taking over his empire at Old Trafford. But insiders at United say it was much simpler than that: the man from Govan had voiced his innermost fears that he would be left bereft without day-to-day involvement as manager of the world's biggest football club. He did not want to end up dazed and confused, looking out on Blackpool's seafront and twiddling his thumbs, as had happened to his friend, the great Bill Shankly, when he retired from Liverpool FC.

Whatever the reason, the decision helped transform United. They had not been their usual confident selves that season. As an example, in a particularly low spell starting on 17 October 2001, they clocked up some poor results: a 2-3 loss to Deportivo La Coruña (home), a 1-2 loss to Bolton (home), 1-1 draws at home with Leeds and away in Lille and, to cap a disastrous three weeks, a 3-1 defeat at Liverpool and a 4-0 hammering at Arsenal, the latter admittedly with a weakened side in the League Cup.

There was a general consensus that the team had lost some motivation because the manager was leaving at the end of the season, plus a belief that some of the less-committed players were taking the mickey because they knew the boss would be gone soon – that, in effect, Ferguson was a 'lame duck' manager.

Naturally, Giggs was not one of those slackers.

But United would also suffer poor form in December when Ryan was out with another hamstring injury. He suffered the setback in training in Germany prior to the 1-1 Champions League draw with Bayern Munich on 20 November 2001. Without him, United were hit with painful back-to-back December defeats in the Premier League – 3-1 at Arsenal and 0-3 at home to Chelsea. They also lost 0-1 at home to West Ham in the league.

He returned on 22 December, coming on as a 65th-minute substitute for Solskjaer as United hammered Southampton 6-1 at Old Trafford. Four days later, he started against Everton at Goodison – and emphasised his importance to the United cause by scoring the second goal on 72 minutes in a 2-0 win. Then he grabbed a double in the trip to Fulham on 30 December as United won 3-2.

In a season of doubt and uncertainty, it was clear that the Red Devils needed their talisman more than ever; that they must have him fit and firing on all cylinders if they were to prosper amid the confusion over Ferguson's supposed exit. Football writer extraordinaire James Lawton said as much in the *Independent* in January 2002: 'He [Giggs] has brought back to the last two weeks of Manchester United's tumultuous season some of the vital qualities which over the years so profoundly separated them from the rest of the pack: certainty, hunger, and a wonderful competitive nerve. If ever a football team needed a sense of renewal, as a result of a serious overhaul of its instincts, it was surely United and no one could have elected himself to the task with more vibrant force than Giggs.

'Of all his team-mates, perhaps Roy Keane has most welcomed the return of Giggs. At times Keane fought almost single-handedly to wrestle United from the edge of dissolution...'

And Ferguson would also pay tribute to the ever-maturing, developing player and man Ryan was becoming. The boss told Jonathan Northcroft of the *Sunday Times*: 'The maturing of someone is a terrific thing, the biggest satisfaction for a manager, because there's nothing worse than unfulfilled potential. I believe Ryan is coming to the stage when a player is most in command of their game. We're about to see the very best of him.'

But Giggsy's return to form after injury and Fergie's U-turn would not be enough to salvage United's season. The defeat – on away-goals after the two matches ended an aggregate 3-3 – by Bayer Leverkusen was particularly painful for both men. It would be the Germans who would play Real Madrid at Hampden Park in Fergie's native Glasgow, and for Giggsy, the defeat simply highlighted what he had feared since winning the Treble: that United might not build on their Champions League win of 1999. Ferguson said Bayern had been lucky, but admitted: 'I think it is the worst defeat losing in the semi-finals.' He added, 'I think in any game you need that bit of luck and there were four opportunities cleared off the line. That's why we needed that little bit of luck, particularly with the last one with Diego Forlan's great lob, and the defender has done fantastically to clear it. Leverkusen got that luck tonight with their equalising goal. That was the decisive moment right before half time and it might have been more than the two minutes. It was the decisive feature and if we had gone in [at half time] at 1-0, we would have won the game.'

Of course, there was a touch of sour grapes in the comments – inevitable really, given the nature of what could have been for the boss. Giggsy was also down and described the result as 'agony' and the 'low point in my ten-year career.' That elusive second Champions League win meant everything to him. Earlier in the campaign, he had explained it like this: 'We've got the potential to be the best United team ever created by Sir Alex, but we haven't gone out and proved that, and it'll mean nothing until we do. The Treble-winning side proved themselves; we haven't put everything together yet. Some of the football we've played this season has been the best I've ever seen, but we've made too many mistakes. We need to get to a higher level if we're going to win the European Cup.'

He went on to say that they'd come too close for comfort in Europe: 'By our standards we should be doing better; we need to be stronger. Because of the standards we've set, people get on our backs when we fall below them, but some of the criticism is understandable. We know the football we are capable of, but when you make mistakes, you get punished.'

Yet now the European dream was over for at least another 12 months, but he knew there was the little matter of the Premier League title and with two games to go, United were still in with a shout. The match directly following the Bayer letdown was Arsenal at home – a crunch fixture and probably just what Ryan needed to emerge from his disappointment. Win – and he was still in with a chance of another league champion's medal. He told the *Sunday Mirror*: 'Now our only hope of avoiding a complete disaster is to beat Arsenal on Wednesday and hope Everton can do us a favour at Highbury on Saturday. United have got the strongest squad I have ever known but we have let ourselves, the manager and the supporters down. And that is unforgivable. There are no excuses for any of us...'

But a complete disaster it was to be. Sylvain Wiltord would break Giggsy's heart by scoring the only goal as the Gunners won 1-0 at Old Trafford to rubber-stamp them as league champions. Arsenal would rub United's noses in it by winning the FA Cup as well, thus chalking up their third double. They had lost only three matches out of 38 in the league; United, in comparison, had lost nine of their 38, more than ever before in a Premier League campaign.

So what now, Ryan puzzled, as he headed off on holiday over the summer of 2002. Would United somehow regain their grip, or might Arsenal consolidate theirs? He thought back to the dark days of 1998, when the team won nothing only for them to lift the Treble the following season. Always a realist, he fully understood that this was another watershed for himself and United. He would be twenty-nine in the November of 2002 and time appeared to be running out if he was to scoop that second Champions League win.

But he was also an optimist and he believed that if anyone could take the club back to the top, it was the boss. Sure, Fergie had made a mistake in announcing that he was going to retire and then prevaricating and finally changing his mind – it had undoubtedly affected the club and the players' form had suffered. But now, he would be focused 100 per cent and determined to make up for the lapse that had benefited the

Gunners. The knowledge filled Giggsy with hope, so it was not all doom and gloom that summer.

Indeed, as soon as he returned to pre-season training there was good news: Ferguson had broken United's transfer record for the second time in as many years by signing centre-back Rio Ferdinand from Leeds in a deal worth £29.1 million. It made him the most expensive defender in the world and left Ryan with a huge grin on his face.

If there had been one area of the team that needed strengthening, it was central defence. The previous season the boss had unexpectedly flogged the excellent Jaap Stam to Lazio for £16 million, much to the dismay of the fans and most of the players. Now, with Rio, Ryan hoped that the ship would be steadied once again.

But even Giggs, who had always preferred to see the glass half-full, was surprised by the extent of the transformation. United emerged from Arsenal's slipstream to steal back their league crown. By May 2003, they had won their fourth title in five years – and their eighth since the Premier League was formed. It was a truly remarkable turnaround, especially if you take into account the fact that the Gunners were eight points clear at the start of March. Two months later, they were five points *behind* United in the final league table, amassing 78 to United's 83.

Ruud van Nistelrooy won the Barclaycard Golden Boot award after scoring 25 goals in 38 league matches and 44 in all competitions. He singled out Ryan for helping him attain the honour, saying the winger deserved a lot of the credit after he and Beckham had set him up for many of his goals that season. 'They are two great players,' the Dutchman remarked.

'I am lucky to be working with them every week. They make my life as a goalscorer so much easier. I would like to thank them both from my heart.'

This was also the season that Giggsy would rack up his most-ever appearances in a campaign for United – playing in a total of 59 matches in all competitions and scoring a highly creditable 15 goals.

The turning point for Giggs and United in the campaign was the 18-match unbeaten run they embarked on from 28 December 2002 to 11 May 2003. It began with a 2-0 win at home to Birmingham and continued right up to the last match of the season, a 2-1 win at Everton.

The Reds would exit the FA Cup at home to Arsenal, losing 2-0 in the fifth round, but Ryan would be more gutted by the Champions League loss to Real Madrid in the last eight. They lost 3-1 in Madrid in the first leg and went out of the competition 6-5 on aggregate after winning the return 4-3. That second leg at Old Trafford would prove ominous for Giggs and Manchester United.

David Beckham grabbed a memorable brace but was outdone by the Brazilian Ronaldo, who stole a hat-trick. Beckham, who had only come on as a substitute after Ferguson inexplicably persevered with the out-of-sorts Veron, showed his true worth to the colours but would be gone within two months after his continuing fall-out with the boss.

United would certainly suffer without him.

Meanwhile, Ronaldo would be fêted for his hat-trick but his brilliance would alert a foreign outsider to the delights of the beautiful game. Soon Giggs and United would have to compete without Beckham – against a Chelsea side buoyed by the arrival of the Russian oligarch Roman Abramovich, who would later admit he fell in love with football the night he witnessed Ronaldo and Beckham's brilliance in that Champions League clash.

The goalposts were moving – if Ryan was to achieve success in the autumn of a sensational career, he would be hard-pushed to do so. As the 2003/04 season loomed United looked weaker and their opponents stronger: Chelsea were about to break up the United/Arsenal dominance in the Premier League.

And Ryan Giggs was soon to face the toughest stretch of what had been up to now a truly glittering career.

CHAPTER 8
THE GOING GETS TOUGH

We've spoken a lot about the seemingly endless glory years that Ryan enjoyed at Old Trafford – but the 2003/04 and 2004/05 seasons were probably the toughest of his career for the golden boy. For the first time since the glory years, United under Ferguson were in decline and Ryan would also struggle on occasion as the team lacked their usual fluidity and decisiveness.

The main problem was in midfield. At the end of June 2003, the boss sanctioned the sale of David Beckham to Real Madrid. Ferguson's relationship with Beckham had broken down and they could no longer work together.

But the sale was an all-round disaster. Madrid snapped him

up for a giveaway £21 million and immediately recouped their money (and more) by selling 1 million shirts at £45 a time within a month. The marketing power of Beckham helped Madrid climb above United in the ranks of the world's richest clubs and also allowed them make inroads into the lucrative Far Eastern market, which United had previously taken for granted as their domain.

The sale also impacted on the club's claim to be the number one team in England, let alone Europe. Much to Ryan's disappointment, it had been four years since United won the Champions League, but at least there had still been the consolation of lifting the Premier League crown. But now, with Beckham gone and Roy Keane no longer his old majestic self, even that could no longer be taken for granted.

United were in transition – Cristiano Ronaldo would arrive shortly after Beckham's departure to replace 'Goldenballs' and the mercurial Wayne Rooney was to follow him to the Theatre of Dreams in 2004 – but some of Ferguson's answers to solving the growing crisis in midfield did not address the problem. In the summer of 2003, he brought in Eric Djemba-Djemba in his first botched attempt to replace Keane, then thirty-one. The Cameroon midfielder was a disaster; he was simply not in the same class as the skipper.

At the same time, Ferguson also signed the Brazilian Jose Kleberson, for £6.5 million, in the hope that the two men could possibly work together to become the new Keane. Again, it didn't work – Kleberson was unrecognisable from the man who had performed so heroically for Brazil in the World Cup of 2002. At best, he and Djemba-Djemba now seemed jobbing journeymen.

Both would eventually be taken away under cover of night to Aston Villa (Djemba-Djemba) and Besiktas in Turkey (Kleberson). The boss iced the cake of mediocrity that summer of 2003 by also bringing in the lightweight French winger, David Bellion. He would prove just as disappointing a signing as Kleberson and Djemba-Djemba. Then, the following summer, Fergie was to hail another midfielder whom he felt would be able to take on Keane's mantle – Liam Miller, on a free transfer from Celtic. The Irishman had become a firm crowd favourite up at Parkhead, but he also struggled to carry his form to Old Trafford. He was a weak imitation of the strongman who had gained ovations in Scotland as he failed miserably to make any real impact in solving the midfield conundrum.

Was it any wonder Giggsy struggled for his best form those two seasons – when the men Ferguson had brought in to strengthen the midfield actually ended up weakening it?

There was also the threat from outside Old Trafford, from Arsenal and Chelsea, to their domination. As already mentioned, Giggs and United would also face a new threat to their power base in the form of the Russian oligarch Ambramovich, who was determined Chelsea would become Premier League kings (and at the same time make a name for himself in Britain) whatever the cost.

The times they were a-changing and United appeared to be being left behind as they battled to emerge from transition against powerful new opponents.

Before Abramovich's arrival in 2003, Giggs had won the Premier League eight times, but now he would have to wait until 2007 to make it nine as Chelsea started to lord it, backed by an initial £100 million of investment in top-quality new players. But even the impatient Russian would have to play the waiting game. That 2003/04 season would ultimately belong to United's traditional rivals of the Premier League years: Arsenal.

Giggs was in confident mood at the start of the campaign. After all, United had regained their league title the previous May and the boss kept his word by bringing in a raft of new players to make up for the loss of Beckham. 'We've got a great chance of doing well again,' he would say. 'It lifted us winning the league title back, now we want to push on.'

Ferguson was to endorse that view, saying, 'The best thing that could have happened to the players last season was winning the league. It brought back exactly where they were as a football team; it reinvigorated them.'

Yet the season would not live up to expectations, as the league crown went to Highbury and they were eliminated from the Champions League in the last-16 knockout stage by Porto, managed by a certain José Mourinho. The flamboyant, self-styled 'Special One' would continue to be a thorn in United's side when, in the summer of 2004, he left Portugal to become Chelsea manager as part of Abramovich's Russian revolution at Chelsea.

The season got off to a good start for Ryan as he collected his fifth Charity/Community Shield winner's medal on 10 August 2003 at Cardiff's Millennium Stadium after United beat Arsenal 4-3 on penalties after the match ended 1-1.

Ryan carried his good form from the Welsh capital into the league opener against Bolton, grabbing a brace (and his team's first two goals of the new campaign) as United breezed to a 4-0 triumph at Old Trafford.

So far, there had been little sign of the struggles that would eventually arrive when the midfield started to splutter and choke like a malfunctioning motorbike exhaust. Keane was still standing up to the rigours of the campaign and Giggsy chipped in with some outstanding work. His best game during the first half of the season came on 9 November 2003, when his two goals single-handedly destroyed Liverpool and United ran out 2-1 winners at Anfield, thanks to Giggsy's powerful second-half strikes.

Some fans were questioning whether he was as influential as he used to be when he hit passes astray or failed to beat a man. They were known as the 'moan brigade' by the real United fans at Old Trafford: they would jump on a player if he made a mistake or appeared off-key, whatever his standing at the club. In their eyes, no one should ever have a bad day at the office. For the most part, Ryan would ignore them and get on with doing his bit for United but even the most forgiving of footballers might have been pushed not to feel a little disheartened when his own fans kept getting on his back. He would later admit that the booing and the critical receptions he sometimes endured did affect his self-confidence. At the time, he was determined not to let it get him down, that he would battle through it and reach peak form again. Never a quitter, Ryan Giggs was always a fighter.

But that day at Liverpool showed he still had what it took to play at the absolute top – and a relieved Ferguson paid tribute to his man: 'It was a fantastic match, really incredible, and every player on the pitch deserved full marks. Ryan was great today – he won the match for us after they had put us on the back foot. They played with a conviction that we did not match; we lacked confidence for some reason. But in the second half we were more like our real selves and Ryan put us 2-0 up before Liverpool started playing well again. It meant a nail-biting finish.'

Ryan also declared himself 'well pleased' with the goals and the outcome, and even Liverpool boss Gérard Houllier admitted that Giggs had torn his team apart. He said, 'I thought we deserved much more from the match – we dominated for long periods and created enough chances. The two goals from Giggs killed us off, they were good goals. If you give Giggs chances like that, he will punish you; he is a world-class player.'

A couple of weeks after the match Giggs would be thirty and you couldn't have blamed him, had he entertained thoughts of finally giving it a go in Italy, maybe at Inter Milan, where he was still fêted. He was getting aggro from some of his own fans and was no nearer sorting out a new deal at United where the chairman, David Gill, was reluctant to hand out contracts for more than one year to players over the big 30. Ryan would soon fall into that category, but he was no ordinary player. You might have thought United would have made an exception to the rule, but Gill was adamant at the time that it was not possible. It's easy to see why Giggsy could have been tempted by an offer from abroad – which would have probably involved a three-year contract – but, to his credit, he stayed loyal to United and eventually earned himself a two-year deal the following year.

Yet his title dream would disappear in the 2003/04 campaign after the New Year. As well as the growing problems in midfield, United were already at a disadvantage from January 2004 when defensive kingpin Rio Ferdinand was banned for eight months for failing to attend a drugs test. The central defender played his last match of the season in the 1-0 league defeat at Wolverhampton Wanderers on 17 January. He left the field after 50 minutes to be replaced by Wes Brown – and 17 minutes later Kenny Miller fired Wolves ahead. It would be the first goal against United in Ferdinand's absence and the first defeat – but it would not be the last. Out of 16 further Premier League matches, United won just seven, and some of the defeats they suffered were real sickeners. They included losses to their biggest rivals – 4-1 at Manchester City and 1-0 at home to Liverpool.

Ryan Giggs was not a happy bunny by the end of the league campaign as United trudged home in third place on 75 points, 15 behind Arsenal and four behind the resurgent Chelsea. It was even more of a bitter taste in defeat as the Gunners were universally lauded 'The Invincibles' after becoming the first team to go unbeaten in the league since Preston in 1888/89. In the modern era, only two other teams have won their leagues in Europe and stayed unbeaten during the campaign – Milan in 1991/92 and Ajax Amsterdam in 1994/95.

Nevertheless, there would be two consolation prizes for Giggs that season as the Gunners gloated about their achievement. The first was that he would lift another FA Cup winner's medal. The second would be that by beating Arsenal 1-0 in the semis he and United would thwart Arsène Wenger's men's chances of winning the trophy for a third successive season and, at the same time, crush their dreams of winning another double.

United ended a five-year wait for an 11th FA Cup triumph

with a 3-0 win over First Division Millwall at Cardiff on 22 May 2004. Ronaldo headed United in front just before the interval and Giggs was directly involved in the two that followed to kill off the Londoners. Ryan was brought down in the box by David Livermore on 65 minutes and Van Nistelrooy converted from the spot to make it 2-0. Ten minutes from time, Giggsy dazzled down the left wing and sent in a perfect cross for the Dutchman to celebrate his second goal of the game. Afterwards, skipper Gary Neville paid tribute to his old mate – and also to United's emerging star, Ronaldo. He told BBC Sport: 'Ryan Giggs and Ruud van Nistelrooy produced some good moments for us, but Cristiano Ronaldo was particularly outstanding. I think Ronaldo can be one of the top footballers in the world. To come with the price tag on his head and at his age, he has been outstanding for us this season.'

Ryan was happy to secure another FA Cup win and celebrated afterwards with the rest of the boys at the dinner and party held at the Vale of Glamorgan hotel, which was traditionally United's base when they played in Cardiff. But there was still a feeling that, OK, he and United had won the FA Cup, but was that real success in the modern era? After all, it had not been that long ago when the club had even opted out of the FA Cup to play in Brazil. There was a general feeling – and it would get stronger as the years went by – that the FA Cup was no longer that much of a prize, that United should be thinking of the Premier League and the Champions League rather than being sidetracked by domestic knockout cup competitions.

It was a view certainly shared by some fans. One, Steven

Hayes, summed up the opinion of many when he said: 'Yes, it was great to see Giggsy winning another medal – and for Ronaldo to get something in his first season at the club – but it all felt a bit of a consolation prize. Ryan was used to picking up league-winning medals – and everyone knew he, Fergie and Keano were all desperate to win the Champions League again. That's what they wanted more than anything else. So, yes, it was hard to believe that any of them were THAT elated just to win the bloody FA Cup! Certainly – and I know this will sound like we are spoiled – the fans weren't. OK, it was a trophy – but it was now becoming distinctly second-rate.'

It was a theme that many other United fans would pick up on. 'Big Bird', of Salford, was one of them: 'A Mickey Mouse cup, our consolation prize for a sickening season. It was a professional performance, nothing else. We played a team frightened of its own shadow with no idea what to do when it got the ball, mostly just kick it up field or kick it out to give their ten-man defence a rest. But credit where credit is due – we still won. Yet let's not get carried away here. On this performance there was nothing to suggest a resurgence or anything to worry the rest of the Premier League about; there weren't any signs that we'll set the Premier alight next season. If Arsenal or Chelsea had have been playing Millwall, the score would have been in double figures. It was a good day out, lovely weather, cool beer – but just a stroll in the park for an ordinary United team.'

It was a fair point for a football club that had become accustomed to being at the very top of the tree for the previous decade. But if Giggsy and the lads thought it was a one-off away from the big-time honours, they were in for a shock. The next two seasons were even worse – as United were once again edged out from the top table by rivals from London.

CHAPTER 9

HAUL OF FAME

'Ryan's record with United is unbelievable. I'm really proud of him. He is a great athlete and a great person. The day he came to Manchester United, I knew he was special.'

Sir Bobby Charlton, 2005

'Whatever the club has paid me in my time as manager was justified at a stroke by securing Ryan as a player for the club.'

Sir Alex Ferguson, 2005

Many at United had dismissed winning the FA Cup in 2004 with a shrug that said, 'So what?' As we have seen, there was a feeling within the club and among the supporters that they should be reeling in bigger fish. But by the end of the following season, they could look back on that 2004 FA Cup win with nostalgia, as Giggs and his team-mates won sweet nothing.

You could argue with some conviction that the 2004/05 season was one of the most disappointing, if not *the* most, for Ryan. Sure, there were plus points – like the signing of Rooney to go with that of Ronaldo in the previous campaign, and an appearance in an FA Cup final (albeit as a loser) – but there was an underlying feeling of gloom, and even doom, within the club.

The manager had famously made his U-turn about leaving a couple of seasons earlier, but now he was in what seemed a perpetual power struggle with two of United's biggest shareholders, John Magnier and his partner JP McManus, whose company Cubic Expression owned more than 25 per cent of the club. The row between the three had rumbled on for months after a dispute over the ownership of the racehorse, Rock of Gibraltar. The United manager believed he had been promised a greater share in the nag – a half-share, as opposed to the 5 per cent of any winnings that the two other men contended they had offered him.

In theory, he could lose his job if they forced through a takeover, but there was also another possible takeover looming – from the hardnosed US tycoon, Malcolm Glazer. Throughout 2004, the owner of the Tampa Bay Buccaneers NFL franchise had been increasing his stake in the club and by October it would rise to 27.63 per cent to take him within touching distance of Magnier and McManus, who owned 28.9 per cent.

The shenanigans and uncertainty behind the scenes, allied with United's struggle to maintain their status as No. 1 on the field, led to a tough season for both team and fans alike. Giggs was to end up without any medals but would at least have the consolation of appearing in another Cardiff final and also enjoy a double boost to his status as a Red Devils legend during the campaign.

The first came in September 2004 when he became only the third man to play 600 games for United. The landmark was achieved in the 2-1 home victory over Liverpool on 20 September. In typical style, Ryan refused to get carried away by the honour, telling manutd.com, 'I'm proud to reach 600 appearances – but I'm still as hungry for success as ever.'

The match was a key one for United, who had stood 10 points behind league leaders Arsenal beforehand. There was surely something about United players making their comebacks against their biggest rivals after controversial bans: Cantona had done so back in 1995 and now, nine years later, Rio Ferdinand was also turning out against Liverpool, after his eight-month ban. Rio's central defensive colleague Mikael Silvestre was to grab the glory – scoring both United's goals, both of which were set up by Giggsy: the first from a free kick, the winner from a corner. It was a win Ryan and United needed after three successive draws looked like derailing their challenge to champions Arsenal and the ever-improving Chelsea.

Ryan's second personal landmark of the season came when he was inducted into the English Football Hall of Fame in 2005. He was honoured by his inclusion, but even more pleased when Ferguson told him shortly afterwards that David Gill had agreed to break United's unwritten rule of not offering players over thirty more than a one-year deal. A delighted Giggsy said at the time, 'I wanted three years, but we quickly settled on two.'

A couple of months earlier there had been conjecture that he might follow his best pal, Nicky Butt, to Newcastle had United continued to snub his pleas for a longer deal. In December, 2004, Neil Custis of the *Sun*, reported that, 'Newcastle are lining up a £4 million New Year swoop for unsettled Manchester United star Ryan Giggs. An approach has already been made and the Welsh winger is aware of their interest. Toon boss Graeme Souness is ready to make his move during the January transfer window.'

Giggsy always maintained it was speculation and nothing else; that he had never contemplated, let alone wanted to leave the club that was close to his heart. He also denied having anything to do with the rumours about a move to the Toon after some hacks claimed he had deliberately set tongues a-wagging in an attempt to engineer a better deal at Old Trafford.

The season started as it would end: badly. And against the same bogeymen: Arsenal. United would lose 3-1 to the Gunners in the Charity Shield and then fall to them in the FA Cup final the following May. Ryan was to score United's first competitive goal of the campaign, in the 2-1 win at Dinamo Bucharest in the Champions League third qualifying round.

He would also grab the opener in the 6-2 thrashing of Fenerbahce at Old Trafford in the first match of the competition's group stage. But even the glorious veteran winger was to be upstaged by a relative novice – yes, Wayne Rooney would signal his arrival at the world's biggest football club by netting a hat-trick against the hapless Turks. At a fee of £27.5 million, the nineteen-year-old Scouser's transfer made him the most expensive teenager ever in world football but his goals against Fenerbahce backed up his claim that he would be worth every penny. Rooney had commented, 'Obviously it's a lot of money and it's a lot of money for a player to be sold for, but I feel I'm capable of fulfilling my potential and hopefully in that time it'll turn out to be a bargain for United. I just want to do the best I can and for the club to do the best they can.' He would go on to be the club's top-scorer for the season, with 17 goals (one more than Van Nistelrooy, while Ryan would get eight).

Giggsy would be back on the scoresheet for what was arguably United's best result of the 2004/05 campaign: an excellent 4-2 win at Arsenal. He claimed the first goal in the Premier League win (although this went down in the record books as an own goal), but it would prove scant consolation as both the Gunners and Chelsea finished above the Reds in the end-of-season table. The Blues, with Abramovich's roubles, won the title with a total of 95 points, Arsenal were runners-up on 83 and United landed third on 77.

At least Ryan was spared the humbling experience of having to be part of the guard of honour that clapped newly crowned champions Chelsea at Old Trafford on 10 May 2005. The boss left him out of the clash that saw Chelsea claim a new Premier League points' record of 94. United lost 3-1 after Van Nistelrooy had given them hope with the opener on seven minutes.

Ferguson was unusually quiet after the defeat and even downbeat. 'Once Chelsea's second goal went in, they were worthy winners. I didn't expect us to get second place after a disappointing result against West Brom on Saturday,' he admitted. 'But tonight was about trying to keep our confidence up and on the whole it was good. That is the one thing I can take out of the game. The tempo was fantastic and anyone watching as a neutral would be thrilled by the football played. I thought we played some good football, the match was very competitive and it was really a game for professionals.'

It was as if he had accepted that the balance of power had switched from Old Trafford to Stamford Bridge, that it would be some time before his team would be able to challenge them properly. Sure, he had Rooney and Ronaldo on board, but they remained boys who needed nurturing. They were not yet ready to take on the world – or Europe – together, although they eventually would be.

Indeed, United exited the Champions League in truly disappointing style: losing 1-0 at home and away in the last 16 to AC Milan. Hernán Crespo scored twice in the double-header as the wily veterans of the Rossoneri made the Red Devils look what they were: a transitional team that still had some growing up and developing to do. Even Giggsy struggled to get out of first gear as the Italian outfit initially smothered United's ambition and then destroyed their dream.

In the return leg at the San Siro, Ryan would come closest of all to getting United back in the tie as one of his shots smashed against the woodwork. Afterwards, Ferguson was to rue their lack of luck, saying, 'We didn't get the break we needed when Ryan hit the post. We needed to score the first goal. That was the key to the whole contest, that was the chance, and unfortunately we didn't take it. If we had taken the first one it would have been a different game. If you look at the two games we had six good chances and we didn't take any of them. The margins at this level are very fine and that is what has decided the tie overall. I'm disappointed to go out, but we've gone out to a very good team. Our decision-making could have been better but you only get that through playing and my players will get better.'

That last line was as close a public admission as you would ever get from the United manager that his team was in transition – and that he needed time and patience from the fans. Yes, they would get better, but it would not happen overnight.

No matter, however far they were from what Fergie visualised as the finished product, this team still had something to play for that season – the FA Cup final on 21 May. United got to Cardiff by thrashing Newcastle 4-1 in the semis in the same city. Ferguson made a big decision on the day of the final – giving Darren Fletcher a run-out at Ryan's expense. The boss didn't reveal his line-up to the squad until 11.30am, and Giggsy was puzzled and angered by his omission.

Later, Fergie would try and smooth it all over by saying he wanted to inject some pace and strength in midfield as he was already carrying two veterans in Keane and Scholes. He felt it was vital to compete with the Gunners in that department and Fletcher would go head to head with the powerhouse duo of Patrick Vieira and Gilberto Silva. In other words, nothing personal: needs must on the day. But Giggs's omission was not that much of a shock to the gathered press corps – Ferguson had been using Fletcher in tough games to do the running for Keano, to do his legwork. Giggs would make a late appearance – an extra-time role after he emerged on 91 minutes – taking the place of Fletcher, who was exhausted after working flat out for himself and Keane.

Beforehand, memories flooded back of the 1979 final between the teams. Then the Gunners led 2-0 with five minutes remaining after first-half goals from Brian Talbot and Frank Stapleton. Gordon McQueen and Sammy McIlory grabbed late goals to make it all square, but, with the match almost over, Alan Sunderland sneaked in for the winner.

Twenty-six years on and there was a chance that the match

could be just as momentous and unforgettable. OK, as already suggested, neither United nor Arsenal now saw the FA Cup as one of the big prizes of football – but that was when they were both winning the league! Now, with the prospect of a trophyless season for one of them, both Ferguson and Wenger were busy building up the cup – emphasising that by winning it, they and their teams would still have enjoyed a successful season. Now the two giants of the game were left desperately scrapping for the leftovers at King José's table – after Mourinho had devoured the main course (the Premier League crown) for himself. Certainly, United were left in no doubt by the boss that this was a game they had to win. Transitional team or not, he didn't want the fans on his back.

The players also had a major incentive to lift the FA Cup – it was claimed that they had lost upward of 25 grand apiece for their failure to finish runners-up in the Premier League, and defeat in Cardiff would cost them further hefty bonuses.

United outplayed their bitter rivals and deserved to have collected their bonuses, but football is never as straightforward or as predictable as that. Giggsy was sent on by Ferguson for the extra-time period, but could not change the outcome of a 0-0 draw. The Gunners went on to lift the trophy 5-4 on penalties.

Ferguson would again stress that this was a developing team – and that they would come good: 'We've always been the sort of team that is galvanised by defeat and adversity. We're that sort of team. We'll get ourselves off the ground – cup football can do that to you sometimes. We are a very good team and in that form we can play against anybody. It was a really good performance and we got our game together today. You could toss a coin for Man of the Match out of Wayne Rooney and Cristiano Ronaldo because they were great, the pair of them. There's a great future for those boys, and Darren Fletcher as well.'

No mention of Giggs, but he hardly expected it. In May 2005, he was on the fringes of the team, playing a sort of senior tutor role to the three aforementioned youngsters and others like them at the club. I, like many journalists and fans, had bemoaned the choice of Fletcher to nursemaid Keane – at the expense of Giggsy – but I had to admit afterwards that it was the right move. Fletcher played a key role in breaking up Arsenal's attacking game and helping United themselves surge forward.

Rio Ferdinand argued that United deserved more and admitted it was a sickener to lose on penalties: 'It's a bit of sucker punch, really. You go into a cup final, you want to win. It's disappointing but I'm sure we'll come back. It was a very good team performance but at the end of the day if you don't score goals, you don't win games.'

The stats backed him up, proving United had indeed been mugged. Arsenal had five shots (one on target) compared with United's 20 (eight on target). The Gunners had one corner, United had 12. Yet it was the Gunners who triumphed.

Typically, with Ryan being involved, there would have to be some record-breaking or history-making fact surrounding the event. And it was this: the 2005 FA Cup final had been the first ever to be decided on penalties – with Paul Scholes missing for United – and the first to end goalless since 1912.

Giggs himself was downhearted – he had not made the starting line-up and had then been on the losing side but he still joined the boys back at their hotel, the Holland House in Cardiff. He sat near to the youngsters, Ronaldo and Rooney, the boys who would eventually take up his mantle as the great entertainers of Old Trafford.

Ryan would later say that he and the rest of the team had decided to go for it that night – so they could get the loss completely out of their system. A source revealed that Ronaldo was determined to be the star of the after-final party – although he did show a surprising naivety that apparently had Giggs and the rest of the lads in stitches. It began when Ronaldo persuaded two girls from the luxury hotel's spa complex to join them during their meal. He couldn't stop chatting to them through a 'boring speech by Meester Fergison' and then asked the girls if they would like to carry on the night at a Cardiff club. Both looked nervously at each other, thinking the tall, spotty-faced lad from abroad was maybe a bit too forward for their liking. As if picking up on their fears, Ronaldo pulled an older woman to his side. 'It be OK,' he grinned, speaking in pigeon English. 'This is my mum, and she come everywhere with me.'

It was an amusing final anecdote to what had been a far-from-happy season. Skipper Keane was to throw true light on how the season had panned out and on his team's failings when, with typical candour, he commented: 'We played quite well and had plenty of chances, but it's about putting the ball in the back of the net and we didn't quite manage it. It's small consolation to say that we had all the chances. We dominated, but I'm sure the Arsenal players won't be too bothered about that – they've got the winners' medals and the cup, and we haven't.'

Harsh, but true: United had failed and there were growing fears among the supporters and within the club that they were on a downward trend. Giggsy had only just signed his new two-year deal, but by the end of the season United would be in the hands of the Glazers. Now the club's future – and that of older players like Giggs and Keane – was suddenly unclear. To finance the massive debts they had accrued to buy the club, the Americans would surely need to cut costs. How would they view men who could be seen as diminishing assets? Men who were drawing big money but not always guaranteed starting, let alone starring, roles? Yes, Ryan had much to think about as he headed off for his summer holiday to Marbella in 2005 – as did his mentor Ferguson. Had the past season been just a blip before the onslaught of further honours – as had been the case in 1998 when a barren campaign was followed by the Treble – or was battling for the FA Cup going to be as good as it got?

Neither Ryan nor his boss would go off on their hols without a care in the world, especially when a few days after their defeat in Cardiff, their most bitter enemies would lift the European Cup. That summer, the names on most football fans' tongues were Steven Gerrard, hero of Liverpool's dramatic fightback against AC Milan in Istanbul, Rafa Benítez, boss of the Kop kings, and José Mourinho.

Was the balance of power in English football moving irrevocably away from Old Trafford? And, after a decade of unbridled glory, were Giggs and Ferguson – the architects of United's dominance – finally becoming yesterday's men?

CHAPTER 10

DARKNESS BEFORE THE DAWN

'I am only interested in playing for a team that could win the Champions League, so there is no possibility of that at Manchester United.'

Juventus goalkeeper Gigi Buffon, 2005

'There's no way that Ryan Giggs is another George Best – he's another Ryan Giggs.'

Denis Law

Giggsy and United would endure a third consecutive tough season in 2005/06. Unlike the previous campaign, there would at least be another winner's medal at the end of it, but it would be the bottom-of-the barrel League Cup, by then known as the Carling Cup – the trophy Ferguson and United had previously considered so irrelevant that they had made a habit of sending out reserve sides to compete in it.

Now, as United's absence from football's top table continued, in a remarkable volte-face, the manager was to begin his spin that the League Cup was worth winning after all. The season would also see Ryan equal his record for the fewest appearances – 37 (which matched those of 1996/97 and 1997/98) – although it would not be an equivalent nadir for his goalscoring skills. He was to hit the net five times, one more than in 1994/95, 2007/08 and 2008/09 (he did score only one goal in the 1990/91 season, but that was his debut campaign and he played in just two games).

As the season played out, it would become a dark one for Giggs – and for United as a football club. There were scenes of anger from fans when the Glazer family took their seats as the club's new owners, despair at the lack of success on the field, shock at the exits of two star men – Keane and Van Nistelrooy – and sadness as the great Georgie Best lost his battle for life.

As if all that was not enough, Ferguson would also see his own position come under scrutiny as United crashed out of the Champions League at the group stage and finished bottom, which meant they did not even have the consolation of a UEFA Cup spot.

It all got off to an uncomfortable start for Ryan and the boys when their traditional holiday break was cut short to accommodate an earlier-than-normal start to the new season. This was to give the players breathing space before they joined up with their national teams for the World Cup the following year. Giggsy packed his bag for the pre-season on 27 June 2005 – just five weeks after they had lost to Arsenal in the FA Cup Final on 21 May.

Or at least the 'breathing space' angle was how United explained it to their players. Over at Stamford Bridge, José Mourinho refused to cut short his own break, or that of his players. He announced that his club would begin their pre-season 10 days later than United, on 6 July. 'We'll enjoy the summer break and will come refreshed into the new season. We are the champions and it is a great feeling,' he grinned.

Alex Ferguson merely shrugged his shoulders when told of Mourinho's decision. He believed the early start would benefit his men; that it would help them avoid the nightmare of the previous campaign when they had begun sluggishly and struggled to keep pace with Chelsea. 'The important thing is for us to improve and learn from the early season attack. It was a bad start for us last season and we lost the League then. We are going to start earlier, much earlier – that will make sure we are ready because it looks to me as if you're going to have to start better than normal. Normally, we start training about 10 July and make steady progress until we get the turn, but it doesn't look as if we can afford to do that.'

The boss was surely being disingenuous. It was not the lack of an early start that had cost United so dearly the previous year: no, it was the fact that United were still a team in transition while Chelsea had bought top-class players who instantly gelled together. Undoubtedly Chelsea were, at the time, the better side.

Some of the senior players were unhappy with the early start and the prospect of a daunting summer boot camp. Certainly, Keane – and, I am told, Ryan – were hardly thrilled by the prospect – and the skipper told Ferguson as much. There would also be a tour of the Far East and a Champions League qualifier against Debreceni VSC. Surely, the veterans argued, it would have been more sensible to follow Mourinho's plan of action and return at a more leisurely pace?

But Fergie would have none of it. 'The four games we play in the Far East will add to their stamina and sharpness before the season starts,' he insisted. Many thought it a poor decision – and the outcome of the season, as United struggled, would bear out the opinion of the countless journalists scratching their heads in the press box.

The grumblings that had already started would reach their peak by Christmas when United crashed out of Europe. It was suggested Ferguson had lost the plot, however temporarily, and that his team had become over-cautious. Playing with a lack of adventure and style, without wanting to entertain as well as win, was anathema to United fans who had been brought up on Sir Matt Busby's brand of attacking, flair-based football.

It was revealed at the time – and would emerge later that season from the lips of Ferguson – that his new assistant, Carlos Queiroz, had been instrumental in the more cautious tactical approach. Roy Keane admitted that he and some other senior players were unhappy with the assistant manager's training techniques and the emphasis on 'safety first'. The Irishman also claimed they doubted Queiroz's credentials. After all, had the Portuguese not been sacked at Real Madrid after a miserable one-year spell?

It was Queiroz's idea to lead United on 'a bonding break' to Portugal that pre-season, ahead of the warm-up games in the Far East. Keane, in particular, took exception to this decision, apparently backed by Ferguson, to invite families along to the Algarve. In his eyes, it was either a training camp or it wasn't. And if it wasn't, why not just let the players continue their summer holidays alone with their families a little bit longer?

Sources close to the club said Keane seemed to smoulder with resentment throughout his final months at United, feeling he had been dealt a bum hand by the boss, who always appeared to put Queiroz's opinions before those of his on-field leader. And Keane's anger would explode with irrevocable consequences after United lost 4-1 at the Riverside to a Middlesbrough team considered no more than middling. That defeat left United 13 points behind Chelsea, and Keane gave forthright and uncompromising views about the team's performance on the MUTV show, *Play the Pundit*. The programme never made it on to air. It was claimed that United ordered the tapes to be burned after Keane allegedly spent an hour picking his team-mates' performances to pieces – with particularly heavy blasts at Alan Smith, Darren Fletcher, Kieran Richardson and John O'Shea.

By 18 November, Keane was gone – much to the sadness of Giggs, who liked, respected and admired the man as an extraordinary footballer and leader of Manchester United. The word from behind the scenes was that Keane had received a pay-off to buy his silence. He would take a little time out of the game and then return in the New Year with Scottish giants Celtic, the team he had loved while growing up as a boy in his native Ireland.

For Giggsy and United, there would be no such breather. Just more distress and problems as the situation went from bad to worse, on and off the field. Just a week after United fans were forced to come to terms with Keane's exit, Old Trafford was in mourning for the loss of another great: George Best passed away on Friday, 25 November 2005. Arguably the greatest footballer this country ever produced, he gave up his fight for life at the relatively young age of fifty-nine at London's Cromwell Hospital.

Best had been treated there since suffering flu-like

symptoms two months earlier. Following this, he contracted a kidney infection and, towards the end, his condition deteriorated sharply with the development of a lung infection that led to internal bleeding. He had been particularly susceptible to infection because of the drugs he was forced to take after his 2002 liver transplant. The final script in the drama that had been the Irish wonderboy's life was not hard to work out: it was always going to end in tears, given his addiction to alcohol.

The news hit United and Giggs hard. Ryan possibly harder than most, given that he had been through the ranks at United hearing constant references to his similarity to Best. A week after his death, an upset and grieving Ryan paid this public tribute: 'When I first came into the Manchester United team, with me being a winger and playing at seventeen, there were always comparisons. But all I ever did was take it as a compliment because of what a great player he was. The tribute the fans gave to George [in the midweek Carling Cup match after his death against West Bromwich Albion at Old Trafford] was fantastic – to honour such a great player, that's what Manchester United fans do. They're great with ex-players, they don't forget, and to see the old players, current players, to be playing against West Brom – who George made his debut against – everything was just so fitting. To win the game as well, everything went so well on the night and I'm sure he would have been proud.'

He then added a personal anecdote: 'I was fortunate to do a video with him when I was about nineteen or twenty. I spent two days with him just going around Old Trafford, going around The Cliff training ground and round some of his old haunts in Manchester. They were some of the places I now go to, and those were two great days and he was nothing but brilliant with me. I was fortunate to have spent time with such a great player and his death is a great loss to Man United and to football in general.'

Of course, Best's death also opened up the old debate yet again about whether he was the greatest ever at United; whether Best was indeed the best – and how Ryan Giggs fitted into the overall equation.

Let's stop a little to consider the question, before returning to the other events that would conspire to make the 2005/06 season such a tough one for Giggsy and the Red Devils.

First, it's important to say Giggs and Best had God-given talent and both will always be towards the top when those lists of United's greatest 50 players are produced every now and then. They were both geniuses on the pitch – yet very different men off it. Best attracted fame and trouble as a light attracts moths, while Giggs played a straight bat throughout his career, keeping himself in tip-top condition by eating the correct, nutritional foods and steering clear of the deadly booze. Yet, contrarily, it was Best who – despite his lifestyle – avoided the injuries that could have threatened Giggs's career and his work on the football field.

It was a point not lost on Sir Alex Ferguson. When the United boss was asked about the similarities between Best and Giggs by Hugh McIlvanney, he told the *Sunday Times* maestro: 'George was unique, the greatest talent our football ever produced – easily! Look at the scoring record: a total of 179 goals for United in 466 matches played. Here at Old Trafford they reckon Bestie had double-jointed ankles.

Seriously, it was a physical thing, an extreme flexibility there. You remember how he could do those 180-degree turns without going through a half-circle, simply by swivelling on his ankles as well as devastating defenders that helped him to avoid injuries because he was never really stationary for opponents to hurt him. He was always riding or spinning away from things.'

It was a fair point – just think how many games George would have played at United, had he followed Ryan's dedication and ideas on fitness, which, since the age of thirty, have even involved following a yoga plan.

But while Ryan mostly stuck to the straight and narrow after walking into Old Trafford at fifteen, George rapidly embarked on a wayward lifestyle. He was a mischievous, immature man, a Peter Pan of football. We would excuse him many of his misdemeanours simply because he was George Best, and because he lived a life that few of us would have been able to survive without some sort of crutch. For George, it would be alcohol. He was football's first superstar, its first pop star. And football clubs at the time simply weren't prepared for helping their players cope with fame and the problems it brings. Sir Matt Busby was to admit as much when he remarked, 'What were we to do, shoot him? I always looked for a cure with George. It would have been easy to have transferred him, but that wasn't the answer. Special rules for George? I suppose so, but only in the sense that he was a special player. I mean, you make it different once you say someone is a good player, and the man next to him is a genius. George is a genius.'

Giggs was lucky in the sense that in Ferguson he had a manager who was able to offer him the sort of help that Busby had not been able to give Best. He threw a protective cocoon around his young prodigy and mapped out his moves early in his career. It was Fergie who decided when Ryan would play and when he would slip back into the shadows, when he would do his first interview, what promotional deals he was allowed and even which agent would best serve his needs. And it was in much the same vein as motor racing supremo Ron Dennis would chart Lewis Hamilton's ascendancy from talented teen to world champion at McLaren – and both lads ended up as world-beaters.

No, it was definitely tougher for George. But you could also argue that Ryan left him standing in terms of his remarkable achievements, which included a long list of honours attained and records broken – including two European Cup wins to George's one, and the most appearances by anybody ever in a United shirt. Giggsy also outdid him in his private life, managing to find a stability and peace and quiet that forever eluded poor Georgie boy. He became a happy family man whereas George remained a wandering, lost soul – for ever searching for the drug of choice that would fix him, including constant booze and women.

Andy Bucklow, a senior journalist on the *Mail on Sunday*, has followed United since the Sixties and thus is well placed to comment. This is what he had to say on how he rated Ryan in the overall pantheon of United greats:

'It's probably a strange thing to say of Manchester United and the Premiership's most decorated footballer, and the current football writers' Player of The Year, but I still feel that Ryan Giggs is, in many ways, still very much underrated. By that I mean he could, and possibly should, be considered as possibly the greatest player the club has had when you measure his overall contribution to United's mind-boggling success over the past 20 years. And I'm not just talking about the sackful of winners' medals alone.

'We have seen three phases of Giggs: from the carefree 17-year-old who burst on to the scene in 1991 to become the Premier League's first poster boy, through to the complete left-sided player who knew how and when to play and release the ball as well as sprinkle a game with genius such as with his 1999 wonder dribble and strike against Arsenal in the FA Cup semi. And now we have the reinvented Giggs, the cute midfielder, still capable of the odd burst of pace and twisted blood dribble, but now more deep-lying, outthinking defences with his astute passing and instinctive movement. And the only player to have scored in every Premier League season after his brilliant free kick at Tottenham in September 2009.

'Yet despite all this, and the fact that he overtook Sir Bobby Charlton's all-time appearance record during the Champions League triumph in Moscow in 2008, the young Giggs was perhaps more appreciated by the fans than the older model is now. In some ways his longevity has worked against him in the popularity stakes. He's been so bloody good over 20 years that we've come to take him for granted.

'That's why in United fans' player polls, Giggs, although always up there, ranks behind the likes of Cantona, Ronaldo, and, yes, George Best. All great

young Ryan Giggs in the early years of his Manchester United career. Giggs n the PFA Young Player of the Year in 1992 and 1993.

Above left and right: Giggs on international duty for Wales. He broke the recor
for the youngest ever Wales debutant on his first appearance in 1991.

Below: Giggs in Champions League action for United against Juventus in 1996.

:gs was a vital part of the United and Wales teams by 1998, and although
npered slightly by injury, he continued to contribute important goals.

On the road to European glory – Giggs celebrates scoring against Brondby (to and his incredible 90th-minute equaliser against Juventus (*bottom*) that would help United book a place in the 1999 Champions League final.

above: Giggs is mobbed by fans as he arrives in Barcelona for the 1999
Champions League final.

below: Giggs celebrates with Teddy Sheringham and David Beckham after
Sheringham's injury-time equaliser in the Champions League final against
Bayern Munich.

Giggs prepares to lift the Champions League trophy – United's amazing 2-1 win sealed their first European Cup since 1968.

though Giggs sadly never made it to an international finals with Wales, he was always incredibly proud whenever he had the chance to play for his country.

Giggs salutes the fans after his testimonial match at Old Trafford on 1 August 2001

players, all world-class players, but the last three are rather more high-profile and controversial than the boy who learned very quickly to do all his talking on the pitch, where he has now performed for just about as long as the others put together.

'Best once said, in tribute to the young Giggs when he was the flying new winger on the block that "One day people might even say that I was another Ryan Giggs." Well, they cannot say that because, apart from the obvious skill factor, Giggs is everything that Best wasn't and in some ways Best's career died so that Ryan Giggs's might live.

'Best was at his peak, and by that I mean his real peak when his heart was in it and before the booze took over, for six, maybe seven years. When Sir Matt left, so, in many ways, did George. Giggs may be playing a different role and more infrequently these days, but you can make a case for him being at or near his peak for more or less his entire career.

'Best was never jeered by his own fans, even in the bad days pre-relegation in 1974 when we were all grateful even just to have him in a poor side when he was clearly a stone or two overweight after one of several abortive comebacks. To many, George never had a bad game, and though we all prefer to remember his true genius through the numerous vintage clips, that is just plainly ridiculous.

'Even in his prime Best had average games just like anyone else. As did Charlton, as did Law. But they were different times, times when a sad 6-1 thrashing away at Burnley didn't create quite such a national commotion as a "calamitous" 1-0 defeat at the same venue in 2009.

'Yet, hard as it is to believe now, Giggs was booed by United fans at Old Trafford in a League Cup semi-final in 2003 and it seemed he was on his way out. His cause was not helped by missing that celebrated sitter against Arsenal in the FA Cup, a match which ironically led to Beckham's departure rather than Giggs's, after Fergie's pinpoint dressing room pass on to Goldenballs' head with a boot.

'But typically, ten days later, after being dropped to the bench Giggs came on for an injured Diego Forlan, no less, to score twice in a 3-0 Champions League away win at Juventus and then, subsequently, helped United to another title triumph by overhauling Arsenal. That Juventus game was one of the few times that the ever-modest Giggs sought to remind the ungrateful of his worth.

'After a typically stunning run, he beat half the Juventus defence to shoot past Buffon with his weaker right foot. In front of the travelling United fans, now in delirious celebration, Giggs turned and pointed to his name and number. This prompted the *Manchester Evening News* to ask fans: "Did Giggs prove his real worth at Juve?" Faintly ridiculous then and still laughable now.

'He shouldn't have had to remind them who he was or what he was about. Most of us already knew, and were getting very twitchy about a possible transfer to Serie A. Thank God it never happened and, with his more customary unassuming brilliance, Giggs has been reminding us of who he is ever since.

'So while you could make out a good case for Best just shading Giggs in the genius stakes, how highly do you rank the fact that Giggs has done it on the pitch for three times as long as George and helped the club to even more success? We can only ponder what George could have achieved had he not been the lone template for today's celebrity footballer. It doesn't take much imagination to believe that in his dotage, he'd have been in a similar role to the one Giggs is deployed in today.

'That's the measure of the achievement of Giggs at Manchester United. The measure of the man is that he would never claim to be considered greater than any other legend, past or present. But give it time, and he just could be. And even now, history says that he already is.'

Back in that 2005/06 season, Ryan and United were to face more moments of darkness in the remaining months of the campaign that followed George's death. The most serious would be the loss of European football by the Christmas of 2005.

The Reds had started with a bang when they crushed Debrecen of Hungary 6-0 in the third qualifying round, but the group stage was a real struggle. It shouldn't have been – United were drawn in Group D against second-drawer opposition from Spain (Villarreal), Portugal (Benfica) and France (Lille). Somehow, they conspired to make life difficult against a trio who hardly inspired fear in the hearts of any of the other European giants who might meet them. For Ferguson and his team, the disgrace that season was that they would finish bottom of this mediocre group, not even qualifying for what was then the UEFA Cup. The campaign started promisingly enough – with a 0-0 draw in Spain and a 2-1 win over Benfica at Old Trafford.

But it started to fall apart when United could only manage a 0-0 draw with Lille at home and then lost the return leg 1-0 in France. Before that first leg against Lille, Ferguson had praised the Champions League, hailing it as more important than the World Cup. To us in the media it sounded as if the United manager was trying to deflect attention away from United's worrying failings around that time in the Premier League. As if he was saying, well, OK, we are struggling a bit in the league, but just watch us go when we pick up our pace in Europe.

An indication of the fans' growing unrest came in the home match against Blackburn at the end of September – which United lost 2-1 – when a section of fans booed off both the team and the manager. The warning bells were ringing four days before that defeat. The *Sun*'s Neil Custis wrote then: 'Alex Ferguson is facing a player revolt over tactics. United have had only five shots on target in their last three games and failed to score in 225 minutes of football. Many players are growing sick of what they see as a negative style of play, with a supposed 4-3-3 formation often turning into 4-5-1. But the tactics appear to be decided by Ferguson's number two, Carlos Queiroz. And he is determined not to budge from what he sees as the right way to win back the Premiership.'

During the Blackburn *débâcle* two thugs had even tried to charge a barrier to get to Ferguson in the dugout. Immediately he was given extra security guards, but was confronted by more fans shouting abuse as he walked off at half time.

So, by the time of the Lille home match, he was much in need of a boost. But if he hoped it would come in Europe, he was miserably mistaken. The goalless draw was indicative of

United's struggles in the Champions League that season. OK, the French team were bruisers – as Ryan, in particular, found out – but they should have been dispatched with ease. What they did was to cynically take him out of the game. He was forced to undergo surgery after fracturing his cheekbone in three places in an aerial clash with Stathis Tavlaridis (ironically, a former Arsenal man) and faced six weeks on the sidelines. The boss was infuriated by the incident and his anger worsened when the referee refused to allow his player to receive immediate treatment.

It was only when Giggs was replaced by Ji-Sung Park with seven minutes remaining on the clock that the full extent of the damage was uncovered.

Ferguson said afterwards, 'The referee is supposed to stop the game when a player has a bad injury. When you see the incident, I am amazed the referee didn't allow the physio on. Our doctor is not happy about it and it is something we are looking at. Ryan has suffered three separate fractures and his cheek will have to be plated. If we had been able to get on the pitch, we would have taken him off immediately because you can see the indentation in his cheek from the TV pictures.'

Fergie believed Ryan stayed on due to his own courage: 'The miracle is he didn't get any more knocks because something really serious could have happened. When he came off and we saw the damage, we realised Ryan had been very lucky. Lille are a very aggressive side who were committed to getting a result any way they could. I looked at the video and I have never seen as many elbows and aerial challenges in all my time in England. You have to give Lille credit in terms of how far they have come as a club since we last played them four years ago, but they certainly weren't prepared to gamble and try to win. They just wanted to make sure they didn't lose.'

After the 1-0 loss in France a fortnight later, United desperately needed a win over Villarreal at Old Trafford on 22 November 2005. With Giggs still out injured, they could only draw 0-0, which meant their European hopes depended entirely on the result in Lisbon, when they faced Benfica on 7 December. Giggs was back, but the United of old were not: they fell to a 2-1 defeat and crashed out of the competition at the group stage for the first time in 11 years.

Ryan had just lost out to Gary Neville in the battle to be United's new skipper and now he was bowing out of Europe, for that season at least, on the worst low imaginable. Ferguson had praised him when he reviewed his options for captain, saying, 'Ryan has worn the armband many times, purely on seniority, and that is quite right. A player who has served this football club the length of time Ryan has deserves to be recognised.'

Now Fergie had to find words to describe his anguish at his team's risible defeat – words that would also keep him in a job as the clamour for his head grew louder on phone-ins and other nationwide debates among United fans.

Asked if he was worried about his future, he snarled, 'I am not going to answer that. I've got a job to do, it's a great job and I've confidence in my players. This club has always risen from difficult situations, and we will again.'

Indeed, his record of achievement at the club quite rightly bought him time to turn things around again – much to the relief of Giggsy, who could not even contemplate working under anyone else at United. That season, the team finished runners-up to Chelsea (by eight points), exited the FA Cup in a demoralising 1-0 defeat to archrivals Liverpool, but won the League Cup, much to Ferguson's relief.

He has always maintained that a trophy a season represented success and now Fergie would 'big up' the one he had written off more than once as an irrelevance in the seasons when the big trophies had been coming thick and fast. On 26 February 2006, United thrashed Wigan 4-0 in Cardiff to lift the trophy.

Rooney grabbed a brace, with Saha and Ronaldo also getting on to the score sheet. It was small consolation for a tough, trying campaign. Yet there would even be fallout from the only real high of that fractious season: Ruud van Nistelrooy was angry that he was a sub and not even brought on when the result was in the bag. Already he had fallen out with Ronaldo during a training session over the other player's closeness to assistant boss Queiroz. Insiders say that Ruud had scoffed at Ronaldo, saying, 'Off you go to see your father then.'

The remarks were hardly well timed – Ronaldo was still mourning the death of his real father. He is said to have replied, 'I can't, my father has died,' before skulking away. Apparently neither Ferguson nor Queiroz were pleased when news of the bust-up reached them, especially given the sensitivity of the comments. It was the final straw – by May, the Dutch striker had joined Keane in leaving United. Ferguson would explain that the decision to offload van Nistelrooy, 'was a result of a couple of incidents in training that concerned me in terms of the spirit of the club'.

As Giggs left for his summer holidays in 2006, he must have wondered how United would ever get back to the top of the pile – in England, let alone Europe. The club no longer seemed able to sign the biggest names as Chelsea outmuscled them in the transfer market and the West London outfit also edged them out as champions once more. Then there was the setback in Europe of December 2005, plus worries about how the team would fare without Van Nistelrooy and Keane.

Twelve years earlier Ferguson had told the world that his kids would pull him through, but were Ronaldo and Rooney ready to step up to the plate?

Against all the odds, Ryan Giggs was to find himself back where he belonged – as a champion – the following season. And Ferguson would have found the perfect response to the critics and fans who had written him off as yesterday's man.

For United would end the dark days with a new dawn in 2006/07, much to the satisfaction of Giggs and Ferguson, the two men who walked side by side for the whole of United's era of dominance. Ferguson was to say that he was not surprised by his team's and his own remarkable renaissance – but he was one of the few who wasn't. From the gloom and doom of 7 December 2005, when United finished bottom of their Champions League group and exited Europe in miserable fashion, to the joy and delight of 5 May 2007, when they celebrated winning the Premier League once again in style with a 1-0 win at neighbours Manchester City, the transformation was truly amazing – even shocking.

Just how had United done it, given the paucity of quality evident in that defeat in Lisbon less than 18 months earlier? Just how had Giggsy emerged triumphant once again – when few would have bet their houses on him winning any more Premier League crowns, let alone the Champions League?

Well, you have to give Ferguson credit. His wonderboys –
Rooney and Ronaldo – finally came of age as he always said
they would. And his transfer market buys proved they were
well worth the money by making vital contributions. I am
thinking in particular of the defensive stalwarts Nemanja
Vidic and Patrice Evra, who arrived at Old Trafford just a
month after the Lisbon *débâcle*. Vidic was a rock, a natural to
partner Ferdinand in the centre of the backline, while Evra
simply got better and better as he settled – and is surely now
the number one left-back in the world.

Plus there was the beefing-up of the midfield that had been
allowed to suffer and struggle since 2004. Finally, the days of
the Klebersons and Djemba-Djembas were over as Ferguson
apparently began to see sense: there was no point in trying to
find a direct one-on-one replacement for Keane – there was
none. Keano was the master, possibly with only Patrick Vieira
in his prime fit to lace his boots.

No, much better to get the midfield singing to a different
hymn sheet.

To his credit, instead of trying to find another enforcer and
power player, Ferguson opted for the artistry and more refined
industry of Michael Carrick. The manager splashed out what
seemed an overblown £14 million. Eventually, the Tyne &
Wear born midfielder would look a bargain as he drove
United back to the top, providing a razor-sharp supply line of
crosses and passes for Ronaldo, Giggs and co.

Ryan had one of his best seasons for the club. He breathed a
sigh of relief as it soon became evident that the grim days were
at last over. Now he, like United, could dazzle again. Along with
several other United stars, he made the PFA Team of The Year.

It read: Goalkeeper: Edwin Van der Sar (Manchester United). Defence: Gary Neville, Patrice Evra, Rio Ferdinand, Nemanja Vidic (all United). Midfield: Steven Gerrard (Liverpool), Paul Scholes, Ryan Giggs, Cristiano Ronaldo (all United). Attack: Didier Drogba (Chelsea), Dimitar Berbatov (Tottenham Hotspur).

United would win the league by six points from Chelsea and finish a massive 21 points ahead of archrivals Liverpool. Ryan was to play in a total of 38 matches and score six goals.

By now he was official vice-captain at the club, but as skipper Gary Neville suffered a series of injury setbacks he would regularly lead the team out in his friend's absence. He would link well with Carrick and his other old mate in the team, Scholes – the Ginger Prince had previously suffered eye problems, but now he was back in business.

Suddenly, from being a lost cause, struggling to put their passes together, United were playing champions-style, champagne football – and Giggs was having a ball. He was thirty-four in November 2006 but was regularly turning back the clock with some fine displays. The excellence of his work was reflected at the end of the campaign when he finished third in The Football Writers' Association Footballer of the Year award for 2007. Team-mate Ronaldo won the award, with Chelsea's Didier Drogba runner-up and Scholesy fourth.

But it was Ryan who lifted the Barclays Premiership Merit Award. He was presented with the special honour in recognition of his record of nine Premier League titles. Appropriately enough, his mentor and boss, Sir Alex, won the Manager of the Year award – fair game after he had transformed his team from losers to winners in the space of 18 months.

Giggs scored the first of his six goals in the 2-1 Premier League win at Watford on 26 August 2006. He grabbed the winner just before the hour mark.

Two weeks later he won another match for the Reds, scoring the only goal in the home league win over Spurs. Coincidentally, the following February, he was to score the final goal in the 4-0 return win over Spurs at White Hart Lane. Clearly, he enjoyed playing the north Londoners – over the years he had made a habit of scoring memorable goals against them at vital moments.

Giggsy also enjoyed some fine form in the Champions League as United reached the semis. The earlier stages of the competition gave them the chance to gain revenge against two of the teams who had played a part in the lowest moment for Ryan and Co the previous season. In the group stage, they beat Benfica 1-0 away and 3-1 at home – with Giggs scoring the second United goal in the 3-1 win – to finally dispel the bitter taste of defeat in Lisbon a year earlier.

And in the knockout stage they would beat Lille 1-0 at home and away, with Ryan grabbing the winner in France with seven minutes remaining. That goal caused uproar among the Lille players – they claimed they were not ready with their wall when he cleverly scored from a free-kick after 83 minutes. Angrily, they walked off the pitch, but eventually returned. Afterwards Ferguson remarked, 'I have never seen that before in all my years in football. That is a disgrace and Uefa have to do something about that because it was pure intimidation of the referee. The Lille staff encouraged their players to come off and that made it a hostile atmosphere inside the ground. Ryan asked the ref if he could take it quickly – and the ref agreed.'

143

Giggs's quick thinking put United in the driving seat, but he sensibly stayed out of the war of words that was developing. Just 24 hours before the return leg in Manchester, Lille were at it again – trying to wind up Ryan and his team-mates and upset their preparations. Of course, it was all water off a duck's back to United, who are wised up on mind games and, in Ferguson, possess the master of them all.

Lille goalkeeper Tony Sylva – the man Ryan caught napping with his quick free-kick – tried to stain the veteran winger's reputation by saying, 'Giggs is very intelligent, but I am not happy with the way he scored his goal at all. Football is a sport and it is necessary to play a clean game, to play without tricks. Giggs didn't do this. If you analyse the rules, I believe that the goal should have been cancelled and that Giggs should have received a yellow card. We are still furious with the referee that night and with the players of Manchester United. The English claim they are the kings of fair play, but that night they demonstrated they are experts in anti-sporting behaviour.'

United would not be distracted as they professionally finished the job and then trounced Roma 8-3 on aggregate in the last eight. But their good fortune ran out in the semis as they lost 5-3 on aggregate to a very fine AC Milan side. There would also be disappointment at Wembley on 19 May 2007. A Didier Drogba goal ended Giggs's hopes of yet another double as Chelsea won the FA Cup final by a goal to nil. As a spectacle, it was a letdown and Ryan felt particularly disappointed as he had led the team out as skipper on the day. He and Ferguson believed he was denied a blatant penalty when Michael Essien fouled him in extra time when he was trying to convert a cross from Rooney. Ryan's effort went straight at Chelsea keeper Petr Cech, who then seemed to lift the ball over his goal line as Giggs fell into him.

Giggs said, 'It was clearly over the line – that's what I was asking for. I could see it was over the line and the referee didn't give a free-kick so it was a goal. I felt I was getting to the ball quite comfortably and felt someone touch my leg. We're disappointed, obviously. The big decisions didn't go for us and if you don't get the big decisions it is going to be hard for you. The referees are picked on merit and how they perform throughout the season.

'The FA Cup is a big occasion and you want the referees to get the big decisions right. They are only human and sometimes they get them wrong, but in the Cup final you hope they get them right and today they didn't.'

Ferguson backed up his captain, saying, 'It's a penalty kick. Then the goalkeeper's spilled the ball behind the line. I think it would have been a difficult one for the linesman to call but the referee should be in a better position. We couldn't see where we were, but when I see it now it's a penalty.'

Giggsy departed Wembley that night thinking about what could have been, but in the disappointment he and his team-mates knew there was a lot to celebrate. After all, they had won back their Premier League crown and had shown they now had a team that could again compete not just at home, but in Europe too.

A new era of optimism – and glory – had definitely dawned for Ryan Giggs in the end-days of his career after that unpleasant, suffocating spell in the darkness. He and United were back in business. And big time, as the 2007/08 season would prove.

CHAPTER 11

MAGNIFICENT SEVEN

After a relaxing summer holiday in 2007, Ryan Giggs packed his training gear into the car and did what he had done for the previous 16 years – headed off to Old Trafford from his luxury home in nearby Worsley to meet up with the rest of the Manchester United squad for pre-season. From a distance you would think he hadn't a care in the world as he laughed and joked with 'the lads' as the boss told them of their pre-season schedule, but you would be wrong. On the outside he might have been smiling, but inside he was feeling the same rush of adrenaline, nerves, hopes, anticipation and excitement that he had always experienced as the boss outlined how training would gradually be stepped up and how he expected his men to be ultra-professional, and winners.

In other words, it was no different to usual as Ryan Giggs entered his 17th season as a Manchester United player. He told friends that he felt as motivated as ever to win the biggest prizes. After clinching his ninth Premier League title the previous May, some pundits had questioned whether he still had any mountains left to climb.

Sir Alex Ferguson had heard the whispers and grimaced. Of course, the star player of his 21-year regime at Old Trafford still had ambitions and personal goals. And to prove it, the boss set Giggs another one, just to ensure he kept the old engine ticking over: the challenge of winning an unprecedented tenth Premier League crown and to play in 30 league games.

And the boy from Wales was to pick up the gauntlet and answer both demands. By the end of the campaign he would have lifted the league title yet again and made 31 league appearances. But he also set himself a little incentive as he joked and laughed with his team-mates that pre-season: to lift the European Cup once more. Of course, he had a medal from 1999, but he felt – like his boss – that if he was to be termed a true great, he would need at least one more.

He was getting no younger – he would be thirty-four by the end of the campaign – and time was running out. Also, he had a feeling that there might never be a better time to achieve the dream. The United team looked as strong as it had at any time during his time at the club – with star men in all departments. Edwin Van der Sar could be relied upon as an extremely safe pair of hands in goal, the centre-back

above: Giggs celebrates after scoring United's second goal against Juventus in February 2003.

below left: Squaring up to United team-mate Gary Neville as Wales take on England in a World Cup 2004 qualifier.

below right: A sight many would like to have seen – Ryan Giggs in an England shirt. Contrary to popular belief, Giggs was never eligible to play for England, though he did captain England Schoolboys.

Above left: Giggs always has time and appreciation for his many thousands of fans. Here, he is signing autographs during a training session with the Welsh national team in Swansea in 2005.

Above right: Celebrating with Wales team-mates Richard Duffy, James Collins and Simon Davies after scoring during their World Cup 2006 qualifier against Azerbaijan.

Below left: Another day, another goal – Giggs salutes the fans after scoring against Benfica.

Below right: A sad day for Welsh football – Giggs announces his retirement in 200

Ryan Giggs's last match for Wales, against the Czech Republic on 3 June 2007. Manager John Toshack and Welsh fans showed their appreciation for the winger after he was substituted during the game.

Above: United players look on nervously during the penalty shoot-out that was decide the outcome of the 2008 Champions League final between Manchester United and Chelsea.

Below: Giggs and the rest of the United team celebrate clinching the Champion League title 6-5 on penalties, after the match had ended 1-1.

1 their way to a second successive Champions League final – Giggs and United ercame Celtic (*top*) and Aalborg (*bottom*) to reach the final again in 2009.

Giggs evades Arsenal's
Alexandre Song during
their 2009 Champions
League semi-final.

dly things didn't go to plan for United in the Rome final, as they were beaten
) by Barcelona.

Still on top form: Giggs remains the backbone of the United team and has pledged his future to the club.

pairing of Vidic and Ferdinand was arguably the best in the world, while the midfield was strong with Carrick, Fletcher, Giggs himself and Scholes, and up front were the exciting talents of Ronaldo and Rooney.

Plus, he learned as he prepared for pre-season, the already top-notch squad would be reinforced by the imminent arrival of new boys Owen Hargreaves, Carlos Tévez, Anderson and Nani.

They were truly exciting, optimism-laced times at the Theatre of Dreams and if United were to bring home that elusive Champions League trophy again, surely now was as good a time as any? The omens were good. Pre-season went well and Ryan picked up his sixth Community Shield winner's medal on 5 August, as United beat Chelsea 3-0 on penalties after the match ended 1-1 at full time. Ironically, the Reds would also end their season – after a nine-month slog – against the same opposition, but then the venue was to be Moscow, not London, and the reward for winning would not be a mere trinket like the Community Shield, but the biggest cup and the greatest honour in world football – the Champions League trophy.

Ryan also grabbed the Reds' first goal of that long but profitable season when he put United 1-0 ahead against Chelsea at the new Wembley on 35 minutes, hammering the ball home. He did not take part in the penalty shootout after Darren Fletcher replaced him nine minutes from time, but declared himself 'very happy' with his goal and the outcome of United's first competitive match of the season.

It may have been termed a friendly but matches between the Blues and the Reds invariably had a hard edge to them, given the fierce rivalry between the clubs to be top dogs since Roman Abramovich took control at Stamford Bridge in 2003. Chelsea had equalised through Florent Malouda – who took a pass from Ashley Cole and lashed the ball past the despairing Van der Sar – and Sir Alex complimented both the Chelsea man and his own player for the quality of their goals, saying: 'I thought the goals were very good – Malouda took his goal very, very well. The build-up to our goal was excellent too; it was a marvellous finish from Ryan. He's slotted it in a gap in the net very well.'

The boss said he expected his new-look United team and Chelsea to be battling it out for Premier League domination yet again – and that his new buys would hopefully help maintain United's dominance. He told the *Daily Mail*: 'We've identified the potential in Nani and Anderson and they can eventually develop into top players. Tévez has the experience of playing in England for a year and he has shown that he can become one of the best strikers in the world. Hargreaves has European experience and will shore up the midfield against counter-attacks. The teams are not at 100 per cent but it's a stepping-stone to next week. Everybody knows we are the two best sides in the country, but Arsenal and Liverpool will play a bigger hand this season.'

A week later United would open up their Premier League campaign with a home match against Reading. Giggs said he felt as fresh and as motivated as ever – and that he considered his decision to retire from international football would also help his game at club level: 'I am getting older – that is fairly obvious. But I am still as enthusiastic as I have ever been and I am excited about the challenge this season presents. Given the squad we have, it is impossible to be any other way. Every season, I just try to look for that extra five or 10 per cent that will keep me involved, whether it is in my preparation for games, or what I do afterwards with the use of ice baths and things like that.

'This year, I am not playing international football, which will give me a chance to get some rest. Hopefully it will help me towards the end of the season when games start to come thick and fast.'

He said that it would be an honour to continue to lead United in the absence of injured club skipper Gary Neville – but that he expected a tough challenge from the likes of Liverpool and Chelsea as he went for that tenth Premier League title, adding: 'The whole league is getting tougher each year and everyone wants to beat the champions, so it is going to be harder still this time around. Chelsea will want to do better than last year, and Liverpool and Arsenal will both want to win it as well. But we have a lot of players who had not won the Premier League before. Now they have, they will want to taste it again.'

Ryan said that the new boys – Carlos Tévez and co – were settling in well and that he had big hopes for them: 'When you sign new players, especially exciting, attack-minded players like the ones we have, it excites players and staff, as well as the fans. There has to be a settling-in period but they have looked good in training and in games, so I wouldn't be surprised if they hit the floor running.'

He said the retention of United's Premier League crown could depend on the team's defence – even though everyone was harping on about the strength in attack that United now possessed: 'We do have plenty of attacking flair – we have at least four or five players who can change a game and take people on. That is what Manchester United is all about. But you cannot lose sight of the fact defences win you championships and that is what happened last year.

'The defenders provide the platform for attacking players to produce the skills they have. We must defend well and be solid as a team.'

And he warned that United would need a good start if they were to see off the challengers: 'You can't give the likes of Chelsea, Arsenal and Liverpool a six- or seven-point lead after a couple of weeks or a couple of months.' But since when did United get off to flying starts? They are renowned for being slow starters and for having to claw their way back into contention before leaving their rivals gasping for breath in the home straight. Much the same way as they play, more often than not in huge games, United seem to thrive on having to come back against the odds; to have to come back from a goal or two down.

So it was no surprise that the team got their season started with the usual damp squib – this time Reading would be the outfit they struggled against in the opener. The Royals held United to a 0-0 draw at Old Trafford on 12 August. Three days later they drew again, this time 1-1 at Portsmouth. And a week after the disappointing home opener against Reading, United blew it big-time, going down 1-0 at neighbours Manchester City.

The loss at City was especially galling for Ryan as it meant the Blues had maintained their unbeaten start, making it three out of three Premier League wins – and that they stood proudly at the top of the table while United struggled in the nether regions. The winner came on the half-hour when a shot by Geovanni took a deflection off Vidic and flew past Van der Sar.

Giggs was the Reds' best player, romping down the left wing and sending over several pinpoint crosses and corners. Carlos Tévez was profligate with several chances and should have hauled United back into the match. Even the then City boss Sven-Goran Eriksson admitted as much: 'United could have scored and maybe they should have done but we defended very well.' He also paid tribute to Ryan, saying the winger was a fine role model for younger players as he continued to defy the years. 'Giggs was outstanding. I have always liked him and his clear love for the game and enthusiasm. He has been a world-class talent for many, many years.'

But Ryan and Sir Alex were in no mood to talk about the ins and outs of the match – both had hated losing to City over the years. It was left to Owen Hargreaves to put United's view across – and to try to explain why the Reds had picked up just two points from their first three games. Hargreaves told BBC Sport: 'In each game we have dominated possession. We have played relatively well, but football at this level is about winning games. We haven't got the points we expected and we just aren't scoring the goals that we need to at the moment.'

On 27 August United finally picked up their first win of the season – a 1-0 victory over Spurs at Old Trafford. Luis Nani was the hero, firing home his first goal for the club. The 25-yard screamer couldn't have come at a better time to lift morale. Spurs hadn't won at United for 17 years, but that hot August day they gave them some uncomfortable moments – as Sir Alex conceded: 'That was narrow, touch and go, nothing to choose between the two sides. They dug in and got forward a bit and there was really nothing in it in the second half. I thought we lacked a little bit of confidence. Players are anxious, there is a lot of expectation here, and what was required was to dig in, show great commitment and we did that.'

Ryan was skipper for the day and was just as relieved as the boss to get all three points. He had certainly led by example, digging in with tackles and driving down the left wing. His commitment to the United cause was illustrated by the fact that he picked up one of his rare bookings – the first yellow card of the afternoon for an ill-timed tackle from behind on Lee Young-Pyo.

A fortnight later, there was a more personal reason to celebrate as Giggs married his long-term partner, Stacey Cooke, in a private ceremony on 7 September. The couple tied the knot at a register office in Manchester and were joined only by close family and friends, including their two children, Liberty (born in 2003) and Zach (born in 2006). They shunned the stereotypical ostentatious footballer's wedding celebrations for a low-key celebratory meal at Salford's Lowry Hotel.

On the pitch, Giggs was back in business for the trip to Everton on 15 September. A traditionally tough place to visit – given the commitment and determination of David Moyes's boys – United showed they were now starting to get their act together by chalking up a creditable 1-0 win. OK, the triumph may have been à la '1-0 to the Arsenal'-style, but a win was a win and three points were three points. Nemanja Vidic was the hero, heading home the decider on 83 minutes, and United were now moving surely up the table.

Another 1-0 win saw the Reds beat Sporting Lisbon away in the first match of the Champions League at the group stage. Giggs was again on from the start and played his part as returning hero Cristiano Ronaldo (who joined the Reds from Sporting) gave United the win to get their European campaign off to a fine start.

United were picking up momentum and wins followed over Chelsea at home (2-0), Birmingham away (1-0) in the league and Roma at home (1-0) in the Champions League. Ryan played in all those matches and had a particularly impressive outing against Chelsea. For the Blues of Stamford Bridge, it was their first match under new boss Avram Grant, after the acrimonious departure of José Mourinho, and they would start badly, with John Obi Mikel sent off for a poor challenge on Patrice Evra.

Ryan set up the first goal for Tévez with a superb cross as Carlos headed the ball past Petr Cech for what was to be his first goal for United. The Argentine also played a part in the second goal. He was pulled back in the box by Ben-Haim and Louis Saha stroked the ball into the net from the penalty spot.

It was the end of United's run of 1-0 wins and, as assistant boss Carlos Queiroz said, everyone was relieved: 'It was a great result but it felt like two games – one before the red card and one after – but before then I felt we played probably our best football of the season. We deserved to be leading when the red card came and Chelsea then became more compact and invited us to attack and make a mistake. But we were patient and clever and never got frustrated as we knew we had the three points in our pocket.'

Now United started to motor – with Ryan at the steering wheel. They scored four goals in four consecutive games in a remarkable 21-day period in October 2007 – with wins over Wigan at home (4-0), Aston Villa away (4-1), Dynamo Kiev away (4-2) and Middlesbrough at home (4-1). And Giggs got in on the goals act in the match at Villa Park, grabbing United's fourth in the rout on 75 minutes. It was a straight seventh win for United and Giggsy said the atmosphere within the camp was great, that the lads had pulled themselves together after an early season stutter and were now committed to making it a season to remember.

But among the fans there were fears that it could all be wrecked by injuries as United had two more men sidelined before the match kicked off against Kiev in the Ukraine. The Reds had already made the trip without four injured internationals – Gary Neville, Owen Hargreaves, Michael Carrick and Louis Saha – and then lost Paul Scholes in a training session and Patrice Evra in the warm-up. Yet they still won 4-2, and that convinced Giggs, stand-in skipper for the injured Neville, that United now had the depth of squad to cope, even in such an injury nightmare situation.

'There was no disruption in Kiev despite the injuries,' he said. 'The manager has chopped and changed this season already, whether that be due to injuries, or suspensions or whatever, and we have coped with it, just as we coped with what happened in Kiev. It just proves the value of having a good squad. I think a few players are due to come back shortly and once that happens, we will start to look strong again.'

And he believed all the signings had bedded in and played some good stuff and that overall, it was looking really good.

He also pointed out that the win in Eastern Europe was United's third from as many games – and that they were spot on for early qualification to the next round of the Champions League. 'You can't ask for any more than three wins from three games. It is the position we wanted to be in, especially with two home games – against Kiev and Sporting Lisbon – to come. Hopefully, we can get qualification sealed as quickly as we can, which will give the manager an opportunity to give the lads who need a game a chance to get fit.'

Early qualification would certainly be a positive step forward – and was more than likely to happen as United had scored four goals away from home, the first time they had done so in nine years. Ryan added: 'To score four goals away from home against any team in Europe is fantastic. Over the last few years, our away-form in Europe has not been the best, but we are on a real run now and we want to carry it on in every competition.'

Something special was happening, that much was clear – the team was firing on all cylinders and there was a feeling they could pull off something remarkable if they continued. It was a similar sense of hope and optimism to the one that had surrounded the camp during the record-breaking Treble year of 1999. Sir Alex said as much in his programme notes before the match against Blackburn at Old Trafford on 11 November 2007, that the squad was one of his best ever, if not the best. 'This is what I have been working towards. I don't like the short-term fix – I prefer to see a pool of players emerge and develop into something special which, believe me, is what is happening at Old Trafford this season. In fact, it is difficult to know where to stop when I am talking about our important players.'

That was real praise from a man who should know, and one who did not generally hand out such compliments. Ryan also knew something special was brewing at Old Trafford and told friends that he was excited by it. After the Blackburn match – which ended in a 2-0 win for the Reds – United had been unbeaten for close on three months and 10 games, dating back to the 1-0 defeat at Manchester City on 19 August. And he had more to celebrate than just the results – for on 16 October 2007, he signed a new one-year extension to his contract that would keep him at the club until at least 2009. Declaring himself 'delighted' with the offer, he said: 'I am delighted to have signed for a further season. I am enjoying football more than ever and I hope to carry on playing football for Manchester United for as long as I can. I would like to thank Sir Alex Ferguson, the fans and everyone at the club for the great support I have received over the years.

'We said a couple of years ago that would look at it season by season – which is what we have done. It is great to get it sorted out. I feel as fit as ever, so I hope there will be a couple more seasons. A lot has changed over the years but I am enjoying my football more than ever. The nearer you get to the end of your career, you want to enjoy it as much as you can.'

His previous deal would have run out at the end of the 2007/08 season so this provided security and proof that the club still rated him; that they saw him as warranting an extension. Sir Alex admitted as much when he said the deal was complete and that Ryan would be staying at the club where he had spent the whole of his professional career since making his debut back in 1991.

Fergie admitted that he had been keen to tie it all up before the end of the season as he wanted to show loyalty was a two-way street – Ryan had proved his, and now Fergie and the club wanted to show theirs, saying, 'Ryan epitomises the word loyalty – he signed as a fourteen-year-old schoolboy and is still with the club 20 years on. Apart from his playing ability, he has a fantastic demeanour and is a great role model to the younger players. I am sure he will be at the club for a long time to come.'

The new deal would also give him the chance to have a crack at overtaking Sir Bobby Charlton's all-time record for appearances at United. The winger had agreed to what would be his 18th season at Old Trafford – an era that had seen him win nine Premier league titles, four FA Cups, two League Cups and the Champions League. He had also made 727 appearances for United and was in sight of Charlton's club record of 758.

The fan sites were buzzing with delight at the news of Giggs's new deal. One United fan said, 'Ryan Giggs has put pen to paper for a new deal at Man United. I don't know the length yet, but this is great news. Great player and glad that he will be playing his last days at a club he has achieved so much for.'

Another fan said he was glad because Ryan was such a brilliant role model and inspiration: 'Every football player should model themselves on Giggs. He isn't flash, flamboyant and is rarely in the papers, and he keeps his head down and just works his socks off on the pitch. He has been a tremendous servant to Man Utd and I believe Old Trafford won't be the same without Giggsy when he does eventually call it a day. The ultimate professional.'

And even a Liverpool fan got in on the act, saying,

'Outstanding player and fully deserves another year at Utd. So many youngsters look up to the likes of Rooney and Gerrard, but for me the most consistent player over the last 10 to 12 years is without a doubt Ryan Giggs – and I'm a Liverpool fan.'

And one fan calling himself 'acerz' summed up the general feeling of goodwill towards so magnificent a servant: 'Giggs is a breath of fresh air in this day and age where money seems to be the only reason people play at certain clubs. I hope C. Ronaldo's recent comments about his intention to remain at Utd and "become a legend" were (and will continue to be) inspired by Giggs.'

By December, United were steaming on and Ryan played no small part in proceedings. He gave fans an early Christmas present on 8 December 2007, when he scored in the 4-1 rout over Derby in the Premier League. Giggs opened the scoring for the Reds five minutes before the interval – and it was not just any old goal, but another landmark for the veteran star. His 100th goal for United – claimed with a tap-in after Derby keeper Stephen Bywater could only deflect an effort from Ronaldo. Giggs was quick to react and after that the floodgates opened with a Tévez brace and a Ronaldo penalty on the 90 ended the resistance of the Rams.

Ryan was typically low-key and unwilling to blow his own trumpet over the goal – even though the feat meant he was joining a club of just 11 that included the likes of George Best, Denis Law, Bobby Charlton and Mark Hughes. 'It's a great achievement for myself. Not many people have done it so I'm really pleased,' he told BBC Sport. 'In the context of the game it was an important goal but now I can enjoy that it was my 100th goal for United.'

Sir Alex admitted he was amazed that the PA announcer did not bother to tell the Old Trafford faithful what the goal meant. 'I am surprised there was no announcement about Ryan's milestone,' he said. 'Maybe no one knew, but I certainly did. It is a fantastic achievement, absolutely marvellous. Not many players have scored 100 goals, but the service Ryan has given us, quite apart from the goals, is outstanding. Ryan is a great character, a great person and a fantastic servant to us all.'

He added that he was also pleased with his player's overall performance and that of his team: 'It was a big win – things can happen in these conditions; they didn't suit us. Carlos Tévez is making a great contribution this season. Cristiano is our regular penalty-taker so I can understand why he wanted to take it, but it would have been great for Carlos if he had scored a hat-trick.'

The love-in with Tévez was not to last, unfortunately. A season and a half later he would be gone – after claiming the boss had not played him enough in the games that mattered and that the club had not 'shown enough love' in their efforts to keep him.

Rio Ferdinand also wanted to add his thoughts to the acclaim that Giggs was receiving for that 100th goal. Typical of the big, opinionated defender, he was forthright – saying Ryan had never got the total acclaim he deserved, and that now was no different. Rio commented, 'I think he's a fantastic footballer who doesn't get the credit he deserves as a player for what he has achieved. He's probably one of the best players I've played with, if not the best, and continues to go from strength to strength.'

Rio believes his team-mate will be appreciated more when he's retired: 'When we go abroad he's respected a lot more in foreign countries than in this country. When people throw names around, saying someone's done this or done that for the Premier League, he very rarely gets mentioned. It's a shame we are not appreciating a player who's been the most successful footballer of our generation, probably.'

Giggs and United were to go unbeaten in December 2007, and with a flurry of wins to match the rain, sleet and snow that characterised the month's weather. There would also be a lone draw – 1-1 at Roma in the Champions League group stage, but by that time United had already qualified for the next stage.

That month, two results in particular made a real statement of intent about how United meant business that season and, much to the delight of United fans everywhere, they brought two victories over the Scousers. The first was a 1-0 win over Liverpool at Anfield on 16 December. Carlos Tévez grabbed the vital goal two minutes from the interval. Ryan was involved in the build-up, his short corner finding Rooney, who teased the ball into the box. Tévez was the man who made contact, lifting the ball over José Reina for the goal that put United nine points clear of Liverpool.

Fergie was purring afterwards, knowing the full implication that the win at one of United's biggest rivals held for their bid to win the league. 'A marvellous day for us,' he said. 'In terms of playing football, we were the better team. It's going to be a long struggle and fight throughout the season. I always said that if we are there or thereabouts at New Year, we have an outstanding chance of winning the title.'

A week later, United beat Everton 2-1 at Old Trafford, thanks to a brace from Ronaldo. Again, Ryan played his part in a big victory: he was fouled in the box by Steven Pienaar two minutes from time, thus setting up Cristiano for the winning penalty. The effect of the two wins combined meant that United now closed the gap on Premier League leaders Arsenal to just a single point. United knew they were starting to hit a bit of form – and the result served as a 'Beware, we are coming to get you' warning to the Gunners. As Reds assistant boss Carlos Queiroz suggested, 'This was a difficult game for us and Everton closed us down well and fought for everything. But, especially in the second half, our performance was full of desire and determination and there was only one team trying to win. It was a special win because it came so late. This is a period when a lot of games come close together and we don't expect it to be easy, so it's good to be up near the top of the table.'

United were coming up on the inside and the talented but naive kids of Arsenal stood no chance, given their experience in this situation. The wins kept coming and the league table changed with them; soon it was United who were leading the pack (as per usual).

In January 2008, the Reds hammered old rivals Newcastle 6-0, but at the start of February there was a temporary (and unpleasant) blip when they lost 2-1 at home to neighbours Manchester City.

Normal service was resumed a few days later when United thrashed Arsenal 4-0 in the FA Cup 5th round, and a 5-1 over Newcastle in the league came just days after that. They also advanced to the quarter-final of the Champions League by beating French outfit Lyons 2-1 on aggregate over two legs. Now Italians Roma lay in wait in the quarter-finals.

In between the two-legged affair against Lyons, United dreams of another triple year perished as the team lost 1-0 at home to Pompey in the sixth round of the FA Cup. Sulley Ali Muntari scored the penalty that ended Red hopes, his goal coming after Milan Baros was brought down by United's substitute keeper Tomasz Kuszczak.

But, as Ryan said at the time, at least United could now concentrate on the two competitions that really mattered – the Premier League and the Champions League. OK, the Treble would have been nice – to complete a set for Giggs after 1999 – but the game had moved on since then. Nine years after that Treble season, the allure of the FA Cup lessened dramatically. Once a must-watch, must-win event, it was now viewed very much as a second-tier event, above the Carling Cup, for sure, but not compelling or even elite to watch or win. Ryan took no part in the loss to Pompey and few at the club mourned United's exit from the competition.

That it was a one-off freak loss was swiftly confirmed as Giggsy and United now embarked on another powerful run of results that would bring the mighty double to Old Trafford. Yes, the Welsh wizard was set to pick up his second European Cup winner's medal – and his tenth Premier League winner's medal.

A week after the FA Cup defeat they played in the first of four consecutive league games – and all were tough prospects, with banana skin potential aplenty. Yet United would triumph in every one of them, with Ryan playing in three.

The first was a 1-0 win at Derby, the goal coming courtesy of Ronaldo. United should have scored many more – indeed,

Giggs should have put them ahead in the first minute but, unusually for him, he spurned a fairly straightforward chance. Maybe he was still rusty with the game only just underway, but he headed over from a cross by Ji-Sung Park.

The following week, it was Ronaldo who led United home again, scoring both goals in the 2-0 home win over Bolton. Ryan played no part in the match, but was back after a rest for the next game – traditionally United's biggest home game of the season – against their bitterest rivals from down the East Lancs Road, Liverpool.

A brilliant 3-0 drubbing of Rafa Benítez's team left United six points clear at the top and well on course to retain the league title. It was an even sweeter win for Giggs and co. (and United's army of supporters) as it also ended any hopes the Scousers may have had of making a late bid for the crown that had eluded them for 18 years. With goals from Wes Brown, Ronaldo and Nani, United won and Liverpool's misery was compounded when Javier Mascherano was sent off for dissent. Ryan was replaced by Nani on 73 minutes and was warmly welcomed to the United bench by his happy boss, his work well done for the day. Ferguson said, 'It was a really good performance – a performance of maturity. Our team has matured over the last six months and today they hit their high peak.'

Next up the Reds crushed Aston Villa 4-0 – making it seven goals scored and none conceded at Old Trafford in two consecutive games. Goals from Ronaldo, Tévez and a brace from Rooney sent Villa into despair. Ryan had a hand in the opener, floating over the corner from which Ronaldo eventually fired home the opener. Giggsy and the boys were on a high; surely the title was now destined to stay at Old

Trafford? The six-point lead at the top of the table was preserved and even Sir Alex began to talk confidently: 'The players reached a peak last week and we've continued that. They realise now it's a race to the line; we need consistency and real focus and we showed fantastic energy. There is great confidence in the way the team is playing and that's great at this time of the year.'

Fergie decided to give Giggsy a break after his efforts in those three Premier League encounters, leaving him on the bench for the first leg of the Champions League quarter-final at Roma. It turned out to be a clever decision: Ryan got the chance to let his legs recover as he watched United storm to a 2-0 victory in the Olympic Stadium with Ronaldo and Rooney playing executioners.

He was back for the Premier League clash at Middlesbrough on 6 April 2008. It was now that time of the season that Sir Alex fondly refers to as 'squeaky bum time' – the time when the going gets tough and only the toughest stay the course. United had been in this position many times, but the prospect of a back end-of-season trip to the Riverside did not appeal. Over the years, Boro had become something of a bogey team and now they were battling for survival. A gruelling battle on the back of the trip to Rome was hardly what Ferguson had in mind for his troops, yet that was just what he would get – but at least Ryan was fresh and raring to go after his enforced rest at the Olympic Stadium, five days earlier.

United took the lead on 10 minutes, thanks – inevitably – to a goal from Ronaldo, but were 2-1 down on the hour after Afonso Alves twice pounced. Fortunately, Rooney hauled the Reds level 15 minutes from time to save their blushes – and maintain their lead at the top of the table. That lead now stood at three points as Chelsea had been piling on the pressure in their games in hand. Probably with that in mind, Sir Alex was more lenient in his analysis of the game and the result than he might otherwise have been, saying, 'We could have lost the game there's no question – they had some chances. At times the defending was a bit haphazard, I thought, but in other ways we could have won the game because some of the approach and football was very good. At 1-0 we looked very strong. They changed their formation to a 4-4-2, got an equaliser and it was a great game of football after that.'

Now the matches were coming thick and fast and Ryan found he was needed far more than many pundits had anticipated. Not that surprising, really – after all, he had the experience and the footballing brain that United so required at this crucial time of the season, the pluses that could make the very difference between success or failure.

He started in the return leg of the Champions League quarter-final with Roma, at Old Trafford. United triumphed 1-0, making it a comfortable 3-0 win on aggregate. Carlos Tévez scored the vital goal to set up a mouthwatering semi-final two-legger against Barcelona. Ryan was replaced by Rooney on 74 minutes: job well done. The win was United's 11th home victory on the trot in the Champions League – a new record – but Ryan and the boss were hardly bothered about that, or the fact they had beaten the Romans. Already both were contemplating the clash against Barca. Giggsy said it was 'the big one', the one everyone would want to play in – and win – while Fergie added, 'Yes, I'm really looking forward to it. I think that we have something special in our team. We cannot go to Spain and be negative, we must be positive. We are pleased to be through. We had to play well, but it was a European quarter-final against the team lying second in Italy and you expect them to play a bit. Our home record has been very good and is something to be proud of, and it will have to remain so because European football is difficult.'

Just four days after helping set up the Barca semi-final, Giggsy would step into the breach at the back end of another titanic battle – this time against Arsenal in the Premier League. United needed to keep on winning if they were to make their dream of another Premier League and Champions League glory season come true – and they did just that against a stubborn Gunners side.

The Reds won 2-1 after going a goal down just after the interval from an Emmanuel Adebayor strike. An equaliser from Ronaldo (from the penalty spot) and a late clincher by Owen Hargreaves did the job. Ryan replaced Hargreaves a minute from time for a cameo appearance. The win put United six points clear at the top and six days later, Giggs was back in the starting line-up at Blackburn.

Rovers also put up a stubborn resistance in a match in which Ryan only lasted the first 45 minutes, before being replaced by Nani. Blackburn took an early lead through Roque Santa Cruz and Giggs's last act in the match came just before the whistle for the interval as he floated over a corner that Ronaldo should have scored from, but instead headed at Brad Friedel.

United were saved from an unlikely defeat two minutes from time when Carlos Tévez made it 1-1 with a close-range header. United had just three Premier League matches remaining – and the first of them was an absolute crunch of a showdown, away at Chelsea. Just when Giggsy and co. needed to keep their cool, they struggled. Two goals from Michael Ballack, one a late penalty, killed off the Reds, whose only consolation on the long journey back to Manchester was a goal from Rooney. The only excuse you could use to justify United's poor showing was that they had an even more important fixture, three days later.

Or, as Sam Wallace, writing in the *Independent*, succinctly put it: 'Let's face it, if Sir Alex Ferguson had to choose between a result against Chelsea on Saturday or one against Barcelona tomorrow, it would be the latter every time. Which must have been the compromise he made with himself when he sketched out a team sheet on Saturday morning that did not include Cristiano Ronaldo, Patrice Evra and, to a lesser extent, Paul Scholes and Carlos Tévez.'

Five minutes from time, Ballack coolly fired home the penalty following a disputed handball by Michael Carrick – the first against United in the league that season. The result meant Chelsea had drawn level with United and the Reds would have to win their final two matches to retain their Premier League title, courtesy of a vastly superior goal difference. Fergie tried to deflect the pressure from his players by raging about the penalty: 'It was absolutely diabolical. It is a major decision. Granted, it hit his hand. But he has not lifted his hand above his shoulders, above his head, anything like that. It is going straight to Rio Ferdinand. The referee should have seen that rather than the linesman. If we're not going to get those decisions, then we are under pressure.

'It's still in our hands. The players and the supporters are really fired up for the next game. Hopefully, we can get the result we want.'

Well, they certainly did that. Ryan came on just after the hour against West Ham on 3 May 2008, United's penultimate league match of the campaign. He replaced Ji-Sung Park and helped keep the Reds' ship steady and on course to maintain their impressive 4-1 lead. The drubbing came courtesy of two goals from Ronaldo and one apiece for Tévez and Carrick. It meant Ryan Giggs was just one win away from his tenth league title.

He told friends he was thrilled and excited by the prospect, but that he would approach the final league game of the season like any other. That summed him up perfectly: footballer extraordinaire because he knew it was important to stay ordinary, to keep his feet on the ground and remain the consummate pro, whatever honours or acclaim might come his way.

United's final league match of the season was at Wigan's JJB Stadium on 11 May 2008. Fergie started Ryan on the bench – it was a big match for the club and the evergreen winger. If he made it onto the pitch, he would equal Sir Bobby Charlton's all-time appearances record.

Giggs had believed that he would be one short of the legendary number nine's record against Wigan – until a club historian discovered that Sir Bobby was credited with playing a 1962 FA Cup tie against Bolton when he actually missed it with flu. So Ryan now knew that an appearance against Wigan would mean he had equalled the 758 appearances of Charlton chalked up before he left Old Trafford in 1973.

Typical of the level-headed and humble man he was, he tried to play down personal glory, saying, 'Yes, it would be a great honour and a proud moment if I do it, but the main thing now is trophies. It would mean more to win the Champions League and the Premier League. Personal records are things to look back on when you finish your career.'

In fact, he came on at the JJB after 68 minutes to equal the record and, in a *Roy of the Rovers*-style sting to the tale, celebrated his big day with the goal that sealed United's retention of their title. The club became champions for the 17th time (and Ryan for the tenth) after Ronaldo set them on their way with a 33rd-minute opener from the penalty spot after Emmerson Boyce had fouled Rooney. It was Rooney who set up Giggs for the second, 11 minutes from time. Ryan took the ball, controlled it beautifully and rifled it home past Chris Kirkland in the Latics goal.

Giggs pronounced himself proud and delighted with the honour and his goal, but did not want to dwell on it. However, others were keen to do so. Sir Alex said: 'He deserves it – he has been a credit to the game. I've known him for 20 years, and for him to do what he has on the day he equalled Sir Bobby's record is fantastic.' Latics manager (and Reds legend) Steve Bruce remarked: 'Ryan scored on his debut and has equalled the appearance record. He is a great, great player. He epitomises what United are all about. He is an absolutely fantastic player.' And Rio Ferdinand added: 'Ryan's amazing, he keeps doing it every season and is an inspiration to the lads.'

A United insider revealed that the reason why Giggs was rather reticent about celebrating the honour was simple: there was still one more match to play in a season that had already been so memorable for the wing legend – the Champions League final in Moscow, against Chelsea. He wanted to stay focused on the game in case he was involved (Fergie had already confirmed to him that he would be in the playing squad) and felt that it would be better to comment more effusively on the record and what it meant to him when he broke it, rather than when he had simply equalled it.

Let's now take a look at the conclusion to the season – how Ryan and United beat Barcelona in the semis and Chelsea in the final. And how Ryan took Sir Bobby's record – and what doing that and winning a second European Cup winner's medal meant to the man who was United's most decorated player ever.

CHAPTER 12

FROM RUSSIA
(WITH LOVE)

In his autobiography, published way back in 2005, Ryan begins by telling the tale of how he was so high on emotion and adrenaline after he collected his first Champions League winner's medal in 1999 that he ended up punching the chairman's son! It happened at the tail end of an all-night party at the upmarket hotel where United were staying.

The Reds had, of course, just beaten Bayern Munich in one of the greatest comebacks in the sport at the Camp Nou. Losing 1-0 with two minutes to go against a German team that had dominated the match, United somehow hauled themselves back into the game and triumphed with two injury-time goals from substitutes Teddy Sheringham and Ole Gunnar Solskjaer.

Was it any wonder Ryan acted so dramatically out of character that night? The night he admitted in *Giggs: The Autobiography* that he was early on 'worse for wear' and later 'bladdered'. The night he clashed with James Edwards, son of then United supremo Martin Edwards, over something and nothing. The night he ended up with a broken nose and the mother of all hangovers.

There is a feeling among Ryan's friends that something was bound to blow that night – although they would never have expected it to end in violence, which was totally out of character for Giggs – because he was United through and through, a lifelong fan, as well as arguably the club's greatest-ever servant, and thus felt the weight of history lifting not just off his shoulders but his club's too.

It really was that massive a breakthrough. Just as in 1968, when United had finally made Matt Busby's dream come true (and his life complete, with redemption, as he saw it, for the Munich tragedy) by winning the European Cup for the first time, so the boys of '99 ended another drought by bringing the trophy back to Old Trafford for the first time since that 1968 victory.

Ryan would later admit that it felt as if they could finally lay to rest the ghosts of the past just as the likes of Georgie Best and Bobby Charlton had done by winning the trophy for the first time. There was also the little matter of the Treble – the win against Bayern saw United attain what no English club had ever achieved (and has not since) – the magnificent treble of Premiership, FA Cup and European Cup.

So it was little wonder the team's celebrations turned a little rowdy as they let off steam after making history for Manchester United FC. Inevitably, given the ever-evolving nature of the game and the fact that the next Champions League triumph would not take 31 years to achieve (it took just nine, in fact), the celebrations after the win over Chelsea in Moscow, on 21 May 2008, were rather more muted and restrained. Certainly there were no punch-ups or broken noses! Maybe a nose or two out of joint (John Terry's in particular after his penalty-miss blunder), but no bones damaged.

Ryan and the game of football itself had now moved on. He was thirty-four and a senior statesman; he was certainly the senior pro at United – it would not have done at all for him to be getting out of his head and behaving badly when younger, impressionable players were watching. Not that he would have wanted to, given the chance. Now he was a family man, much more reserved, pensive and earnest in his outlook on football and life in general. Winning still meant a lot, but it no longer meant everything. United still meant a lot, but they no longer meant everything. The Ryan Giggs in Moscow in May 2008 was a man who could have walked away from football that very night and have still achieved more than probably any other footballer in the English game can *ever* hope to achieve. He had done the lot and won the lot, but he was still 'over the moon' after United put old rivals Chelsea to the sword and he finally overwhelmed Sir Bobby Charlton's appearances record at Manchester United.

Giggs and United had made it to the final after overcoming the mighty Barcelona in a tough two-legged encounter. Ryan played in both legs of the tie – coming on as a late sub in both. The first leg was at the Camp Nou, and he had replaced Carlos Tévez five minutes from time in a match that had seen United launch an almost total rearguard action. They left with a 0-0 draw under their belts, but this was no guarantee of progress in the modern game. An away goal and a draw would have seen Barca through.

Having said that, United should have won 1-0 at the Camp Nou – Ronaldo missed from the penalty spot – and they would hopefully have defensive powerhouse Vidic (who was absent with injury) back for the second leg at Old Trafford. Indeed, you would never have guessed that United's hopes were still on a knife-edge after they failed to score in the away leg if you listened to boss Fergie after the 0-0 draw. 'Going to Old Trafford at 0-0, we have a marvellous chance. The game now starts at Old Trafford – it's the decider. At home, with the atmosphere, we'll be quite different to the first game,' he roared defiantly.

Giggs was overshadowed by another United 'old codger' at the Nou Camp – Paul Scholes had rolled back the years to mark his 100th Champions League appearance for his only club, with Fergie saying, 'He never gave the ball, his reading of the play was terrific and his interceptions were marvellous.'

Scholes would keep his place for the return leg against Barca at Old Trafford on 29 April 2008, with Fergie intimating the pace of what was expected to be a frantic fixture could prove too much, both for Scholes and Giggs. In the end, Paul would play for 76 minutes before being substituted – with Ryan then coming on for the last 14.

But Scholes had certainly done his job well – grabbing the decisive goal on 14 minutes that would see United through with a 1-0 aggregate win. The goal was particularly poignant for the man dubbed by the fans 'the Ginger Prince'. Nine years earlier, he had missed out on the Champions League final because of suspension and now here he was, sending United into another final courtesy of his 25-yard special hit and giving himself the chance to atone for his personal heartbreak of '99.

After the win over Barca, Ferguson confirmed straight away that Scholes would, fitness permitting, be the first name on his team sheet for the Moscow final. Fergie had been forced to tinker with his team after Vidic and Rooney both failed to make the match because of injury. Ferguson had said he wanted pace, but for many it was still a surprise that he didn't start with Giggs, especially as he chose the arguably inferior talents of Park and Nani instead. A United insider told me the manager had decided against Ryan, 'because he wanted to play Paul [Scholes] and wanted Nani and Park in to do the running and keep Barca busy on the flanks.'

The ploy worked, but so did bringing Ryan on with 14 minutes to go. Nani had tired and was giving the ball away too easily; Ryan shored things up and ran the clock down with his experience and know-how. It might have been only 14 minutes, but it was a vital 14 minutes as he used his experience to help Michael Carrick keep the ball and frustrate the opposition.

Ferguson was delighted that he would be leading his team into the second Champions League final of his tenure. He said: 'We are bouncing into that final now. If this team now goes on and wins the European Cup, it will be my best ever.' Again, he played tribute to his 'old codgers' Giggs and Scholes for their part in the glory win, but added that he also owed a debt to his wife, Cathy: 'That wife of mine just bullies me – she kicks me out the door at 7am. I will not risk her wrath.'

So now it was on to Moscow – and the final against Chelsea at the Luzhniki Stadium, home of Vidic's former team, Spartak.

Giggs prepared for the big match by making it clear that he and his team-mates would be giving everything to make the team on the night. After the win over Wigan that confirmed they were League champions for the 17th time, he said, 'In the next week we'll be kicking lumps out of each other to make the team for Moscow. When we get back to training for the Champions League final, everybody in the squad will be bidding for a place and that includes me.' He said that just because he had managed to achieve what he had, it meant nothing when it came to the line-up for the final with Chelsea: 'The final, literally, will be a whole new ball game and with everybody fit and desperate to play, the last thing that will be happening is that we relax after winning the title. Far from it! Becoming champions again is good for the team, it is good psychologically. And if I were in Chelsea's shoes right now, I reckon I would be down.'

At the same time, he added an ominous warning for those who might have believed the Moscow showdown with Chelsea could represent the end of his and the current United team's ambitions: 'Whatever we achieve this season will only be a start – this team has now won two titles and is in the final of the Champions League but that is really only a start. We will go on to bigger and better things.'

Giggs still meant business. He might have become a more rounded, earnest and mature individual who realised there was more to life than football but the flames of ambition still burnt as brightly as ever within.

Sir Alex Ferguson led a 24-man squad as his team flew out

of Manchester airport at lunchtime on a private charter on Monday, 19 May, two days before the crunch match against Chelsea – only three had been part of the match-day squad that touched down in Barcelona a decade earlier for the 1999 final against Bayern Munich. Giggs and Gary Neville were in the starting line-up, while Wes Brown was on the bench. Scholes had been with the squad in Barca, but of course missed out on the game itself – he and Roy Keane were both suspended.

Chelsea arrived in town the same day – with an entourage of 44. It was their first European Cup final but they were also brimming with confidence, convinced their moment of destiny was nigh. But United's destiny was linked to the event that had devastated the club – yet at the same time had also made it the best known in the world – 50 years earlier.

The Munich air disaster of 1958 was in the minds of many United staff and fans as United prepared to do battle: eight of the team's players had been killed as they returned from a European Cup game. United boss Ferguson was more aware than most of the significance of the 50-year anniversary and said, 'We won't let the memory of the Busby Babes down.'

He was spot on. With Munich survivors, including Sir Bobby Charlton, in attendance, the 2008 United side would not let them down. Giggs and co. earned the right to have their names mentioned alongside those heroes of 1968 – Best, Charlton and Stiles – and of 1999 – Beckham, Schmeichel and Stam.

'It was only fitting,' Fergie would tell the press ranks after the match. 'It was such an emotional occasion. I said the day before the game that we would not let the memory of the Busby Babes down. We had a cause and people with causes are difficult to play against. I think fate was playing its hand today.'

Before the game, Ferguson was convinced he now had a strong enough squad to lift the trophy – but added that the winning team would also need a bit of luck. He also admitted that he took a certain pride from the fact that the final would be between two English clubs – that it was a brilliant advertisement for the strength of the Premier League: 'Two European Cups over the history of the Premiership is not a lot, but there are reasons for that, and the balance has been between Milan and Madrid anyway. But the Premier League has improved, the quality of players in England has improved and, although English clubs have no divine right to succeed, we have a better chance of consistency in Europe now.'

The Moscow extravaganza was the third Champions League final between clubs from the same country in less than a decade. Spain's Real Madrid defeated Valencia in 2000 and AC Milan beat Juventus in an all-Italian final in 2003. The build-up was colourful and noisy – as 25,000 fans from each club converged on the city the day before the big game, massing in Red Square, where special tents and entertainment had been lined up to keep them occupied. They mixed amicably for what one newspaper dubbed 'the biggest invasion since Napoleon'. Of course, there were problems getting into the country and finding somewhere to stay. Queues at immigration were long, tiring and testing, and all the hotels in Moscow – which had cashed in anyway by putting up their tariffs – were full.

Even Wayne Rooney's fiancée Coleen suffered at Moscow airport, as her luggage went missing. She said, 'I am looking forward to the game but I could have done without having to spend all that time filling in a load of forms about a lost suitcase.'

By the day of the game itself, the atmosphere had turned more serious, not because of the fans but because of the Russian authorities' fear of the fans. Shops were banned from selling alcohol and some were closed completely. On the journey from the city centre to the Luzhniki Stadium – which hosted the Moscow Olympics in 1980 – police and militia were employed by the Russians, who were wary (and, as it turned out, oversensitive) to the threat posed by their English visitors.

The match itself was evenly contested and would end 1-1 after extra time – but United would triumph 6-5 on penalties to earn Giggs his second Champions League winner's win and United their third. Ronaldo had headed United 1-0 up on 26 minutes with Frank Lampard equalising just before the interval. Ryan came on for what had looked a cameo role three minutes from the end of normal time, but would prove to be far from that. He was to play for the 30 minutes of extra time and have a key role in the penalty shootout – netting himself and spreading his confidence and encouragement among the others in what was, inevitably, a tension-gripped finale.

The match turned on Didier Drogba's red card for an assault on Vidic four minutes from the end. It left Chelsea short of a top penalty taker and then England skipper Terry, taking his place in the spot-kick line-up, missed the penalty that would have won the trophy for the Blues.

It was Ryan who converted what would turn out to be the winning penalty (Chelsea's Nicolas Anelka would miss the final penalty). In doing so, he joined Steve McManaman and team-mate Owen Hargreaves in becoming the only British players to have played in and won more than one Champions League final.

Of course, at the same time he also broke Sir Bobby Charlton's appearances record for United – making it 759, thanks to his great late show. Afterwards he celebrated with the team back at the hotel and made it clear that he did not want his personal glory run to end there in Russia: 'I want nights like this again. We deserved it; we've been the best team. The first half, we dominated. The second half, they had chances but we held our nerve in the end. Penalties can be a lottery – it's how close the teams have been all season,' he remarked.

'The appearances record is a proud achievement for myself and my family but in the end, it's all about winning trophies. The Champions League is the number one competition. It is where you get tested as an individual and as a team. You are up against the best players in Europe and the best teams in Europe. Having tasted success in 1999, you want to go back and get that feeling again. It has been nine years, so our success has been overdue, which is why I am very happy.'

Boss Ferguson took his most loyal lieutenant to one side at the after-match celebration and told him that he was right to want more, that he still had a big part to play in a United team that had more big nights within its grasp. He congratulated him on his appearances record and hugged the boy who had become a man under his tutelage – the boy he now referred to in private as 'my special player'.

In public Sir Alex was also glowing about his team's display, Ryan's achievement – and his future at United. 'It is a fantastic achievement,' he said. 'That is the first shoot-out I've won in a big game. When Cristiano Ronaldo missed his penalty we thought we were in trouble, but we deserved the win. We had the better chances: in the second half they had more control, but in extra time we were better.

'We have the issue of Scholes and Giggs getting to the twilight of their careers. They will contribute in a big way next season, as they normally do, but not as many games. They will be eventually be phased out, as you have to do in life.'

Of Giggsy he said: 'Ryan will be thirty-five in November. I think he'll play until he's thirty-seven, with maybe 25 to 30 games a season. I think Paul Scholes is thirty-four in November – 25 to 30 games next season, because we have the back-up now.'

Giggs had achieved so much that season – what with the appearances record, his tenth Premier League crown and his second Champions League winner's trophy – but there was still one more accolade to come to put the icing on a truly great year. A few weeks after the Moscow final, he was honoured at Salford University when he was made an honorary master of arts in recognition of his contribution to sport and charitable causes in a ceremony at the Lowry Theatre.

He himself was delighted with the honour: 'I'm really pleased to accept this degree. When I started my career as a professional footballer I didn't envisage that one day I'd be made Master of Arts. I grew up in Salford and it's been a big part of my life for 30 years and it's great to be a part of Salford University now.'

It was a fitting end to a remarkable year for Giggs, who campaigns regularly for children's charities and who is an ambassador for UNICEF. The previous year he had been awarded an OBE – now he was being officially recognised in the world of learning. The boy had come a long way from those tough days in Cardiff: he had become one of the most famous and decorated footballers ever, yet at the same time he was a thoroughly decent, likeable guy and still 'Mr Ordinary' even though his feats were most definitely extraordinary.

And there was much more to come from the Welsh wonder – even though the years were rolling by. As the next campaign, the 2008/09 season, would more than testify.

CHAPTER 13

PLAYER OF THE YEAR

ew pundits would have suggested that Ryan Giggs would end up as the PFA Player of the Year when the new season dawned in August 2008. It wasn't so much that he was considered over-the-hill, but the rival candidates – Stevie Gerrard, Frank Lampard, Wayne Rooney and Cristiano Ronaldo – and the limitations necessitated by age (mainly a lack of first-team opportunities) meant that he would never have been in the top five, even if you'd organised a ballot among sports writers.

Sure enough, when the result was announced in April 2009, there were gasps galore. The main two questions were these: just how had he scooped the award when he had started only

12 league games? And how had he won, given the fierce level of competition (including team-mates Rooney, who had a scorching season, and Nemanja Vidic, who was crowned Player of the Year by United's own fanatical supporters)?

And there was another question, one that would be debated after the first two: why had it taken 18 attempts for Giggs to be granted the honour? With regard to the first two questions, it is easy to imagine that the third probably had something to do with it. After all, the men who had voted for him were his fellow pros, the players who worked with him and against him, many of them over many years. They probably felt – as many sportswriters did – that it was perhaps a case of now or never for the veteran winger. Of course, many believed he should have won the award in previous campaigns – no doubt about it, time was now running out. The previous season, he had already hinted that he might be approaching the time when he would hang up his boots for good as a player and maybe turn to coaching.

But surely pure sentiment itself would not lead to Giggsy winning the award? Those pros who voted for him may have had a soft spot for the boy, but they were no fools, were they? I spoke to a couple who did vote for him and they told me that it wasn't just about how many games he played (or would play, as they decided on their winner back in December), but the influence of the man on Manchester United and the way that Giggs, in his 18th season at the club, helped United to their 18th title and his 11th title as much by the work he did off the field as on it.

Clearly he had helped and encouraged the youngsters to become better players and pros, and he himself was the model professional. Ryan would describe the campaign as 'the most enjoyable season of my career'. Little wonder because although he wouldn't make as many starts as he might have liked, he had a big role to play: he would be used by Sir Alex as a creator in central midfield as well as up front and, less often now because his legs tired, out on the wing. It is worth noting that although he had only started in those 12 league games, he had been a regular in the squad for all competitions.

During matches the tremendously positive impact he had on the squad was clear. He cajoled the younger players – like the Brazilians Anderson and Rafael and the inconsistent Portuguese winger Nani – both from the sidelines and when he was on the pitch. In that sense, he was taking on a new role, one wholly encouraged by the boss – that of senior statesman to the new generation of young imports at Old Trafford.

One player at United said he saw Giggs as 'a vintage wine that got better with the years', but insisted his identity should remain a secret in print. 'I don't want him giving me a load of earache for saying he's ancient!' the young man added.

Ryan himself was understandably delighted to win the award – it had been virtually the only one missing from the full collection of honours that he'd accrued over a glittering career. He had picked up the young player award twice but this was a different level and he admitted it meant so much because his fellow pros had voted for him. 'It's right up there with personal accolades – it's the best to have as it's voted by your fellow players,' he said. 'I've been fortunate to win a lot of trophies. I won the young player award twice, but this is the big one. It's an exciting season – I think it is going to go right to the wire; there's big game after big game now. That's what you want and need at a club like Manchester United.'

Giggs saluted his manager Sir Alex when he picked up the honour at the plush ceremony in London, saying: 'The manager has been massive in my career, from when I first met him when I was thirteen. That's over 20 years and he knows me better than anyone, and our relationship has been brilliant and just gets better. I've been so fortunate to have such a great career in so many great teams, it's not even worth thinking about what it would have been like without the manager.'

He admitted that he had started taking his coaching badges and was thinking about the future. Although he hoped to play on as long as he could, he accepted that time was running out: 'As long as I'm getting picked, enjoying it and injury-free, I'll carry on as long as I can. At thirty-five you can't look too far into the distance, you just can't.'

And he also admitted that he was proud to have been a one-club man – even when the likes of the Milan giants AC and Inter had circled for his signature – and that he had never even considered walking away from United. Indeed, he said he felt the stability of being at Old Trafford for so many seasons had contributed to his success and longevity: 'It was never a consideration to leave. I was linked with a few clubs, but it was never really close. Why would I think about it when I was always happy here?'

But he still felt it was possible for someone to overhaul his record number of games for the club. He wasn't convinced that he would always remain untouchable in that sphere. 'They probably said the same thing when Sir Bobby Charlton retired,' he observed. 'But I wouldn't be surprised if someone went past my record. The way players look after themselves now, if they get into a first team at eighteen or nineteen and stay relatively injury-free, they can do it. It is a long time and a lot of games, but you have other big players at big clubs who have stayed for a long time. They are getting challenged all the time, so there is no need to move on and improve yourself.'

In an interview with the *Daily Telegraph*'s respected writer Henry Winter, Giggs told how the award had been the highlight of a special season: 'A lot of people said I couldn't top last season, breaking the appearance record of Sir Bobby Charlton, scoring against Wigan [to win title] and the Champions League final, but it's been better this season. I have enjoyed this season more than any other.

'Personal awards come second to winning leagues but I was really pleased to get that PFA award – at thirty-five. Over the last couple of weeks, I've got "How have you won the PFA Player of the Year?" I got it at Middlesbrough. Just as I was taking a corner, the whole stand sang: "Player of the year? You're having a laugh!" Brilliant! I scored straight after, so I gave them a wave! I get opposing fans saying they respect me, which is great to hear. I was at Chester Races the other week and a couple of people came up and said, "We're Scousers, we're Liverpool fans, but we respect you and the way you play."'

Of course, there were a few pros and ex-pros that moaned and groaned about Giggs winning the award. Some critics would later try to demean the PFA honour, saying it was irrelevant because the votes were cast in December, using the result of the PWA (Professional Writers' Award) announced the following May as substantive proof of that viewpoint. The PWA Player of the Year award went to Steven Gerrard, with Giggs as runner-up, but even the Liverpool skipper pronounced himself stunned that he had won: 'I'm delighted, but I'm a little bit surprised. When you look at the quality of the players there are in this league, it's a great privilege to win this kind of award.'

The PWA award was voted for in April, four months after the PFA, and so Giggs can't have done that badly throughout the whole season. In one campaign, he was just one spot away from winning a coveted double of the PFA and PWA awards. Yet still the snipers claimed he had not done enough to earn either gong. Former 'hardman midfielder' Steve McMahon commented: 'I think "The PFA Player's Player of Five Months" should be a more accurate title. During my time as a professional footballer, you get a letter and then you can vote for anybody you want – but not yourself, of course. You have to pick the player and also the Young Player of the Year. The only problem is that it comes in December and you have to submit the letter back in January, so I don't really know how accurate that can be because the last time I checked the league season only ends in May.'

He believed it was nonsensical that the players were asked to vote for the best player in the league when it was only half-finished, claiming it wasn't fair as the players compete for nine months of the season and not from August to December. 'The voting system should be changed to reflect the whole season or most of it,' he said.

And McMahon wouldn't have voted for Ryan: 'As for Ryan Giggs, I can understand the clamour for one of the most successful and experienced players in the English Premier League to win this award. But honestly, has Giggs been as fantastic as say, Vidic – week-in, week-out? I don't think a sympathy vote should count as a vote. I certainly won't push for him. To be honest the criteria for the Player of the Year is not just about the talent or reputation that the players have, it's about somebody who has had a fantastic season. I would give the award to Steven Gerrard as he has ticked all the right boxes this season. It doesn't matter if Liverpool do not win the league title, winning this award has never had anything to do with it.'

Some contended that McMahon's gripe was mere sour grapes from a Scouser. I would certainly take issue with his view that the award 'has never had anything to do' with winning the title. He would say that, wouldn't he, given it had been 19 years since his beloved Liverpool had won the crown (1989/90 being the last time the Anfield outfit lifted the trophy)? Surely, the best player of any season is likely to have been involved in the best results of that season – thus helping his team to the top honours?

Gerrard may well be the best midfielder in the world, as McMahon also argued, but he was not superhuman enough to help his team win any trophies in 2008/09. That was a flaw – and many would argue that both Giggs and Rooney had better seasons. Certainly, they inspired their side to more trophies – in this instance the Premier League title and the Carling Cup – plus, they both played in the Champions League final.

Website writers were similarly baffled that the press corps could vote Gerrard their main man while dismissing Giggs because he had only started a smallish percentage of league games. Even a Kop regular wondered why Gerrard's own number of starts had not been mentioned, saying: 'I am a Liverpool supporter, so happy for Gerrard, but he has been out for about a third of the season so I don't think he should have really got it.'

And a United fan added: 'Yet again the confusion as to this being for the YEAR 2009 as Giggsy's was rears its head. Yes, Gerrard has had a good season, but if this award runs from Jan 08–Jan 09, then no, I don't think he deserves it. United won the double in that time, so surely the player should come from our team? It's a bit like Ginola (who won the award) in '99 (but no club trophies that season).'

Another football fan claimed Gerrard had not even been the best player at his own club, let alone in the Premier League: 'Clearly Stevie G is a good player – but this is another lazy award by the press hacks. Gerrard hasn't been as effective as in previous seasons, nor has he been the best midfielder in his own team this season – that award goes to [Xabi] Alonso. I suspect that the vote for United players was split between Giggs, Rooney and Vidic.'

And one man said he believed Gerrard had been honoured as compensation for losing out to Giggs in the PFA vote: 'Giggs got his PFA in recognition of his wonderful service to the game. I agree, but I think he should have got a special award that said, "for your wonderful service to the game". Gerrard then got his award to compensate for the PFA award, although being the media darling, he was always odds-on, anyhow.'

PFA Chief Executive Gordon Taylor was one of the first to speak out on Ryan's behalf when the veteran won the PFA award, saying he believed that he fully deserved the honour despite the relatively small number of games he had started. He added that he could not understand the dissenting voices.

Taylor said, 'As far as I am concerned, Ryan Giggs was a worthy winner and I can't think of any footballer in the country who would deny him that trophy in his cabinet.

'He is a top professional in every respect, a role model to be looked up to, and we are proud to honour him as our Players' Player of the Year.'

And, of course, they closed ranks behind him at Old Trafford itself. A few days before the ceremony, Sir Alex voiced his hopes that Ryan would be voted No. 1, at the same time defying anyone to say his man had not played in enough games: 'I hope Ryan gets the PFA award. He has played 30 games this season and the way we use squads nowadays, no one plays in every game. Hopefully, he is rewarded for his contribution to the game – he thoroughly deserves it.'

He also spoke of the May night in 2008 when Giggs broke Sir Bobby Charlton's club record of 758 appearances in Moscow as being indicative of the love and respect felt for the winger by everyone at United. That night – after United won the Champions League by beating Chelsea – the players presented him with a watch to mark his landmark. 'We gave Ryan all the accolades in Moscow,' Fergie said. 'The players' presentation was very emotional and it was a great representation of how the players feel about the boy; it was fantastic. He is the most respected player in the club and what he has achieved is an example to everyone. It is unbelievable to think he has been at the top for so long.'

He added, 'We are a very special club and we are lucky that players have chosen to spend their entire careers here. Being local boys does help, but they are not here on sentiment – they are here on ability.'

The manager was similarly effusive after Ryan won the PFA award, saying that he was the right man to be chosen at the right time. Others from Old Trafford then joined in the praise, led by the excellent comment on the official United website, which proclaimed: 'The only surprise about Ryan Giggs being named PFA Players' Player of the Year in April 2009 was that it had taken so long for him to win the prestigious award.'

Goalkeeper Edwin Van der Sar also congratulated his evergreen team-mate. The big Dutchman said he had come across few pros as dedicated or as likeable as Giggs. He added that he rarely had disagreements with the man who had been United captain in the enforced injury absence of Gary Neville – but that he did beg to differ on one subject: he simply could not see how anyone would ever beat Ryan's appearances' record at Man United.

Van der Sar, who himself had made more than 650 club appearances in a long career, observed: 'It would be hard to beat Ryan's record. There are so many changes now with transfers and everything else, and Ryan started out early. You will not see anything like that in future. And the thing is he is still going strong – it is as though he was only thirty-one. It is a joy to see how he trains as well as plays; how he controls the ball, how he sees a pass and the runs he makes. He can read a game and adjust the way we play. He shows such dedication every day and sets the example for everyone.'

Backers of both Giggs and Gerrard could at least be pacified by seeing their men included in the PFA Premier League team of the Year, which lined up like this: Edwin Van der Sar (Man United), Glen Johnson (Portsmouth), Rio Ferdinand (Man United), Nemanja Vidic (Man United), Patrice Evra (Man

United), Ashley Young (Aston Villa), Steven Gerrard (Liverpool), Ryan Giggs (Man United), Cristiano Ronaldo (Man United), Nicolas Anelka (Chelsea) and Fernando Torres (Liverpool). However, it did not go unnoticed by United fans that Gerrard was one of only two representatives from Anfield, while United had six.

So what were the Giggs' highlights from that campaign that propelled him to the Player of the Year award? Let's take a look...

Well, the 2008/09 season began with our Ryan in a reflective, almost nostalgic mood, but one that was also underpinned with uncertainty. Just days before the big kick-off, he said that he wondered if the campaign might be his final one at United.

He was thirty-four and had not (yet) been offered a new deal at the club (although he still had a year left on his current contract) – and he had been making tentative steps towards becoming a coach. He said: 'For each of the last couple of seasons I've gone into it as if it's my last. I'm not getting any younger, so this one could be. That's my motivation to stay in the team. I have good players around me, and I want to win and experience things like we did last season. Winning trophies motivates me.

'I went to Lilleshall with Gary Neville and Ole Gunnar Solskjaer. It brought me back down to earth after the Champions League in Moscow. I enjoyed it, although it's hard work looking at things from the other side of the fence. It was tough as I've been used to playing and just concentrating on that. There are so many other things to concentrate on as a coach, so I suppose I appreciate what the coach is doing a lot more now. I think I'll pursue it. I have to finish it off this season then go for my Pro Licence. I want to be prepared for when I finish playing.'

Always earnest, always the realist and a pragmatist, Giggs was never going to leave anything to chance in case the boss called him aside to tell him that his playing days were drawing to a close. With his character, he knew full well that Sir Alex would never keep him merely out of sentiment and that he would be put out to grass if the boss considered him over the hill. But he also knew that Fergie did have a soft spot for former players who had the capacity to add to his coaching staff at United – men like the aforementioned Solskjaer, whose intelligence, positive attitude and ability to easily digest and use information meant that he was an immediate success in coaching the reserves at United.

In June 2009, the Norwegian told manutd.com that he was delighted with his first season in the job – and spoke with enthusiasm about it in a way that had attracted Giggs to think about following a similar path. 'My first year in charge of a team was a challenge, a new challenge for me,' the former United striker Ole said. 'But I felt I was ready for it and it was a good experience – very enjoyable indeed. By starting my coaching career at United, I have stayed in the same familiar environment.

'Some of the players I played with come down and play for me once in a while. Gary [Neville] and Wes [Brown] for example, so that's enjoyable. It's also great to see the young players, with the talent they have and their whole careers in front of them, and we just try to give them a little bit of advice and help along the way.'

Ryan could certainly relate to all those sentiments – especially the phrase, 'the same familiar environment'. After a lifetime at Old Trafford, he did not want to move to another club; his heart was there, he had been a Stretford Ender in his teens and he was a fan of Manchester United as well as an employee. He loved the club. Also, like Ole, he got a real kick out of watching the kids come up through from the ranks of the youth team and the reserves, just as he had done as a lad. He said it always gave him a lift when he watched talent fulfilled – and that he would like to be involved in nurturing and encouraging that talent.

In February 2009, he was called aside by the boss and informed that he would be awarded the new deal that he had feared might not come the previous August. Sir Alex also told him that he wanted him to continue with his coaching qualifications as he had a role in mind for him when he did hang up his boots as a player.

The new deal would take him to the summer of 2010 and put his mind at ease after all those months of worry. Plus Ferguson's encouragement was just what he needed, what he wanted to hear – that he would have a future with the club he loved when it all came to an end. After signing the deal that guaranteed him another 18 months as a player at United, Ryan said, 'I feel fit and I'm enjoying my football more than ever. This is an exciting young team and the spirit is great in the dressing room. I want to be a part of that and achieve even more success.'

And Ferguson added, 'His lifestyle, the way he looks after himself, his desire to always want to win are a credit to him and also an inspiration to any young kid who wants to become a footballer. He is like a young boy in the way that he plays. And although he wants to take part in every game, he understands that using his experience when it matters is a benefit to him and the team.'

And former United youth director Eric Harrison, the man who knew a bit about nurturing and bringing on young lads after doing just that with Giggs and others of the so-called Fergie's Fledglings in the 1990s, told the *Daily Mail* that he also believed Ryan would be a star coach – or even an ambassador. 'When the day comes for Ryan to finish, and it's a while away yet, he will be great as an ambassador or as a coach because he has always been prepared to help younger players out,' he observed.

'Ryan is a fantastic role model for kids – his behaviour is impeccable. As a player, his has been a God-given talent. He has natural pace and balance, and that is something you are either born with or you are not; you cannot teach that. He has looked after himself very well over the years and that shows now. He has always had that intelligence and the capacity to learn and absorb things very quickly.'

Perceptive words from both Ferguson and Harrison. Certainly Giggs's experience and know-how had helped and inspired United as they galloped towards an 18th top-flight title that season. Surprisingly, given the furore over his 12 starts when he was acclaimed PFA Player of the Year, he would make 47 appearances (the eighth highest), score four goals and top the assists table with a total of 18 (five more than runner-up Rooney).

Ryan started the campaign where he belongs – in the first 11, as United entertained Newcastle at Old Trafford on 17 August 2008. It was a balmy summer's day and Kevin Keegan was still in the Newcastle hot seat (though not for much longer) and Ryan contributed by setting up the equaliser on 24 minutes for the hosts. His left-wing cross was well met by Darren Fletcher, who rifled the ball home, the goal cancelling out the opener from Obafemi Martins, a couple of minutes earlier.

But Giggs's afternoon was to end in pain when he was forced off with a hamstring injury just after the hour. The match fizzled out into a 1-1 draw and Ferguson made it clear that he thought the loss of Giggs and Carrick to injury had cost United dear and helped explain their poor start to the season. Fergie said: 'We played well in the first half, and their goalkeeper made several good saves to keep them in the match. Our attacking play in the first half was good but as soon as we lost Ryan Giggs to a hamstring injury and Michael Carrick with an ankle, which is swollen up badly – he'll be out for two to three weeks – we lost a bit of our experience in midfield. We had possession of the ball, but didn't make it count at times – but in light of the people we had missing, it was a creditable result for us.'

It would be a month before Ryan finally shook off the injury and worked his way back into the first-team picture – he would miss three games, including the 2-1 loss to Zenit St Petersburg in the European Super Cup. And his return to action was to be a far from happy one: United would travel 35 miles up the East Lancs Road, but come home with nothing after a 2-1 loss to their bitterest rivals, Liverpool. Giggs had earlier admitted that Liverpool were the team he 'got most pleasure out of beating.' No surprise there – he was a United fan first and foremost, after all, and he had been involved in a few savoury scraps against the Scousers.

His first match against them was when he was nineteen – in April 1992, at Anfield when United lost 2-0. It led to the incident that probably sums up best the fiery relationship that developed between Giggs and Liverpool FC. After the match he was asked by a young lad for his autograph. He duly obliged, only for the Liverpool fan to gleefully tear it up in front of him. 'That was a shock,' he would later admit. 'I mean, when someone asks you for your autograph. For the first couple of years of my career it was the biggest disappointment. I'd had such a rise into the first team and everything had gone well, and that was my first real slap. You grow up quickly in football and the important thing is how you react.'

But Giggs being Giggs was big enough and intelligent enough to see that the actions of one fool should not prejudice his views of an entire football club and its supporters. Although he still wanted to beat Liverpool in every match, he tried his best not to antagonise their staff or fans (unlike, say, Gary Neville, who makes no attempt to hide his distaste for the Scouse nation). 'I think I've always shown the right respect to Liverpool and the history they have and great team they are, but I also know that it's the team I get the most pleasure out of beating,' Ryan conceded.

And he certainly had beaten them many times. In the 37 matches against Liverpool he had played in prior to the fixture in September 2008, Giggs was on the winning side 17 times, the losing side 10, and had experienced 10 draws. By the end of the 2008/09 season, he was easily the man who had put in most shifts for Man United against Liverpool – with Arthur Albiston in second place with 26. Giggsy scored his first goal against them in January 1994 – a 3-3 draw at Anfield.

There would be no goalscoring feats in September 2008, though. At the interval, Ryan came on for Carrick but struggled to impose himself. Clearly, his fitness was still not 100 per cent after the hamstring injury he had suffered against Newcastle and Liverpool stole the show with a later winner from Ryan Babel. Carlos Tévez put United ahead after just three minutes, only for a Wes Brown own-goal to send the teams in level at the interval. To add to United's woes, Vidic was sent off on 90 minutes for a second bookable offence (he would also be dismissed in the return fixture at Old Trafford the following April).

Afterwards Mike Phelan, Carlos Queiroz's successor as United assistant boss, admitted the whole team, not just Giggs, had been out of sorts: 'We were only in the game for seven or eight minutes, and after that we didn't perform. They bossed us out of the game and their tactics worked as they put us under pressure. We never responded and we didn't react after the break, and we succumbed to the pressure. We did not take control of the game and we struggled and now we have to get back to basics.'

Four days later and nine minutes from time, Ryan would come on for Tévez in the similarly uninspiring 0-0 home draw with Villarreal in the Champions League group stage. Both he and United had made a stuttering start to the season, but things would improve – and quickly.

A week later he was in the starting line-up for the Carling Cup clash with Middlesbrough at Old Trafford. So you might say, that's no great shakes – it's the second-tier tournament in which Fergie gives the kids a run-out. Maybe so – although Ronaldo, Vidic, O'Shea and Anderson were also on at the start – but the kids still needed inspiration and leadership and Ryan Giggs was just the man to help them out.

Skipper on the night, he made it his mission to guide and support boys like Rafael, Danny Welbeck, Darren Gibson and Ben Amos against a virtual full-strength Boro (who included England winger Stewart Downing in their starting line-up).

United triumphed 3-1 and Ryan grabbed his first goal of the season on 79 minutes – a fine shot that outfoxed keeper Brad Jones – and set up the first goal of the night for Ronaldo, who was making his first appearance of the campaign. Giggsy's wonder goal would attract the headlines the day after – along with the horror tackle by Emanuel Pogatetz that sent Rodrigo Possebon to hospital – and it made the veteran winger think back 17 years.

Then, in 1992, he had also left Boro stunned and confused in the very same competition. After the first leg of the League Cup semi-final had ended 0-0, Giggs tore the visitors apart at Old Trafford on 11 March 1992, scoring the first goal and helping United to a 2-1 win that took them to Wembley. He would go on to start the final and lift his first professional winners' medal with the Reds as they beat Nottingham Forest 1-0, thanks to Brian McClair's winner. And, yes, let's not forget Giggsy even set up the likeable Scot for his winner that day.

And so it was little wonder that he had fond memories as he helped United dismantle Boro 17 years later in a win that would kickstart both his and United's season. The Reds were to embark on a nine-game unbeaten run with Ryan featuring in six, including the 2-0 win at Blackburn and the 4-0 victory at home to West Brom. He would also score in the 1-1 Champions League group stage encounter at Celtic. Ryan started the match and was United's saviour six minutes from time when he headed the equaliser after keeper Artur Boruc deflected a shot by Ronaldo into his direction. Scott McDonald put the Hoops ahead after just 13 minutes with a clever lob, but United had them on the back foot for much of the game, with Giggs forming an effective partnership with Tévez up front until Berbatov and Rooney appeared from the subs' bench. He then drifted out to his traditional left-wing role, but continued to cause the Hoops problems.

Afterwards, Sir Alex praised Ryan's contribution and goal, while observing, 'We obviously deserved a point, but with minutes to go, you think you're going to lose it and it's not going to be your night. That's football sometimes. But, credit to the players, we kept persevering, kept at them, and got our rewards in the end. The second half performance overall was very good and we created a lot of chances, a lot of openings, and so I'm happy to have come away with a point.'

Giggs too was beaming, delighted with his goal and joking that he might be getting on, but he was not senile yet – as his reaction to the parried stop by Boruc for the goal proved. 'It's always worth following up because when Ronaldo hits the ball, it generally moves all over the place,' he said.

But the feeling of optimism would fall by the wayside – albeit temporarily – in the next match. United were to crash 2-1 at Arsenal on 8 November 2008. Two goals from Sami Nasri would condemn them to defeat with Rafael's late goal for the visitors a mere consolation. Ryan had come on 18 minutes from the end (replacing Anderson) and got stuck into the new central midfield role that boss Ferguson had devised for him. But he and partner Carrick could not change the outcome – much to the disappointment of all the players and 5,000 fans that had travelled down from Manchester.

United posed the bigger attacking threat throughout and believed they should at least have come away with a point. Assistant boss Mike Phelan summed up the feeling within the camp when he said: 'Yes, we are disappointed – we made enough chances to score a couple of goals, but that wasn't to be. It was an open game and very end-to-end, but we came out the wrong side of it.'

The win had lifted the Gunners into third place in the table above United and set alarm bells ringing at Old Trafford. After all, they had now lost to title rivals Arsenal and Liverpool, and only managed to draw at Chelsea. Would they be able to pull themselves up off the floor and reignite their domestic and European campaign? Or would they slump and throw it all away?

Ryan Giggs simply smiled when he heard the voices of doom. He had seen it all before – many times. Whenever United lost a match it was the cue for 'United in crisis' headlines. Then they would invariably go out and do the business and now would be no different: Giggs and United would embark on an amazing unbeaten run in the Premier League and put down a global marker in another incredible season.

The extraordinary winger would soon be on top of the world – as he and United claimed the title of world champions.

CHAPTER 14
WORLD CHAMPION

Realistically, he would never ever be a World Cup winner with Wales. Like George Best with Northern Ireland, Giggsy was his country's most outstanding footballing talent ever – but given the lack of equal talents in the valleys and a paucity of resources and no centre of excellence, Wales, like Northern Ireland, were always destined to dance around the lower grades of international footballing achievements.

So, when Ryan got the chance to become a world champion at club level, he did not view it with the same disdain or complacency as certain of his United team-mates did. In his eyes, it was a genuine opportunity to stamp his mark on the only truly global footballing achievement within his boundaries.

Again like Georgie Best, he took the competition very seriously and was determined to win it. In 2008, he and United would do just that – and he would be delighted by it – as they came back from Japan with the so-called FIFA Club World Cup.

Nine years earlier he had won the title in its first incarnation – when it was a one-off match rather than a mini-tournament and was known as the Toyota Cup. Previously, it was called the Intercontinental Cup – and it was in that guise that Best and United battled gamely (with battle being the definitive word) to bring the trophy home. Best had also been desperate to be crowned a world champion, albeit at club level – but it was not to be. He and United had come up against a cynical team called Estudiantes, from Argentina, and they were kicked off the park, taunted and the victims of dreadful tackling and provocation. United would lose the first leg 1-0 at Boca Juniors Stadium, going down to Marcos Conigliaro's 27th-minute header. Nobby Stiles was sent off for dissent, but it would be Best's dismissal in the return at Old Trafford that would hog the headlines.

United would draw 1-1 – thus losing the match 2-1 on aggregate – after Georgie was sent off when the provocation proved too much for him too handle. In fact, both sides finished a man short after George and José Hugo Medina were sent off for fighting. Estudiantes scored first through Juan Ramón Verón and Willie Morgan's last-minute equaliser was not enough to save the Reds. Ironically, Estudiantes' goalscorer Verón was the father of Juan Sebastian Verón, who would join United as their then most expensive signing at £28.1 million in July 2001. His son would achieve only patchy success at Old Trafford – with the consensus being he never truly lived up to his obvious natural potential – before he was shipped out to Roman Abramovich's Chelsea two years later for a cut-price £15 million.

Of course, there was little likelihood Giggs would suffer George Best's fate of being sent off in his two world club final appearances. In the 1999 Toyota Cup, as it was then known, Ryan was the star of the show, dazzling down the wing and inspiring United to their 1-0 win over Brazil's Palmeiras in Tokyo. The winner may have come from skipper Roy Keane, but it was Giggs who set him up for the shot, and he who claimed the Man of the Match award. The win meant United became the first British team to claim the coveted trophy. Their team that day read: 1 Mark Bosnich, 2 Gary Neville, 6 Jaap Stam, 27 Mikael Silvestre, 3 Denis Irwin, 7 David Beckham, 16 Roy Keane, 18 Paul Scholes (10 Teddy Sheringham), 8 Nicky Butt, 20 Ole Gunnar Solskjaer (19 Dwight Yorke) and 11 Ryan Giggs.

Some line-up: formidable, tough and yet full of talent and ability – and, apart from Mark Bosnich in goal for the now retired Peter Schmeichel, easily a stronger line-up than the one that had secured United's second European Cup triumph in Barcelona six months earlier. Certainly the return of Keane and Scholes (after suspension had cost them the chance of appearing in the Barcelona final in May 1999) more than compensated for the loss of the big Danish keeper.

The winning goal in Tokyo had come on 35 minutes and Giggs did all the hard work, leaving Keano to finish the job. Denis Irwin fed Ryan from the back and the winger set off on one of his trademark runs, leaving Júnior Baiano for dead and driving in a cross that left the Brazilian backline floundering. The ball found Keane unmarked and he had the simplest of tap-ins to secure the trophy.

Giggs, who also won a Toyota car after being voted Man of the Match, admitted that he had been surprised when his cross beat keeper Marcos and found Keane for the winner. 'The balls have been flying about in training and they definitely seem to be a lot lighter,' he said. 'I didn't know if it would beat the goalkeeper when I first crossed it and I thought he would reach it – so I was surprised when it went over him and Keano got on the end of it.'

He added that he was delighted to be a world cup winner and also with his award for being the best player on the park. It was another big moment in a career already littered with major awards and honours. Boss Ferguson was also ecstatic that he and his team had made footballing history: 'We wanted really badly to win the world championship. We wanted to win firstly because no British team had won it and secondly because it makes us world champions – and we are proud of that.'

But, in typical 'let's keep our feet on the ground' mood, he also claimed it was not the biggest deal in town. 'I'm very pleased to win the world championship and to become the first English team to win it. The world championship is very special, and I'm very proud of what my players have done,' he stated. 'But you've got to win the European Cup firstly to get here, and no matter how you place this the European Cup is always going to be the golden goose for us. It got us here tonight by winning it, and we've come here and won again, which makes us very proud.'

But it would be left to the beaten boss of the Brazilians to sum up the massive influence that Ryan Giggs had had on the night. The man then becoming known as 'Big Phil' said Giggs had been the difference between the two teams – and that if he had had Ryan in his line-up, it would have been him, and not Ferguson, who was celebrating. Luiz Felipe Scolari – who would go on to manage Brazil, Portugal and Chelsea – was full of admiration for the Welsh wonder. Big Phil, who had also lost the Toyota Cup with Gremio in 1995, observed: 'Ryan Giggs is some player – he made it difficult for us throughout the 90 minutes. He is not easy to contain or control, and he was a constant danger. He is one of the greatest players in the world today.'

Scolari shrugged his shoulders when asked if he was hurting. 'We gave our all,' he said, adding, 'but we learnt once again that Manchester United are a great and a tough team, who can fight. Congratulations to Manchester United, and maybe it will be my turn next time. Maybe Giggs will not be playing then!'

A few months later, it would be Ryan's turn again as 1999 became 2000. This time the event morphed into what would be the prototype of the current tournament and would become known as the Club World Championship. It would run under that banner from its conception at the start of the new millennium until 2006, when it finally took on the moniker, World Club Cup. United would, controversially, miss out on the FA Cup in 2000 to concentrate their energies on the competition, which took place in Brazil in January.

It would not be too dramatic to label United's involvement as an all-round disaster. They missed out on the FA Cup for nothing, flopping in Brazil. It wouldn't have been so bad, had they won the event but their participation was a shambles and an insult to the good name of the world's biggest domestic cup.

The tournament featured eight teams – United, Real Madrid, Necaxa, Corinthians, Vasco de Gama, South Melbourne, Al-Nasr and Raja Casablanca. The format saw a group stage, a final and a third and fourth place play-off. Disgracefully, United finished third in their group – just above minnows South Melbourne, but below Necaxa and group winners, Vasco de Gama.

If the previous year's triumph over Palmeiras took United to the summit of world football, this poor showing in Brazil had many questioning just how good they actually were. After all, they had arrived in Brazil full of beans and determined to prove the knockers back home in the UK wrong for lambasting them for choosing the competition over the FA Cup.

I was told by a United insider that the feeling after the event was that the club had approached it too casually – without the usual commitment and professionalism you might expect from a United side under the auspices of Alex Ferguson – that they had let the success they had achieved over the previous 18 months go to their heads. Sure, it was a fab sightseeing and tourist trip, and the sunbathing at the hotel pool was enjoyable, but United's heads were not tuned in for business – as they had been the previous year and as they would be, eight years later. They began the event badly and could not get out of their rut in time to save themselves. The starting point was a scrappy, scrambled 1-1 draw with Mexican outfit Necaxa – after David

Beckham was sent off – and then they lost to Brazilians Vasco 3-1. By now the game was up, leaving the last match – a perfunctory 2-0 win over South Melbourne – irrelevant.

Ryan was largely anonymous in the opener and guilty of missing relatively easy chances against Vasco as United slipped to defeat. He also suffered the ignominy of being subbed, with Jordi Cruyff taking his place.

It left United open to accusations that they had wasted their time travelling to Brazil, especially as now they would not even be parachuted into the FA Cup at a later stage. But Giggs was down though not out after the loss to Vasco in the legendary Maracanã Stadium. He insisted the trip had been worthwhile – for the experience and know-how the team would gather – and that they would return to England refreshed and ready to launch a full assault on winning the Premier League again.

It was a view backed up by boss Ferguson, who was in typically defiant mood. Fergie dismissed the doom-mongers, who were now laughing at his failed attempt at world domination. He told the BBC: 'It's been fantastic here – what a chance for us to come out and get some sun! Back home, we would have been freezing our toes off.'

Ryan was on the bench in the largely irrelevant final tie against South Melbourne, in which an experimental United side coasted to a 2-0 win, thanks to two goals from Quinton Fortune. The Brazilian odyssey was over – and United headed home, their tails between their legs.

But Giggs would make amends when the chance came around to enter the event, now called the World Club Cup, eight years later. United's win on penalties over Chelsea in the

Champions League final in May 2008 set them up to take part in the tournament. It would be staged in Japan over a 10-day period in December 2008. United were parachuted into the event at the semi-final stage – along with South American champions, Liga de Quito. The two teams were judged to be the top seeds as they had won what were considered the top Continental competitions: United with the European Champions League and the Ecuadorians with the South American Copa de Libertadores.

United headed out to Japan on Sunday, 14 December, the day after the 0-0 Premier League draw at Spurs.

Boss Ferguson's squad indicated just how seriously the manager was taking the event, too: Goalkeepers: Van der Sar, Kuszczak, Foster; Defenders: Neville, Evra, Ferdinand, Vidic, O'Shea, Evans, Rafael. Midfielders: Ronaldo, Anderson, Giggs, Park, Carrick, Nani, Scholes, Fletcher, Gibson. Strikers: Berbatov, Rooney, Tévez, Welbeck.

They were at full strength, with all the top men making the journey to the Far East.

The boss was happy that United would enter the competition at the last four stage in Yokohama on Thursday, 18 December and that their opponents would be Japanese outfit Gamba Osaka. The final, if they made it, would be three days later at the Yokahama Stadium – the venue for the 2002 World Cup final between eventual winners Brazil and runners-up Germany.

United touched down in Japan at Tokyo's Narita airport at 4pm on the Monday – and Sir Alex got straight down to business. Just hours after the boys had booked into their hotel, he had them out training! But he also allowed them to do a tour of the sights and some shopping over the next couple of days – although he stressed to the squad that United were here essentially for business, not as idling tourists, and they would fit in two more training sessions and then it was time for the first match: the semi-final against Gamba Osaka.

Gamba had won the Asian Champions League, but they were not of the same calibre as the teams that United had met in the later stages of the European Champions League. The team, who finished 8th in their last J League campaign, had beaten Adelaide United in Sunday's quarter-final to earn the right to meet the only United that counted – but they never expected to beat United, who ran out 5-3 after a spirited display by the Japanese.

Wayne Rooney was the big name missing from the starting line-up – he had suffered a knock in training – but the team that Ferguson put out was a strong one: Van der Sar, Neville, Ferdinand, Vidic, Evra, Nani, Anderson, Scholes, Giggs, Ronaldo and Tévez. Rooney was on the bench, along with Michael Carrick and Darren Fletcher, among others.

United, who knew victory would bring them face to face with Liga de Quito in the final (after the Ecuador outfit's win over Mexico's Pacucha 2-0 the day before) – would strike first and it would be Ryan who played a key role in setting them on their way. He floated over a pinpoint corner and a grateful Nemanja Vidic rammed the ball home with a header after 28 minutes. On the stroke of half time Ronaldo made it 2-0 with a fine header from another excellent corner from Giggs.

Masato Yamazaki pulled a goal back for the hosts before sub Rooney scored with his first touch. Fletcher headed home the fourth and Rooney made it 5-1 – after some great running and ball control, once again by Giggs. United eased off, Yasuhito Endo scored from a penalty and Hideo Hashimoto made it 5-3 to give the scoreline some respectability.

Afterwards, Ryan said that he had enjoyed the match and was pleased with his contribution, especially the setting-up of two of the goals. By Friday morning United were not only preparing for the final on Sunday, but also the Stoke match that would follow the following Friday!

From 9am that Friday morning in Japan, the players, management and staff started to switch back to UK time to allow their bodies and minds to be in sync for the return to England and the build-up to the Stoke match at the Britannia Stadium on Boxing Day. Tokyo was eight hours ahead of Manchester, so although 9am there, it was 1am in United's world in the Far East. For the next three days, it certainly meant an upside down existence for Giggs and the others.

Their day would begin at 3pm in Tokyo – as that was the equivalent of 7am in England. They would have their breakfast and later go out training under floodlights as night fell in Japan. Then they would have their lunch at 9pm – the equivalent of 1pm in England – and take dinner at 3am (7pm back in England). Finally, they would retire to their rooms for a good night's sleep at 7am, the equivalent of 11pm in England.

This was repeated on the Saturday and Sunday, and meant that when they arrived back in England on the Monday, they were fresh and alert, their bodies in tune with local Manchester time.

This was all possible because the club had their own chef travelling with them, as well as a nutritionist and medical adviser. Plus everyone on the trip was keen for it to work as they knew the importance of the Stoke match – a potentially tough, bruising encounter. United knew they needed to win at Stoke at whatever cost if they were to put the pressure on table-topping Liverpool.

The World Club Cup Final kicked off at 6.30pm local time in Japan – 10.30am GMT. So Giggsy and the boys would not have to play in the middle of the night in their own peculiar time zone! United's nutritionists supplied them with energy bars and drinks to help them through the confusion – although some of the squad later admitted they had felt a bit dazed about kicking off in the night when their bodies believed it was morning.

The gamble paid off: United beat Liga de Quito 1-0 in the final to lift the World Club Cup trophy, thanks to a late winner from the irrepressible Wayne Rooney. But Ryan would not appear in the match – although he still received a medal. Initially, he was disappointed to be left out, but accepted Sir Alex's reasoning. The boss had told him that he needed him fresh and raring to go for the difficult match at Stoke when they returned to England. At thirty-five, he could not expect to appear in too many games on the run.

United then received a setback when Vidic was sent off four minutes after the break for elbowing striker Claudio Bieler. It would lead to him being banned from the first leg of their next Champions League match, the tough last-16 clash with Inter Milan. Rooney won the game with a fine shot low into the net after 75 minutes. United had become the first English club to win the event in its revamped format – and they were now champions of England, champions of Europe and champions of the world!

'The sending-off made it difficult for us,' Fergie admitted. 'It's a soft sending-off, but he swung an elbow. When you do that in front of the referee, you've got no chance – he gave the referee no option. Half an hour to go is a long road with 10 men, but Wayne scored a magnificent goal. After Vidic was sent off, it was important that we didn't lose the ball. It was important to keep passing and hope Ronaldo or Rooney did something special. The collective spirit of the team won the day. With 10 men, we played with great expression and tried to win. It is a measure of the players' ambition.

'In 30 years you'll look back and see Manchester United's name on the trophy, although I won't be around to enjoy it.'

Afterwards, Ryan and the boys enjoyed a glass of wine with their meal as a celebration, but there was no wild bingeing because the challenge of dealing with Stoke, five days later, still remained. They knew they needed to be in tip-top condition for that one.

CHAPTER 15
LEAGUE OF HIS OWN

After the heady success of winning the Club World Cup in Japan, Ryan and his team-mates headed back to the cold English winter and a reality check with Stoke City's dogs of war. The players were granted a bit of time to be with their families at Christmas, but as always, United came first.

No sooner had he seen the delight on his children's faces as they opened their Christmas presents than Giggsy was back training as Sir Alex planned the best gift of all – beating Stoke and Middlesbrough so they could hopefully claw back Liverpool's lead at the top of the Premier League.

Indeed, they made it six Boxing Day wins on the bounce as they completed the first part of the job, chalking up a 1-0 win at Stoke. Carlos Tévez's 83rd-minute winner saw the Red Devils consolidate third place in the table. Giggs was left on the subs' bench for the Middlesbrough match, coming on six minutes from time as United kept up the pressure on Liverpool and Chelsea by 'doing an Arsenal' and winning 1-0 again, with Dimitar Berbatov grabbing the vital goal. More importantly, a statement was made at the top of the table – look out Liverpool, here we come.

United were now just seven points behind the Anfield outfit but had two games in hand. Things were hotting up and the big question was: could Liverpool handle the pressure? It certainly seemed to be getting to Rafa Benítez – almost a fortnight after United beat Boro, he would have his 'Keegan moment' in public.

On 9 January 2009, he blasted Sir Alex in a five-minute rant – in which he said that he was only 'talking about facts' – claiming the United boss was above the law and was 'killing referees'. It was similar to the rant that had upset Newcastle United's title hopes' applecart during the 1995/96 title race – when Kevin Keegan told Sky TV that he had lost respect for Ferguson after the United boss had said that teams tried harder to beat Manchester United than Newcastle. Keegan ended his tirade with the infamous words, 'I'd love it if we beat them! *Love* it!'

Now Benítez was falling into the same trap after Fergie had lured him in like a spider with a fly. And Liverpool would suffer for his instability just as Newcastle did because of Keegan's. By 29 January, United would lead the Premier League by two points.

The day after Benítez's outburst Liverpool could only scrape a 0-0 draw at Stoke. Two points dropped, and it got worse for them: the day after United, with Giggs putting in a fine 80-minute performance on the left wing, comprehensively outplayed and outclassed nearest rivals Chelsea.

The 3-0 win marked the death knell for Blues' boss Luiz Felipe Scolari's reign at Stamford Bridge and spelt major trouble for Benítez. United were now on 41 points, five behind Liverpool, and Fergie responded to Benítez's claims with a classic putdown from his mind-games manual: 'He was obviously a very angry man and he's been disturbed by something or other. The things he said aren't facts and that's well documented, but that's all I want to say about it.'

I was told by a United insider that Ryan and the United lads found the contretemps 'amusing' but they steadfastly refused to allow it distract them from the mission of overthrowing the Kop at the top of the table.

And they certainly kept their heads while some at Liverpool were losing theirs, chalking up a 1-0 win over Wigan at Old Trafford on 14 January, and following it with another 1-0 win, this time away at Bolton. The victory at the Reebok put United one point ahead of Liverpool, sitting proudly at the summit of the Premier League on 47 points. A crushing 5-0 win over West Brom followed at The Hawthorns and by the end of the month United were two points clear at the top as Liverpool's slump continued (with two 1-1 draws against Everton and Wigan).

Ryan was rested when United beat Wigan, but played his part in the wins over Chelsea, Bolton and West Bromwich Albion. Indeed, his performance against the doomed Scolari's Chelsea was arguably his best of the season. And it came not out on the left wing or in the role of supporting striker, but in the middle of the park – in the engine room, where he stroked the ball around beautifully in central midfield. He also had more inspirational skipper duties for the match after the man who would have helped him as his deputy cried off with the recurrence of a back injury. Rio Ferdinand's loss was young Jonny Evans' gain, with Rio's absence providing him with another chance to further his case to one day be a long-term fixture in the backline.

With Darren Fletcher proving an excellent holding midfield foil, Ryan turned back the years and was rightly judged to be Man of the Match. His passing and vision were top-rate and he had the experience to back it all up, calming down the players around him as Chelsea hit their hosts hard with their own brand of powerful, on-the-break attacking football for the first 20 minutes or so.

Inevitably, it was Giggs who set up the first goal, floating over an inviting corner that was gratefully nodded on by Berbatov for hardman Vidic to ram home with his head. Wayne Rooney made it 2-0 just after the hour mark and Berbatov wrapped it all up by grabbing his second and United's third on 86 minutes.

Giggs's display was all the more remarkable when you consider the men he was up against – the powerhouse midfield of Chelsea comprising Michael Ballack, Frank Lampard, Deco and John Obi Mikel. He had just Fletcher and Ji-Sung Park for company in United's midfield.

Afterwards, he was on a high: delighted to have been voted Man of the Match and that United, under his leadership, were edging ever closer towards Liverpool at the summit of the

Premier League. 'It was a big victory. It's been documented that we've got all the top teams at home in the second half of the season. We know we didn't do as well against them in the first half of the season as we could have done, but we're hoping to put that right and this is a good start,' he declared.

'The first goal was always going to be important in a tight game like this,' he added, 'and it came at just the right time for us, just before half time and changing everything going into the second half. Chelsea didn't get many chances – we were superb in defence and we did well in midfield and upfront. I was very pleased with my own performance in midfield but the most important thing is that we won and closed the gap at the top. We've had a tough first half to the season in the league but we're usually always strong in the second half. If we perform like we did today, we'll have a great chance.'

The 1-0 win at Bolton six days later took United to the league summit for the first time that season. Giggsy came on 17 minutes from time (with fellow sub Paul Scholes) to notch yet another landmark as he made his 550th league appearance for United. He and Scholesy sparked the Reds into life after a low-key match – and Berbatov headed home the winner in the last minute.

Giggs was jubilant after the match – he could see United were now getting into their stride: winning matches they could have drawn, showing grit and determination, and heading into the final stages with the experience no other team possessed. Boss Ferguson summed it all up for him, saying, 'Being top is not decisive at this stage but it is always nice because it is the best place to be. We have been playing catch-up in terms of fixtures for a while now. We still have another game in hand against Fulham on 14 February. Only after that will we have a good idea of where we stand between Liverpool, Chelsea and ourselves.'

At the end of January 2009, few doubted Giggsy and United were on their way to yet another title. The key was this: while Ryan and the creative midfielders and forwards were still unlocking defences, their own backline was impregnable. In fact, after the defeat at Arsenal on 8 November 2008, United would embark on one of the most remarkable runs in football history: they would go 16 matches unbeaten in the Premier League – until 14 March 2009 – as they marched unrelentingly towards retaining their title.

The 5-0 win at West Brom also meant United kept a clean sheet for an 11th successive Premier League match – a new record. That, in turn, also opened the way to another record – for Edwin Van der Sar had not conceded a goal for 1,032 minutes, beating Chelsea keeper Petr Cech's previous English best of 1,025 minutes.

Van der Sar then went on to claim the British record for clean sheets. The United keeper managed that one when the Red Devils won 1-0 at West Ham, eight days after the Everton match. The shutout at the Boleyn Ground on 8 February meant the Dutchman overwhelmed the achievement of Bobby Clark, a former Scotland international, who went 1,155 minutes without conceding between the Aberdeen posts in the 1970/71 Scottish first division season.

United would finally concede in a Premier League match, 13 days later. Unlucky for some – a 2-1 win over Blackburn at Old Trafford – but not Van der Sar. He missed the game, with Tomasz Kuczcsak deputising. Giggs, as vice-captain (and often skipper), was proud of the men at the back who had held the fort so safely and resolutely. He knew that without them United would have struggled to keep pace with Liverpool and Chelsea. 'They've done really great,' he said. 'They're a real rock for the rest of us to build on.'

Ryan did his bit for the cause in the match at West Ham, grabbing the vital goal that secured the points. His brilliant winner put United two points clear at the top in what was their eighth 1-0 win in their last 11 league games. Just after the half-hour, Ryan scored: he dribbled into the box, beat Scott Parker and then hammered the ball home with his right foot. Afterwards he would joke about it being a rarity as it had come off his right foot, not his natural left, but it was no laughing matter for West Ham. It took a man who was also once a sublime player to put into context just how good was Giggsy's effort.

In his new role of West Ham manager, Gianfranco Zola – the little Italian who used to mesmerise the English top-flight in a Chelsea shirt – spoke in awed terms: 'Ryan Giggs is a genius, a true great. It was also going to take something special to win the match, and Ryan came up with it. It was a wonderful goal, but I would much prefer it was ours! It was a close match. Unfortunately for us they have some great players and if you make a mistake, they punish you.'

United assistant boss Mike Phelan also paid tribute to Giggs and Paul Scholes, his partner-in-creative-crime in midfield that day: 'The result was important. We felt we needed to come here with the experience and with those two [Giggs and Scholes] you don't get much more experience. The match was great value for money. Both teams attacked and we managed to get the win.'

Ryan would score one more league goal that season as

United went on to claim their 11th Premier League title. He opened the scoring in the 2-0 win at Middlesbrough on 2 May 2009. Once again Sir Alex paired him with Scholes at the heart of the team and both men combined to inspire United and edge them ever closer to the crown they craved. Ryan netted on 25 minutes, driving the ball low and hard into the back of the net. That left him two short of 150 goals for United – and ripped out the heart of Gareth Southgate's battling youngsters. Ji-Sung Park ended the contest on 51 minutes with a confident shot after Rooney set him up.

Afterwards, a demoralised but generous Southgate heaped praise on Giggs and Scholes as the architects of his downfall. 'For any youngster playing against them, it's not just what they do on the field, but the way they've lived their lives at the top of the game for more than 10 years,' he observed. 'They're shining examples of how to let your football do the talking. They've both shunned the celebrity lifestyle when, particularly for Ryan, it would have been easy to go down that route. They're judged on the honours they win, their performances on the field, and nothing else.

'I'm sure they've earned a fair amount of money, but that isn't uppermost in their minds, and I'm sure for Sir Alex to have professionals like them and Rio Ferdinand and Gary Neville in his club must help enormously with young players.'

Ryan admitted that he had 'really enjoyed' his goal and that he personally thrived on the pressures and expectations as the season reached this stage – the run-in and the finale: 'The challenge keeps me going, especially at this time of the season when there are so many big games. Coming to Middlesbrough to get a result is the sort of test I relish.'

Just four fixtures now remained between United and glory – three of them were crucial, the final one irrelevant to the outcome of the battle. Giggs played in the first three, but was rested for the final one (along with many other key men).

The first of the quartet was at Old Trafford and it was a huge match: the second of the annual league encounters with neighbours Manchester City, the derby game. Giggs was on for the full 90 and played his part, directing operations from central midfield with Darren Fletcher, as always a willing co-worker. Goals from Ronaldo and Tévez saw the Reds home and left them needing just four points from their remaining three games to clinch the title.

Next up was the JJB Stadium in Wigan and Ryan emerged in the 75th minute as a sub for his old mate Scholesy. When he came on, the score was 1-1, with Carlos Tévez cancelling out Hugo Rodallega's opener. Giggs was lively and involved immediately; he helped up the tempo of United's play and it was no surprise when Michael Carrick earned all three points for the visitors with a fine goal from 20 yards out, just four minutes from time.

Giggs and United now needed just one more point to secure the title – and had two games left, the first coming three days after the win at Wigan: against Arsenal at Old Trafford. Sir Alex promised there would be no complacency: 'We'll approach the game the way we always approach a game; we still have a job to do. It is against a very good Arsenal side – I don't take any notice of what is written, they are a very good side.'

The importance of thirty-five-year-old Ryan Giggs to United's cause was emphasised when he started against the Gunners on 16 May, and lasted the whole 90 yet again. Age may have been creeping up on him and the old legs might not have been as nimble or swift as they once were, but in the opinion of the man who mattered – the boss – he was still up to the job. In the event, the match was a letdown, a real anti-climax, but the result was what counted and United let no one down in that department. The fans may have come hoping to see their team equal Liverpool's record of 18 top-flight titles in style, but at least they witnessed the end of their most bitter rivals' long-term dominance.

In a first half beset by nerves and attrition, United had only two efforts of note: from Ryan and Rooney – with Arsenal putting safety first after their defeat by the Reds in the Champions League. Ryan's was a half-chance that he failed to convert four minutes from half time. The second half was just as attritional and every Manc Red breathed a huge sigh of relief at the final whistle: nil-nil, but point – and 18th title – taken.

It also meant United had become the first club to twice achieve a hat-trick of titles. They had equalled the record of Huddersfield, Arsenal and Liverpool after also achieving it once between 1999 and 2001.

Ryan was the first to embrace with his mentor Sir Alex. The two hugged and Ferguson whispered something into his ear – apparently it was, 'Congratulations, and you are not done yet!' – as they celebrated their own personal Premier League titles' haul, a remarkable 11 each.

Giggsy then celebrated with the team, sipping some champagne as it all finally sunk in. But, typical of the man and his quest for perfection and eagerness for glory, he now announced that he wanted to celebrate what would be a record-breaking fourth consecutive title in the 2009/10 campaign: 'I hope we win another one next year! No one has ever won it four times on the trot, so that is another record for us to break.'

He was also keen to help United close the gap on Liverpool in terms of European Cup wins – they had three to the Merseyside outfit's five. Ryan was aiming to add a fourth to his club's collection and what would be a personal third in Rome later that month as United looked to overcome Barcelona in the Champions League final.

But he was not to play in the final Premier League game of the season at Hull City's KC Stadium for Sir Alex opted to use the game as an opportunity to give his fringe and younger players a run-out. Even at half-strength the Reds won 1-0 with a goal from young midfielder Darron Gibson. Giggs and the likes of Ronaldo and Rooney were told to put their feet up and relax so they would be fresh and fit for the Champions League final, three days after the match.

It was turning into some season for Ryan. He had just pocketed yet another Premier League winner's medal, a Club World Cup medal, a League Cup medal and hoped to make it a quartet in Rome. The League Cup medal (his third in the competition) had come at the start of March as United battled to beat a spirited Spurs side at Wembley.

Ryan did not start in north London – Sir Alex explained that he would be leaving him and other regular first teamers out to reward those who had played in the competition in earlier rounds. That left Giggs and the likes of Nemanja Vidic scratching their heads as they had most certainly played in earlier rounds to help settle down the kids that Fergie usually started in the tournament. Indeed, Ryan had played in three of the four ties that took the Reds to Wembley – and scored one of his four goals that season in their first Carling Cup appearance, the 3-1 win over Middlesbrough in the third round.

After coming on as a late substitute as the match went into extra-time, replacing Darron Gibson on 91 minutes, he earned his winner's medal. And it would be Giggs who was handed the task that demanded an ice-cool temperament and a gunslinger's finish – the first penalty. No problem, Ryan told Fergie, smiling as he headed to the spot and smashed the ball home for United.

Ronaldo and Anderson also scored for the Red Devils from the spot in the shoot-out, but only Vedran Corluka converted a penalty for Spurs. The Carling Cup was on its way to Manchester: it might not mean much in the echelons of modern-era football honours, but it brought another medal for the Giggs' mantelpiece. It was his third League Cup medal – after also claiming the award in 1992 and 2006 – and he set a record as the only player to win the competition three times.

Ryan told friends that it had been another great day in his career at Old Trafford. As they celebrated their win in London before heading back to Manchester, he let his hair down with the other lads, but the celebrations did not last long. After all, they were hardly going to go overboard at winning the Carling Cup: they had much bigger fish to fry. With almost three months of the campaign still remaining, Giggs would put major celebrations on ice, just as he had done the year before, funnily enough.

Even defeated Spurs boss Harry Redknapp said he could see United going on to win the Champions League, the Premier

League and the FA Cup: 'They have got a big chance – they are the team to beat. They have a fantastic squad, it looks as if the league is going their way and you wouldn't bet against them in the Champions League and the FA Cup.'

But they would win only one of the three – leaving Ryan disappointed at the end of the season. Disappointed at only claiming the Premier League, the Carling Cup and the World Club Cup? Well, that was the nature of the boy and the club he played for.

The FA Cup dream would disappear on 19 April 2009, when United exited at the semi-final stage at Wembley. They lost 4-2 on penalties to Everton – and many pundits claimed it was all Sir Alex deserved after sending out a team that was arguably not as good as the one he paraded in the Carling Cup final. Ryan Giggs, Wayne Rooney, Cristiano Ronaldo and Edwin Van der Sar were not even on the bench. Almost inevitably, it ended in tears for United's revamped line-up in the penalty shootout.

So, what happened in the Champions League final? Well, Ryan and co. were certainly confident they could win it. In his pre-match Press comments, Giggs said there was no reason why the team could not continue its run of success – and indeed, added that he felt victory would prove this team was the best United side that he had ever played in: 'I have played in some really good teams. In 1999 it was obviously the Treble side, while the 1994 team sometimes seemed unbeatable. But this season we have won the league for a third successive time and I think if we win the Champions League as well, you will not get very many people arguing against it being rated as the best-ever United side.

'Nobody has ever defended the Champions League. To accept that challenge and succeed would, on its own, be brilliant. But to have won a hat-trick of leagues as well, you have to talk in terms of this being the best team the club have had. It is hard work winning the Champions League. Mentally and physically, it's draining. It's about going again and having the desire and hunger to do it all again. This season there has been the same desire at the club because we recognised that nobody has defended it and the players look for those challenges.

'Everybody wants to beat the champions, whether it is the league or Champions League, that is why it is so difficult to retain.'

In the previous year's final, Ryan started by coming off the bench in place of the unlucky-to-be-suspended Darren Fletcher. He said he was in good shape and looked forward to adding that third winner's medal to his collection (after 1999 and 2008). But the match against Barcelona in Rome did not go to plan. Why? My view, and one shared by some of the United players, was that the team froze after a cracking 10-minute opening. They were like Ivan Drago in the movie *Rocky IV*, thinking they were unbeatable and immortal until they got cut. When Rocky caused Drago to bleed, the big Russian looked stunned and began to lose his nerve. Similarly, when Samuel Eto'o turned Nemanja Vidic to fire Barca ahead on 10 minutes, United fell to pieces. They bought into the nonsense that Barca were unbeatable and almost looked on in awe for the remaining 80 minutes, allowing them to run wild and dictate the game.

Which was a mighty pity – as Chelsea would tell you, Barca are far from invincible as the Blues showed by outscheming them over two legs in the semis and only going out because of the incompetence of referee Tom Henning Ovrebo.

After the first goal United didn't turn up and it was an incredibly disappointed Giggs who led them up for their losers' medals. Ryan had earned his place in the final line-up – he had played and made major contributions in all of the last 16, quarter- and semi-final matches. Indeed, before he starred in the last-16 home win over Inter Milan, José Mourinho took time out to salute the Welshman. 'What can you say about a man who has won 10 Premier League titles? The proof is in his medals,' Mourinho said. 'Yes, maybe we are talking about the greatest Premier League player of all time. At the very least, no player has contributed so much to a single Premier League club as Ryan Giggs has to Manchester United.'

The Inter boss, once manager of United's main rivals of the last decade, Chelsea, told the *Sunday Mirror* that he believed the move from the wing to central midfield had lengthened Ryan's time at the top: 'He has found new life in central midfield this season, and I think that has been very important for United's season. At thirty-five, he is going to have lost some of his pace, of course – but Sir Alex has been very clever, playing him in a new position and like we have seen in the past with players like Zola, Bergkamp and Zidane – quality shines through beyond age.

'United have their young, wonderful players like Cristiano Ronaldo and Wayne Rooney. But who knows, maybe it will be Giggs who makes the difference for them in the Premier and Europe this season.'

United beat Inter 2-0 at home in that last-16 second leg after drawing the first 0-0. They then beat Porto 1-0 away after drawing the first leg of the quarter-final 2-2 at Old Trafford. In the semis, they saw off Arsenal 3-1 at the Emirates after winning 1-0 in the first leg at Old Trafford.

The stunning double over Arsenal raised hopes that Giggsy and the boys would be able to replicate that form against Barca and that was what was so disappointing when they did not play to their true strengths. Lionel Messi escaped the clutches of Rio Ferdinand to head home and make it 2-0 to Barca.

Before the final Ryan said that Ronaldo could swing the game United's way; also that the winger would be mad to leave the Reds for Real Madrid: 'He is at the best club now. Cristiano has proved he is the best player in the world over the last couple of years and he has done that at United, so why leave? He's still a young player, still learning the game, and can still improve. He can do that at United.

'Real Madrid will come back purely because of the club they are and the history they have got, but United are more stable in the fact there are no presidential elections and the manager's been here so long. Ronaldo is a big-game player. He was brilliant last season in the final and scored, and he thrives on these kind of games.'

But Ronaldo did not thrive – like the team he faltered after the first 10 minutes. It could have been worse, as Giggs and the rest were honest enough to concede afterwards. But Ryan also pleaded for leniency and respect for the way United had won three trophies that season. 'Everyone is disappointed and no one wants to lose a final, but we will try to get back there next year,' he said. 'Barcelona played very well and we were not at our best, but we have got to keep improving, that is what great teams and great players do, look forward to the next challenge. We will look to get to a third consecutive Champions final. That is the challenge we have got next year. It has been a fantastic season and we must not forget that. We have achieved so much. To win three Premier League titles on the trot is an unbelievable thing to do and now we must look to make it four.'

Sir Alex also stood up and admitted his team had been outplayed: 'I think the first goal was a killer for us; it was their first attack and they scored. We had started brightly, but we got a bit nervous after that and of course with a goal lead, they could keep the ball all night.'

He went on to say that United were beaten by a better team: 'We weren't at our best – after the first goal it was very difficult for us. They defended quite well actually, we thought we could get at their back four better than we did. Losing is the best part of the game, because in adversity you always move forwards quicker. Of course we are disappointed, but we are a young team and we can improve.'

A young team, yes, but time was running out for United's greatest servant of all time (and arguably player of all time). As Ryan Giggs approached the 2009/10 season, he knew full well it might be his last: his contract ran out in June 2010 and he would be thirty-six. Would there be one final hurrah to the glorious Ryan Giggs' fairytale?

CHAPTER 16
20:13

Mondays have traditionally got a bad press. Think of the financial meltdown in 1987 when the world's stock markets crashed. Or the song 'Blue Monday' by Manchester band New Order, which the band have said was written as a retort to their fans who tended to be 'blue' because they never played encores!

But black and blue Mondays would be old hat by 2013, thanks to a similarly shattering yardstick in the world of football and, ironically, in Manchester too. For on Monday 22 April, Ryan Giggs would win his thirteenth Premier League title medal after Manchester United routed Aston Villa 3-0 at Old Trafford. That victory meant United had won the title back from neighbours City with four weeks of the season remaining. The win put them 16 points clear of second-placed City and also meant that Ryan's total honours had now reached a remarkable 23 major titles.

Not bad for a lad who had spent his entire career with the same club. His personal haul also included four FA Cups, four League Cups and two Champions League crowns.

Both his manager and team-mates were quick to pay homage to the man who had just cemented his position as the most decorated player in British football ever.

'He's a unique freak,' boss Fergie said of Giggs, who was now in his 22nd season with the club. 'He'll play for another two years, trust me.'

And midfielder Michael Carrick, who had enjoyed his best ever season at Old Trafford – perhaps not uncoincidentally because Giggs had spent a large part of the campaign as his central midfield ally – led the praise from the players. Carrick said, 'I keep talking about him but what else is there left to say? It is sensational that he is still able to do that after all this time. It is not just physical, it is mental, having the drive and desire to do it every day. Ryan is out there training every day. The standard he has set is unbelievable. He is a legend. It is a throwaway comment too often. But he is the legend really. It is a pleasure to play with him and work with him every day.'

Even UEFA president Michel Platini – not usually renowned for his praise for British football or its stars – wanted to add his congratulations to Ryan and United's achievement on that wonderful Monday night at Old Trafford. Platini said, 'His loyalty and dedication to United is beautiful. I like the people that fight for their colours and don't change clubs every two months to make business. He's a guy who would never change clubs.'

At the end of the last chapter, we had asked whether Ryan had one last hurrah in him as he approached the 2009/10 season. The answer – as that 20th top-flight title win for United proved on 22 April 2013 – was a resounding 'yes'. Since 2009, he had proved he could indeed play a key role as a central midfielder, as well as still turning out down that left wing when needed. He had maintained his fitness and guile thanks to his devotion to training and yoga. And he had earned the one-year contracts offered to him at the end of each season since the summer of 2009.

A month before winning his 13th top-flight medal, Ryan had signed another one-year deal – which ensured he would still be playing at the highest level at the age of 40! The deal, signed on 1 March 2013, meant he would be at United until at least June 2014, taking him through his 23rd season as a first-team player. After signing Ryan admitted he was relieved and delighted to be tied to the club for at least another season.

'I am feeling good, enjoying my football more than ever and, most importantly, I feel I am making a contribution to the team,' he said. 'This is an exciting team to be part of, with great team spirit, and we are again pushing for trophies as we head towards the business end of the season.'

Fergie was also delighted, saying, 'Ryan is an example to us all – the way he has and continues to look after himself. What can I say about Ryan that hasn't already been said? He is a marvellous player and an exceptional human being. He has fantastic energy for the game and it is wonderful to see. Ryan seems to reach a new milestone every week, and to think that he now has 23 unbroken years of league goals behind him is truly amazing in the modern-day game. I don't think it will ever be achieved again by anyone.

'His form this year shows his ability and his enjoyment of the game are as strong as ever and I am absolutely delighted that he has signed a new contract.

'He still has that wonderful youthfulness in the way he plays, he still has great balance and a change of pace. He still has his fitness and still gets you a goal. I told him this morning I expect a bill from his mother for all the sandwiches and teas she used to make for us when we went to his house every week when we were trying to get him to sign schoolboy forms.'

In signing that deal, Giggs showed his intention to become a member of the small, elite club of players to star on the top-flight stage at the age of 40 and above. Giggsy would become only the third outfield player to play in the Premier League in their 40s, following Teddy Sheringham at West Ham and Gordon Strachan at Coventry.

And boss Fergie made it clear that he expected him to stay on at United way beyond his playing career.

'The plan is for Ryan to stay on after he's hung up his boots,' he said. 'Involvement after they've played here is important for our players, whether that be as a coach or assistant manager or working with the youth team. If anyone has ambitions to be a manager they should take on different roles before you get there, almost as a preparation. Ryan has got to take his badges and spend time with the young players in the academy and prepare eventually to be a manager.'

Giggs had chalked up yet another milestone in 2013 – when

he scored in United's 2-0 win over Everton on February 10. That meant he had scored in each of the last 23 seasons, including all 21 Premier League campaigns.

Casting our eyes a bit further back, we see that he also made many more significant contributions to the game and his own career after May 2009. In the summer of that year Ryan would score his first Manchester United hat-trick in a pre-season friendly against Hangzhou Greentown after coming on as a second-half substitute. It might have only been a friendly in China but Ryan was clearly overjoyed at knocking over another hurdle in his wonderful career. The Welshman was on target in the second half of a match in which Michael Owen also grabbed a brace, with Nani, Zoran Tosic and Dimitar Berbatov completing the 8-2 rout.

In September 2009 Ryan made his 700th start for United as they triumphed 3-1 at Tottenham. And he marked the occasion by curling home a great free kick to put the Red Devils on level terms at 1-1 after Jermain Defoe had put the hosts ahead.

There were more milestones to come as the year progressed. He scored his 150th goal for United, only the ninth player to do so for the club, against Wolfsburg in his first Champions League game of the season at the end of September. His free kick for the goal needed a deflection before beating Diego Benaglio – but Ryan then completed his night's work by setting up Michael Carrick for the winner as United edged home 2-1.

Then, at the end of November 2009 and on the eve of his 36th birthday, Ryan was in the right place at the right time for his 100th Premier League goal – scoring the final goal in a 4-1 victory over Portsmouth at Fratton Park, and becoming only the 17th player in the Premier League to achieve the milestone. Ryan said he was 'proud' of the achievement while Fergie added, 'Ryan Giggs is an exceptional player. A rarity. He will play for two years yet. His goal was the icing on the cake – so many things were happening and it is a great result for us and some of the football was good. In the second half we kept our discipline and the ball very well and deserved the win in the end. I am delighted for Ryan.'

One month later he was named United's player of the decade by manutd.com – a wonderful way to see out the year. Adam Bostock, of manutd.com, explained exactly why he and his team had plumped for Ryan. He said, 'It was a close call – but the team eventually settled on Ryan Giggs OBE as United's Player of the Decade. The Welshman's extraordinary length of service was certainly a factor, but longevity alone would not have been enough to see off the challenges from Ronaldo and Rooney. Giggs' enduring ability to undo the opposition with a killer pass, a majestic finish, even a nostalgic jig past hapless defenders, means he's every bit as important to United at the end of this decade as he was at the close of the last. He's an inspiration to others – even without the captain's armband he often wears, always with distinction. The only surprise in him winning the PFA Player of the Year and the BBC Sports Personality of the Year awards in 2009 was that he had not done so before.

'Three titles in the last three seasons have taken Ryan's haul of league winners' medals to an English-record eleven – and few would bet against him reaching a dozen in 2010.'

Adam would be wrong in the latter assumption. Much to Ryan and United's disappointment, they missed out on a fourth consecutive league crown – and that dozen for Ryan – as Chelsea pipped them to the league by a single point. Ryan and his team-mates also fluffed their chance to be the first team to reach three consecutive Champions League finals since Juventus in 1998 – as they crashed out in the quarter-finals in April 2010 to Bayern Munich. They also lost to Leeds in the FA Cup and the only consolation for the campaign came with the 2-1 win over Aston Villa that ensured they retained the League Cup.

It was United's fourth League Cup title, and their third in five years. It was also the first time they had ever successfully defended a domestic cup. Ryan was pleased the Red Devils had not ended the season with nothing, but even that consolation had a sting in the tail. He would have expected to have played in the final against Villa – but was sidelined after breaking his arm in a league match 18 days earlier…ironically against Villa.

If the 2009/10 season had been something of a letdown for Ryan, the following would be the exact opposite. For United would win their record 19th top-flight title – an achievement that meant they had finally surpassed Liverpool's record of 18 titles. The 2010/11 campaign would also see Giggs appearing in another Champions League final – but once again the dream team from Barcelona would wreck his own dream of a third win in the competition after the joy of 1999 and 2008.

On January 17, 2011, Giggs hit the magical figure of 600 league appearances for United in a goalless draw against

Tottenham at White Hart Lane. A fortnight later he was named United's greatest ever player in a worldwide poll conducted by United's official magazine and website. Ryan, who beat off legends like Eric Cantona, George Best and Sir Bobby Charlton to win the honour, said, 'Obviously it's all down to opinion and everyone is going to have a different view, but when I got told I genuinely couldn't believe it to be honest, especially because there have been so many great players here. I'm not finished yet though – I feel great and I hope I can carry on for a while longer.'

Boss Fergie paid a personal tribute to his favourite footballing son, telling *Inside United* magazine, 'Longevity always comes into play in these things, and Ryan's been around for more time than any other player here. He recently appeared in his 600th league game, which is an exceptional achievement. That won't be done again, not by one player at the same club. And then we can talk about his performances, which have been top class for 20 years. Even now, at the age of 37, he's amazing.

'It's quite something to be named number one, isn't it, considering the competition? When you look at the galaxy of stars that have been at this club, this is a huge honour for Ryan.'

Indeed it was. But Giggsy has always been very much a team player rather than an egotist out for personal glory: the good of Manchester United has always come first with this very humble, likeable man. Not for him the tricks of Cristiano Ronaldo or the 'look-at-me' antics of past Premier League idols such as Mario Balotelli.

While he was always grateful and delighted for the personal honours that came his way in a glittering career, he was always more on a high when his endeavours meant United had won a major trophy (again). So when he picked up still more accolades as the 2010/11 season drew to its close, they were very much a sideshow to the bigger picture – the dream of everyone at the club to win that 19th league title (and, as Fergie once so famously put it, 'knock Liverpool off their f*****ing perch') and gain revenge on Barcelona in the Champions League final at Wembley.

Giggs helped the club achieve the first part of that dream, but was unable to prevent the brilliant Barca from overwhelming United as they won 3-1 in the Champions League final at Wembley. As part of that record-breaking 19th title for the club (and 12th for Ryan) he surpassed the Manchester United league appearance record of Bobby Charlton by playing his 607th game, against Liverpool. Unfortunately, it would end in a 3-1 defeat for the Red Devils, but it would prove to be only a temporary blip as Giggsy and the boys went on to lift the Premiership trophy.

They had gone to the top of the table on November 27, 2010, and stayed there until the last game of the season – a remarkable run of results ending with a 4-2 home win over Blackpool. Yet Ryan's joy at that win would be tempered by the disappointment of the loss to Barca at Wembley six days later.

Giggs had played a key role in helping United reach the final. On April 26, he grabbed the first goal from a Rooney pass as the Reds beat Schalke 04 in the semi-final first leg – at the same time earning himself another place in the record books as the oldest goalscorer in Champions League history.

The scene was certainly set for a classic final at the end of

May. United had reached the final after a comfortable 6-1 aggregate win over Schalke and Giggsy was relishing the match with the Red Devils' old foes Barca in the showpiece in London. Of course, the crack Spanish team had beaten United 2-0 in the corresponding match in Rome two years previously, but United boss Fergie reckoned they had nothing to fear this time, even though many pundits were now openly describing Barca as 'the greatest club side in world football ever'. Fergie said, 'I don't think we should be going there lacking in confidence. We are playing a fantastic team but we can't be frightened out of our skins. Their form is there for everyone to see. Our job is to find a solution. I think we'll be quite well prepared for the final.'

Even his opposite number at Barca admitted his fear that Fergie could indeed 'find a solution' for the Wembley final. Pep Guardiola pointed out that United had a number of great players – including, of course, Giggsy.

'They have a great squad with two great teams and extraordinary players,' he said. 'United can field five teams that are competitive. I can't make nine changes to my team because we have a small squad, but they have so much quality – [Dimitar] Berbatov, Chicharito [Javier Hernandez], [Wayne] Rooney, [Paul] Scholes, [Ryan] Giggs – they have so many players to choose from.'

United were booked into the Landmark Hotel, their regular base when playing at Wembley. Ryan and his team-mates settled into the rooms and suites the club had taken over in the luxury Victorian establishment in Marylebone, Central London. 'It certainly lived up to its reputation as one of London's few 5-star establishments!' a source said.

'United were delighted with it. Ryan knew it from previous stays and neither he nor his team-mates suffered sleepless nights. There was no noise from the trains and Giggsy and co were cocooned away from the public and the inevitable gaggle of fans who congregated outside when they learned the team was staying there.'

Everything was set up for the *coup de grace* – a win that would avenge the runaround Barca had given United two years previously in Rome. Unfortunately, Barca refused to comply with the script – ensuring Ryan would suffer what he later admitted was 'one of his most disappointing nights in football'.

The teams had lined up like this, with Giggsy working in tandem with Michael Carrick in the midfield engine room:

BARCELONA: 1 Valdes, 2 Alves, 3 Pique, 22 Abidal, 6 Xavi, 8 Iniesta, 14 Mascherano, 16 Busquets, 7 Villa, 10 Messi, 17 Pedro.
MAN UTD: 1 Van der Sar, 3 Evra, 5 Ferdinand, 15 Vidic, 20 Fabio Da Silva, 11 Giggs, 13 Park Ji-Sung, 16 Carrick, 25 Valencia, 10 Rooney, 14 Hernandez.

But the Red Devils would once again come up short – it would be the Spanish giants who once again, gave United a footballing lesson, emerging victorious 3-1 with goals from Pedro, Lionel Messi and David Villa, with only Rooney's wonderful strike providing any consolation for the Reds.

Sir Alex's team had proved not quite good enough and Fergie was honest enough to admit afterwards that they had, in all honesty, been 'given a hiding' and that they were distinctly second best to the team who notched their third Champions League success in six years. They were honest words from a proud man.

Similarly, Ryan doffed his hat to the Barca players, admitting they had been the better team on the night and adding that he believed no one could have lived with them on that form. They were simply the best.

I was at Wembley that day and sensed a tension among United fans even before kick-off. It was as if they knew that this was going to be a struggle against a team that was simply too good. The United hordes weren't as noisy or as humourous as usual; indeed they were drowned out for much of the match by their Catalan rivals. An unusual state of affairs, given that United supporters are among the most partisan and fanatical in the world.

Two days after the drubbing, a staunch United fan emailed me with the following fears. 'Can't really believe I'm daring to ask this, and I am feeling very low, but I will: Has Sir Alex Ferguson reached the end of the road? He is the greatest manager on these shores. But, even if he kept plugging away for the next ten years, would he overcome Barca? Even when the likes of Xavi and Iniesta have packed it in they will still have enough to shaft us (because Messi will still be there) unless the Glazers dig deep. And we know the answer to that, don't we? God, I feel gutted today. Awful, awful, awful.'

It got me thinking, too. That maybe some good would indirectly emerge from the defeat – that maybe the United boss and his team, led by the still inspirational Giggsy, now had the necessary carrot needed to keep Sir Alex and Ryan battling and inspired for another few years?

The answer during the next two campaigns – the 2011/12 campaign and the 2012/13 season – would be a resounding YES!

Giggsy seemed to go from strength to strength. By the end of the 2011/12 season, he would be 38, and 39 at the conclusion of the 2012/13 term. Yet his performances continued to defy belief. It was as if he had been given the gift of a second youth as he powered through games in central midfield, but with the addition of the wisdom and vision all those years at the top had brought. Certainly for United and Fergie his continued excellence was wonderful news – especially as the boss had still not found a solution to the central midfield dilemma that had plagued him since Roy Keane had been shown the exit in 2007.

United were short of class in that vital area. Darren Fletcher had improved dramatically but had been laid low with an illness during both those latter campaigns and the Brazilian boy Anderson had not managed to plug the gap. The situation was so troublesome that when Paul Scholes offered to come out of retirement, the boss nearly bit his hand off!

So Ryan's Indian summer was a massive bonus at Old Trafford as United attempted to move through a transitional phase without too much damage.

After that Wembley defeat by Barca, UEFA also paid tribute to Ryan's overall contribution during the season, saying, 'He excelled in United's run to the 2011 UEFA Champions League final, setting up all three goals in the last eight against Chelsea FC and scoring in the semi-final at FC Schalke 04 – and ended the campaign with his 12th league championship medal after United surpassed Liverpool's record of 18 English titles.'

But after the summer break in 2011, that was all consigned to the history books as Giggsy and the team returned for another tilt at the Premier League and the Champions League. But the 2011/12 campaign would prove to be somewhat transitional as new players – including Phil Jones, Chris Smalling and Ashley Young – tried to find their feet at the world's biggest football club. It would be a season of disappointment as Ryan and the boys lost their Premier League crown to local rivals Manchester City and were knocked out of the FA Cup by Liverpool and the League Cup by Crystal Palace.

The loss of the league crown to City caused particular pain – even more so as the Blues only won it on goal difference, in the final minute of the last game of the season. It was the last straw in a season of heartache as United had earlier crashed out of the Champions League at the group stage. Their subsequent involvement in the Europa League saw them exit at the hands of Athletico Bilbao.

On a personal level, Giggsy did notch up another few milestones during the season. In October 2011, he was honoured with the Golden Foot Award for that year. He received a trophy at a ceremony headed by Prince Albert II of Monaco night after winning a vote on the competition's website. Ryan beat nominees David Beckham, Didier Drogba, Samuel Eto'o, Iker Casillas, Gianluigi Buffon, Javier Zanetti and Carles Puyol to the award. As part of his triumph, he would have a mould of his feet added to Monte Carlo's 'Champions Promenade'.

'I have been fortunate to play alongside great players, play for the greatest manager and play for the best club in the world,' said Giggs at the cermenony. 'When we lose he is scary but Sir Alex is hard but fair. He demands a lot from his players, as he does from himself. He is the best manager and it's great to have had him there throughout my career.

'It's a great honour to win such an award and to have my footprints alongside some of the greatest football players is a real privilege. I suppose I will have to start thinking about retirement soon but at the moment I am still enjoying my football. If it all finished tomorrow I could say that I have had a fantastic career and wouldn't swap it with anybody. I'm enjoying it now just like I was when I was 17, that's one of the main reasons I'm still going.'

Two months later, he maintained his record of scoring in each of the past 22 top-flight seasons by grabbing United's third goal against Fulham at Craven Cottage in a 5-0 win. The goal was also his first of the season in the league. Then, at the end of February 2012, Ryan made his 900th appearance for United in the 2-1 away win against Norwich City. He celebrated in typical style – by scoring the winner in the final minute! After the match, Fergie paid Giggs yet another tribute, telling BBC Sport, 'For a player to play for one club for 900 games is exceptional and it won't be done again.' And Ryan added, 'To play 900 games for this club, who I've grown up supporting, is special – it's a great day for me.'

But by the end of May, Ryan was low when asked for his views on the season. He was clearly disappointed that United had blown up on all fronts, but he said his anguish was slightly relieved by the fact that he would be playing Olympic football during the London 2012 Games that summer. Not only playing – but captaining the Great Britain team. On 28

June 2012, Giggsy was named as one of the three over-aged players selected for Great Britain at the Olympics – alongside Craig Bellamy and Micah Richards – and was subsequently named skipper. Ryan led the team out for their first group match against Senegal at Wembley on 26 July. Earlier he had made it clear how much his selection had meant to him.

'As a footballer, you don't start out in your career hoping to win the Olympics. You want to win leagues, FA Cups and European Cups. But to get the chance to play in a tournament at such a late stage of my career is obviously one I'm excited about and looking forward to. Of course, you want to win every game and win the tournament. We know it's going to be tough – but having seen the quality of our team over the last few weeks, we're hopeful of going a long way.

'An Olympic gold would be up there with my European medals. I don't like to prioritise any medal or trophy, because it's always a good feeling when you win. It's always a challenge – no matter what you win – and this is a big challenge.'

It was – and there would be no gold medal. Instead the adventure would end in the anguish of defeat in a penalty shoot-out in the quarter-finals in Ryan's native Cardiff – after the match against South Korea had ended 1-1. A disappointed Ryan said, 'We weren't good enough, that's the bottom line.' But, as always, he tried to see the positives from the experience and added, 'I would like other players to experience what I have experienced – the whole Olympic attitude. It can only be good for players' development. I will always cherish this.'

Indeed he would. But in the next 12 months Ryan would

also be cherishing that 20th title for United – and his 13th. With Giggsy in top form, the Red Devils stormed to that record breaking number. Perhaps 23 April should be renamed Red Monday by United fans! The Monday on which Ryan Giggs confirmed – if confirmation was needed – his legendary status at the world's most popular football club. And the extra good news for United fans was that it wouldn't be the end of the story for Giggsy.

Let's now wrap up our look at Giggsy's glorious career by taking a look at his international career and assessing the ongoing debate over where he stands in the annals of United greats – and how he compares one-to-one with the late, great Georgie Best.

CHAPTER 17

PRINCE OF WALES

'Any manager in the world would like a player like Giggs in their side, and I am no different.'

Dunga, manager of the Brazilian national team

'If only he'd played for England.'

Sir Bobby Charlton

'It's ridiculous when people say he should have played for England. He's Welsh and that's it.'

Robbie Savage

It's the area of his career – like George Best's, given his relatively similar level of failure at international level – that always gives some the stick with which to beat Ryan Giggs; to say that, yes, OK, he was a Manchester United great but he wasn't really a *world* great because he never lorded it on the international stage.

It was hardly Ryan Giggs's fault that he was eligible by birth to play for a country that, if not among the world's minnows, could certainly never be relied upon to qualify for the World Cup finals, let alone win.

Just as irritatingly, some pundits will drone on about how he should have played for England and then he really could have shown how big a star he was on the world stage. Again, there was never the remotest chance of him doing so. Ryan Giggs is a proud Welshman, who loved turning out for his country and who would have hated any attempt to try and get him into an England shirt. He did not want to play for England. Sure, he played for England schoolboys, but that was a different matter altogether. The eligibility issues are different in the U-21 and senior teams. All schoolboys in England are eligible to play for England schoolboys – regardless of nationality. Scots who attended English schools have, like Ryan, turned out for England schoolboys.

He also went on to captain England at schoolboy level, but let's do away with this debate once and for all – Giggs was never eligible to play for the senior team and only played for the schoolboy team because he was at an English school. He explained it like this to the *Sunday Times* in 2002: 'There would never have been any confusion had I not played for England schoolboys, but I wasn't going to turn down the chance to do so because it was a great experience. I was captain and played nine games alongside people like Nicky Barmby, yet I always knew the next year I'd be in the Welsh youth team. In fact, I played for Wales Under-16s against an England side that was more or less the one I'd captained the year before.'

Giggs was born in Wales, both his parents and his grandparents were Welsh. He could not have played international football for any country other than Wales. Or as he himself said, 'I was born in Cardiff, my mother and father are Welsh, my grandparents are Welsh. There was never an issue who I'd play for, never a doubt in my mind.'

Twenty-eight days after he made his Manchester United

debut in March 1991 as a sub at home to Everton, he stepped out for the Welsh U-21s in their match away in Poland to play his part in a 2-1 triumph.

In fact, his full international career would span 16 years and 64 caps, from 1991 to 2007. During that time, the wonderboy was to score 12 goals for his country, but he never played in a single European Championship or World Cup finals match because Wales failed to qualify.

Naturally, that was frustrating for the man who had won everything there is to win at club level, but he accepted it as his lot – and it wasn't a bad lot, was it? Some international stars never win anything at club level – for Ryan it was the other way around, but he was level-headed and patriotic enough to accept the situation. Indeed, he thanked his lucky stars that he had enjoyed such a glittering career at United – he could have been at a lower-league club, winning nothing and playing for Wales, as some of those playing alongside him at international level did.

There were also claims during his long, international career that the Welsh did not truly appreciate his talents or his efforts for the national team; that he sometimes hid behind injuries to avoid meaningless games for Wales, but he would then be fit to turn out for United. I see much of this as mischief-making among the Press who, as usual, were desperate for stories to fill endless pages.

Ryan was as patriotic as any Welshman and was so proud to pull on the red jersey, and even prouder when he was made Welsh skipper. And the Welsh footballing public adored him; he was their hero and their inspiration. They knew he was a special gem and appreciated his efforts. One fact confirms this was the case and also highlights the fondness with which he was viewed by the Welsh population as a whole: in January 2009, it was announced that a portrait of Ryan Giggs had been acquired by the National Library of Wales for £10,000 and that it would go on display at their Aberystwyth headquarters. Giggs would be in very fine company – his likeness is alongside those of two of the greatest Welshmen ever, NHS founder Aneurin Bevan and poet Dylan Thomas. It was painted at a studio near Old Trafford in 1998 when Ryan was twenty-four by artist Peter Edwards. Mr Edwards, from Oswestry, Shropshire, had already done a portrait of Sir Bobby Charlton, which is on display in the National Portrait Gallery in London. He wanted to do a similar work of his hero Ryan and got Sir Bobby to set up the sitting. It was completed after three sittings totalling about four hours.

Edwards remarked: 'He was very down-to-earth and quietly spoken, but very friendly. You sometimes worry that you are going to be disappointed [when you meet a famous person] but I thought he was a very nice young man.'

The gallery has only one other Welsh sporting hero in its collection – rugby legend Barry John – which serves to emphasise the respect that Giggs had gained within his homeland for his achievements. 'Ryan is an example of one of our great Welshmen and it is a lovely portrait,' said Dr Paul Joyner, head of purchases and donations for the library.

Always a record breaker, it would be no different for Ryan Giggs when he started out on his international career with the Wales senior side in 1991. He became the youngest-ever player to appear for the seniors when he made his debut as sub in a European championship qualifier against Germany in Nuremberg on 16 October 1991. Ryan was 17 years and 332 days old. Wales lost 4-1. He had four more caps as a sub while the management team tried to break him in gently.

His first full appearance would be 18 months later – at home to Belgium in a World Cup qualifier on 31 March 1993. He scored his first goal in the 2-0 win. That was the beginning of his odyssey with the Welsh national team – from that game on (and if fit), he would always start: he had truly arrived on the international stage.

Now, he was determined to make a go of his international career. He had been made aware of the inevitable comparisons between himself and George Best – how George never found success on the international stage because Northern Ireland never reached the finals of any major competitions. But he was adamant it would not necessarily be the case with him – and that if it was, he might have to consider moving abroad to test himself against the best players in the world.

He told *Sunday Times* writer Hugh McIlvanney in December 1993, 'I feel this Welsh team we've got right now is probably the best we are going to have for a long time and some of the most important players are at a late stage of their careers.' But what he said next made a few people sit up: 'Maybe I won't be fortunate enough to go to the World Cup with Wales, and signs of that happening would bring Italy more into my thinking. Nobody can question my commitment to Manchester United: I know how special the club is and how lucky I am to be part of it, but I wouldn't want to finish my career without convincing myself that I had realised every ounce of my potential. I do have a dream of proving my worth among the very best footballers in the world and most of them play in the Italian League. When the present deal is completed, I'll only be twenty-five. I should be just approaching my prime and it could be that it will be right for me then to go to Italy.'

Imagine the fright that interview gave boss Fergie and United's army of fans back in 1993! The idea that Giggs was seriously contemplating a move to Italy (where Inter Milan would become perennial suitors) if he didn't achieve success with Wales was a major worry. In the event, of course, Wales would not make the 1994 World Cup finals and that disappointment would underpin the whole of Ryan's international career. But as he matured, he would see that he had no reason to leave United because of his homeland's failings in international football: he would simply beat the world's best players on the European club stage in the colours of the Red Devils.

It was a crying shame that Wales did not make it to the 1994 World Cup finals – they had arguably their best team ever in terms of attacking and creative intent. There was Giggs, Dean Saunders, Ian Rush and Mark Hughes – four forwards who could walk into most national team squads and three of them arguably genuine world-class talents (Giggs, Rush and Hughes). Yet they were let down by a lack of quality balance at the back and in midfield.

In that qualification campaign for 1994, Giggs and Wales were just a win away from making the finals. They needed to beat Romania at home, but went down 2-1 (with Paul Bodin missing a penalty when it was 1-1). Ryan would describe the defeat and missing out on the World Cup finals as 'the biggest disappointment of my career', admitting that he was 'completely gutted.' The defeat and failure to qualify would also cost the hard-working Terry Yorath his job as manager.

The Football Association of Wales turned to John Toshack, then manager of Real Sociedad, to replace him. But the omens were hardly favourable – he would be coming in as a part-time boss and admitted that he did not see eye to eye with some of the folk at the FAW who had employed him. Initially, however, it looked a promising appointment – especially when 'Tosh' spoke of his admiration for Giggs and how he planned to build his team around the then wonderboy. The aim was to get Ryan and his team-mates in the finals of the 1996 European Championships, which would have special significance as they would be held in England.

The day of his appointment, in March 1994, Toshack revealed, 'The closest I've come to seeing Ryan in the flesh was when I was invited over to London by the BBC to watch Wales's last two World Cup qualifiers from the studio. I do remember watching his dad, Danny Wilson, play fly-half for Cardiff Rugby Union club before he switched to Rugby League with Swinton. Obviously, I've seen a lot of Ryan on satellite TV and I'm very excited at the prospect of working with him. We are fortunate to have a player like him in the side and what we have got to try and do is to make full use of his talents.'

He continued: 'Although it's 11 against 11, he's the type of player who can win a game for you on his own. He's had a lot of attention and that's always a problem with a gifted young player, but from a long way off it looked to me as if he's been handled well in that respect by the people responsible for him at his club. He's obviously very positive in his play and is a very exciting player with a bright future ahead of him. I just hope for his sake, for Wales's sake and for Manchester United's sake, he can fulfil completely the potential he has shown up until now.'

It was encouraging stuff and Toshack would meet up with Ryan the following week as Wales met Norway in a friendly match in Cardiff. Even then, some pundits questioned the wisdom of employing a part-time manager – especially when that manager would commute from Spain, where he was managing a La Liga club side, and would be keeping tabs on his players via satellite TV.

Tosh aimed to quash the jibes when he said, 'I wouldn't have taken the job on if I didn't think that Wales could reach the European Championship finals. I've not been chosen to look after the grass roots of Welsh football or manage the under-18s or under-21s. My task is solely to get us to those finals and if we don't make it, I'll be the first person to tell the Welsh FA to start looking for someone else.

'But I'm too proud to allow either my club, Real Sociedad, Wales or John Toshack to suffer. I've got more to lose than anybody. Football is a hard, cruel and calculating business, and if you survive as I've done in the atmosphere out in Spain, it gives you confidence not only in your work, but not to be concerned about the problems others might see.'

Tough words, but the reality was somewhat different. Tosh resigned after just 47 days in charge, following the match with Norway, which Wales lost 3-1. He claimed he could not work with the FAW, but his critics alleged he was also upset at being booed off by the Welsh fans after the defeat, and that they had chanted the name of his predecessor, Terry Yorath.

Ryan was used to stability at Old Trafford, but while still a youngster, he now prepared to meet and greet his third international boss in a year.

Mike Smith took over from Tosh for the start of the Euro '96 qualifiers, but defeats against Moldova and Georgia brought about his exit and the arrival of a fourth manager for Giggs and Wales in just over two years, with Bobby Gould's arrival in the summer of 1995.

Smith may have been downcast at the manner of his exit, but he had no doubt that Wales had a chance to make the 1998 World Cup finals – as long as Giggs was fit and playing. Injuries meant he had been able to call on Ryan just twice in the Euro '96 qualifying campaign that ended in failure. Smith believed Giggs could be Wales's talisman, much as Paul Gascoigne had been for England in Euro '96: 'Like Eric Cantona he is an instinctive player, but Ryan also has so much pace. There are so few players around like him. Wales have to make him their key player in the way England have tried to do with Gascoigne. He offers goals from dead-ball situations with his free kicks and he can also tear defences apart by running at them. He will be such an influential player in this campaign for Wales they have to shape things around him.

'The key factor will be to get all the other players around him to produce quality performances, too. If they don't, then again Wales will struggle.'

But under former Wimbledon boss Gould, Wales would fail to qualify for those finals. For Ryan, the only consolation was that he would become captain of the national team for the first time in October 1997 – when Wales lost 3-2 in a World Cup qualifier in Belgium. The second time he skippered the team – four years later in a World Cup qualifier in Oslo – had an even worse outcome, as Giggs was sent off for the only time in his career after picking up two yellow cards in another frustrating 3-2 defeat.

Gould left his post in 1999 and was replaced by the legend that was Mark Hughes, the man Ryan would admit he most enjoyed working under at international level. 'Sparky' admitted some years later, to BBC Sport, that he had been nervous when he took on the job, but was grateful to the likes of Giggs for helping him to ease into it: 'It was difficult to begin with – not just for me, but for the players, too. For example, I'd played alongside Ryan Giggs at Manchester United as well as at international level. One minute the players are your team-mates, the next you're telling them what to do. I went from sitting among the players, criticising the manager to actually being the manager!

'I can understand how some people have found it a difficult transition to make, but I was lucky with Wales because the players wanted me to succeed. They could have made things a lot more difficult for me than they did.'

In 2004, when the reign came to an end, former Chelsea chairman Ken Bates paid tribute to the change that had come to pass under Sparky, saying, 'With Wales, Hughes inherited a set-up reminiscent of a pub team and left it disciplined, organised and on a sound footing.'

Sparky himself would say that he felt those were the main qualities he bequeathed to the Welsh national team. 'I have tried to instil a team spirit into the squad similar to that which I experienced and benefited from at club level.'

That sounds a fair enough analysis to me. Certainly, when

Sparky took up the reins, Ryan and the boys were full of optimism after the uninspiring reign of Bobby Gould. It was a time of hope and some little glory as Sparky and Giggs took Wales to the brink of qualifying for Euro 2004. They had fallen short in the 2002 World Cup qualifying campaign, but Euro 2004 would be generally described as 'a glorious failure' as Welsh hopes went right down to the wire.

The highlight of the campaign came in October 2002 when Wales beat Italy – one of four straight wins that got them off to a blistering start in their qualifying group. That win left Wales at the top of Group 9. A 70th-minute winner from Craig Bellamy made it seven games without defeat for the Welsh and led to delirious scenes of celebration on the streets of Cardiff.

Simon Davies had put the Welsh ahead only for Italy to equalise through Alessandro del Piero. Then Bellamy stole the limelight, beating Gianluigi Buffon with an inch-perfect shot to seal victory for Wales.

And it was a win that was thoroughly deserved. Wales set about the Italians with a brave forward line of Giggs, Davies, John Hartson and Bellamy – a gamble that paid off. Mark Hughes said, 'I went for the win, I felt we had the weapons that could really worry them, and that's how it proved.'

But their valiant efforts early in the campaign would be undone later. It would all end in tears as they lost to Russia in a two-legged play-off showdown.

Wales guaranteed the play-off spot by drawing 1-1 with Finland in their final group match at the Millennium Stadium. There was gloom in the camp that they had not qualified automatically, but Ryan was still optimistic. He said, 'We're a bit disappointed about drawing 1-1, but on reflection, I am sure we'll all go back to our clubs and think it is something we should celebrate. The champagne may be on ice for some people, but I think we can all be proud – the players, the staff and the supporters – that we are in the draw in October.

'If we'd said a year ago that we would be one point behind Italy and still have a game to play, no one would have believed us – they'd probably have laughed. I can understand why some people are a bit down, but we shouldn't be; it's just a measure of how far this group of players has come over the last couple of years. It is one of those things where we should be celebrating, but we are not. Nevertheless, I am confident that we will be celebrating after the play-offs.'

Unfortunately, on this occasion his confidence would prove misplaced. The first leg was played in Russia. Ryan and the boys left in confident mood, after holding their hosts to a 0-0 draw in a display that exemplified the discipline and professionalism that Sparky had brought to the team during his tenure as boss. Wales were under siege for most of the match, with Giggsy having to slip back and help out in midfield for the majority of proceedings, but they held out in a commendable defensive performance.

They headed home confident they could complete the job, the following week in Cardiff. But it was not to be and, in a match that Ryan would later describe as one of his 'most disappointing at international level', they allowed the Russians to score after the 20-minute mark and were beaten at the final hurdle. Giggs saw a shot hit a post and his misery was compounded when Vadim Evseev – the tough-tackling defender who chopped him down in the first leg and caused a storm that led to Ryan confronting him and to several bookings – nipped in to head the decisive goal.

Naturally, Ryan was peeved that Evseev and his team had won the game. Evseev then poured petrol onto the fire by running towards the TV cameras at the end of the match and verbally ridiculing the Welsh for their loss. He shouted at the camera, '*Khui vam! Ponyatno? Khui vam I ne Evropa!*' As author Marc Bennetts in his book *Football Dynamo: Modern Russia and the People's Game* says, roughly translated that meant: 'You get fuck all! You understand? You don't get Europe, you get fuck all!'

The coarse Spartak Moscow defender had killed off Welsh dreams of ending a 45-year wait to appear in a major finals. Now Giggs and the Welsh nation were united in their grief and disappointment. After the match, Ryan admitted that it was one of the lowest moments of his career: 'The only way to get over disappointments in football is to look to the next challenge, which is to qualify for a major championship. This is as low as I've felt in football, but I'm already looking at the World Cup campaign. I hope we can stay together as a team because we have worked hard to achieve so much. There are older players in the squad, though, and you would have to put the question to individuals.'

BBC pundit Alan Hansen spoke for most people when he said Wales had been unlucky: 'Ryan Giggs was desperately unlucky to hit a post right on half-time, and then Gary Speed missed a header not long after the break when you would have put your life on him hitting the target.'

But the fact was Ryan had lost out again.

There was a glimpse of hope that he and Wales might still

get there via the back door when it was revealed that Russian midfielder Yegor Titov had failed a drugs test after the goalless first leg of the November play-off in Moscow. Wales challenged Russia's inclusion in the Euro 2004 finals, but their appeal was thrown out by an unsympathetic UEFA. Their disciplinary body said Wales had failed to prove that Titov was still under the influence of the drug in the second leg in Cardiff four days later, when he played for the first hour, as Russia won 1-0.

It was a decision that enraged Mark Hughes. 'Obviously I am disappointed,' he stated. 'I had hoped they would have taken the opportunity to send a message to everybody in our sport, but they have not taken that opportunity, rightly or wrongly – wrongly in my view.'

But the resentment over the dispute did not solve the problem facing Ryan Giggs. There he was, thirty, with time running out if he was to achieve that dream of making a major finals.

A year later boss Sparky would be gone, with John Toshack returning to the helm. Sparky's attempt to maintain the belief the team had in the Euro campaign seemed to desert him as the World Cup qualifying group got underway in earnest in the autumn of 2004. Wales began with a disappointing 1-1 draw in Azerbaijan and followed up with another poor result, a 2-2 draw in Cardiff against Northern Ireland. It did not help Sparky that Ryan missed out on both matches – his absence only served to underline his importance to the team in terms of inspiration, discipline and leadership (especially as the Welsh had a man sent off against Northern Ireland).

Giggs was forced to serve a two-match ban – a result of his being found guilty of elbowing Russian Vadim Evseev during that tumultuous first leg of Wales's Euro 2004 play-off tie in Moscow the previous year. But he was back for the qualifier away to England on 9 October 2004. Before the match he admitted that it would be a special day for him – and not just because it was a chance to get one over on England (the first time he had played against them for Wales). No, he was looking forward to playing the match at Old Trafford, his beloved club ground – but he admitted to being haunted by the fear of continuing failure at international level: 'Everyone is striving to get the team to qualify for a major championship. The way I look at it is that in your international career that would be viewed as success. If you don't qualify then a lot of people and also the players would see that as failure because that is what we are all playing for.'

He was used to success at club level but said it hadn't happened internationally and that he could rectify that, starting against England: 'It was frustrating to miss the first two matches, so it is good to get back into the swing of things. I was disappointed to miss those games [against Azerbaijan and Northern Ireland], especially because it was through suspension and not injury, and it happened so long ago.

'It wouldn't have been quite as frustrating if we had more positive results but we didn't, so we are looking to get a result on Saturday. It is a big occasion, there's no bigger game than playing England, and it's great for me to play against the lads from Man United, plus guys like Nicky Butt and of course, David Beckham. It will be a bit strange to be playing at Old Trafford against them, but I will be going out to enjoy it.'

He said he was confident Wales could pull off a major shock: 'We know that we are capable of doing it and we have got the players who can hurt them. If we play to our potential, like we did a year to 18 months ago, then we can get a result.'

But even his presence could not prevent the Welsh from slipping to a 2-0 loss. He did set up their best chance of the day – a cross met by skipper Gary Speed that he should really have nodded home past Paul Robinson, rather than placing straight into his grateful arms.

It would be unlucky 13 for Sparky as he took his men to Poland on 13 October for his final game as Welsh boss before leaving to become Blackburn manager. Even though the match was at the Millennium Stadium, Wales could not raise their game sufficiently to match the eager Poles – and lost 3-2 on the night. The defeat left them struggling in fifth place in Group 6 with just two points from four games; they trailed second-placed Poland by eight points.

A miracle was needed if Ryan was to achieve his aim of reaching a major final. But it was not to be, and his only real consolation for the remainder of his international career would be that he would take the captaincy permanently on Gary Speed's retirement after encouragement from new boss John Toshack.

He got on well with 'Tosh', but still success would prove elusive.

There are some who say Ryan could have done more for Wales – particularly that he should have turned out for his country in friendly matches. They point to him frequently pulling out of such games through injury and moan that he missed 18 consecutive friendlies (and did not play in one until nine years after his debut, in 2000) and 50 games in total through withdrawals, often blamed on hamstring trouble by his club boss Ferguson. That first friendly appearance would come on 29 March 2000, when Wales took on Finland in Cardiff. Ryan admitted that he was upset by the constant jibes over the years, telling the *Guardian* the day before the match, 'When people say you don't want to play for your country, it hurts. Then you find people having polls asking fans whether I should be picked to play for my country in future, and that's just stupid because I always give 100 per cent when I play for Wales.

'I hope that by playing on Wednesday it will finally kill off the thing about me not playing in friendlies for Wales.'

Though it didn't 'kill off the thing', it helped to sideline it. Ironically, Giggs would score Wales's goal in a historic match, as the Welsh went down 2-1 in front of a massive crowd of 66,000 in the first football match at the Millennium Stadium. Jari Litmanen took the honour of becoming the first player to score a goal at the stadium; Ryan was the first Welshman to score at the new home of Welsh football.

Giggsy's former United team-mate Ruud van Nistelrooy once tried to get those Welshmen who refused to stop criticising him off his back by saying they should realise they were lucky to have him – and that Ryan, 'would have been an even bigger player in the world if he had played for England.'

That remark earned van Nistelrooy a verbal lashing from Ryan's Welsh team-mate, Robbie Savage: 'Ruud is entitled to his opinion, but I can tell you that Ryan Giggs is as proud as we all are to play for our country. It's ridiculous when people say he should have played for England. He's Welsh, and that's it.'

My feeling is that, OK, Ryan did not have a very convincing

friendlies record, but that Wales still got excellent service from him when you look at his efforts in competitive matches. He was their most consistent performer in the matches in which he did play – and certainly their best hope to inspire victory in what were sometimes mediocre squads. He did his best, but like Georgie Best, would ultimately have a nagging feeling that his international career had not been what he hoped because he did not reach a major final.

When I think of Ryan and Wales I like to think of the good times, scarce as they were. I look back to Wales's 2-0 World Cup qualifier win over Azerbaijan in October 2005. He scored twice and could have had a hat-trick as his class showed. His second was the pick, a wonderful solo run that left three defenders for dead, followed by an oh-so-clever curling shot that piled into the top corner. Boss Toshack summed up his skipper's magic when he said afterwards, 'Ryan has become our pied piper, and he deserved a hat-trick after the best move of the game. We took him off near the end because he felt some pain in his back, but it is nothing serious. He had certainly given a Man-of-the-Match performance.'

Ironically, given the furore over the years over Giggs's absence from friendly games, it would be in a friendly that he would give another of his best performances in a Welsh shirt – the one that would have the legendary Dunga purring over his skills. It would happen at White Hart Lane, home of Spurs, in September 2006 when Wales faced Brazil. The Samba kings would run out 2-0 winners, but Giggs was to be the star of the show, turning in a fine display that left Brazil coach Dunga – and many others – gasping with admiration. Indeed, Dunga is said to have paid Ryan the ultimate compliment: that the

Welsh wonder would not have looked out of place playing for the five-times world champions alongside the likes of Kaká and Ronaldinho.

The *Independent* summed it up like this: 'If Ryan Giggs was a Brazilian. Even the South Americans' coach, Dunga, was asked to muse on that proposition after the Welsh captain produced the compelling performance during last night's defeat. "Everyone would like to have a player like him," the World Cup-winning midfielder smiled. "But I have nowhere to put him."' Indeed. Wales stationed Giggs in the centre of midfield and for the first half, before being withdrawn by prior arrangement, he caught the eye against Ronaldinho, Kaká, Arsenal's Julio Baptista and so on.

The Brazilians – and the crowd – would have liked to have seen Giggsy on for the second half, but time was fast catching up with the genius. Welsh boss Toshack admitted he was wrapping his star in cotton wool, saying, 'It is in Manchester United's interests, but it is in our interests as well.'

For Giggs, the end on the international stage was drawing ever closer and would arrive 18 months after his wonder show against the Brazilians. And he would go out on a high – named Man of the Match in the Euro 2008 qualifier against the Czech Republic in Cardiff, in June 2007.

Giggsy paved the way for an emotional farewell by announcing his decision the previous Wednesday. He said he wanted to say goodbye in front of the Welsh fans so he could thank them for all their support and encouragement over the years; he also admitted that he hoped the decision would be beneficial to his club career – that it would allow him to extend his time at Manchester United. In retrospect, given that he was still going strong at Old Trafford by 2010, it was the right move at the right time.

He said at the time, 'I feel this is a good time, the right time to retire, and it's a difficult decision for me. I have loved playing for my country and I have loved captaining my country. It wasn't an easy decision, but I'll get those breaks in the season and obviously, it will help Manchester United because I'll be playing less football.

'It will also help Wales – I don't feel that I've been performing as well as I could have. Whether it was the amount of football I was playing, I don't know, but I think all three parties will benefit from this. Hopefully this will not only prolong my career, but allow me to be fresher and allow me to enjoy the last two or three years.'

At the press conference to announce his exit, he summed up his international career in this way: 'I've had such a successful time at club level, but obviously that hasn't been the case in my international career because we haven't qualified. That is something I've always wanted to do because you want to play against the best players, you want to play in the best tournaments, whether it be the World Cup or European Championships.

'I'm disappointed not to have done that, but many players go through that and I've been fortunate to have had such a successful career, so I'm not going to grumble. My highlights are my debut, coming on against Germany, and then starting against Belgium at Cardiff Arms Park, and also when John Toshack announced that I would be captain.'

It was a gracious way to go out – accepting his lot in a national team that had never truly hit the heights in his era.

Let's not forget even the great Eric Cantona, Ryan's one-time team-mate and long-time hero at United, never made it to the World Cup finals with his native France. Giggs, Cantona and Best – whoever would have guessed the legendary trio would have such a disappointment in common?

There was shock at Giggs's decision – and tributes, led by then Wales boss Toshack. Tosh said: 'Ryan came to see me and I could see he was a little bit disturbed. I had an idea what might be coming. I would like to say it has been a privilege to have him as my captain; he has always set a terrific example to all the young lads in the squad. We shall certainly miss him. I think we are talking about a very special person here, 16 years on the international scene under quite a bit of pressure when he plays for Wales – probably more than when he does for his club. I would like to wish him all the very best and say just how much he has helped me.'

And former Wales striker Dean Saunders was also surprised – and dismayed. He felt Ryan could have gone on another three years and he praised him as, 'the best player I've played with.'

The Football Association of Wales paid tribute, saying he had been an exemplary ambassador, a great player and a great influence on the younger players in the squad in his role as captain and senior statesman. However, a FA of Wales' source remarked: 'Maybe Ryan has come to accept that the chances of qualification for Euro 2008 are all but gone. It is a great shame – he has been an outstanding servant to Welsh football and since being made captain under John Toshack, he has been a major influence on the young players.'

So, what of the final game itself? Well, it started with lots of fireworks and hope as Ryan appeared intent on taking on the Czechs all by himself, but fizzled out into a 0-0 draw. In the 88th minute, Giggs left the field to a standing ovation and applause from both teams – and signalled the changing of the guard by trotting over to Craig Bellamy and placing the captain's armband on his team-mate.

Giggs could have scored – he will tell you he *should* have – when he went on a dazzling run from midfield, but he could not beat Petr Cech. There was to be no *Roy of the Rovers* finale, just a general appreciation that one of football's true greats had done his best for his country and deserved one final round of applause.

Always the perfectionist, he was typically self-critical after the match at his final Welsh national team Press conference. 'Yes, I should have scored,' he said, when asked about the one-on-one with Cech. 'I did all the hard work, but I put too much whip on the ball. It was just disappointing that we couldn't get a win. It was a great performance and we need to keep doing that in the future. That's the benchmark, to be playing well against the best teams.

'It has been a very emotional week saying goodbye to everyone but I have enjoyed it. The fans have been great from day one right to the end. The players are a good age and there are others coming through. The future looks really good.'

'*Diolch yn fawr*, Ryan,' one banner read. 'Thanks very much, Ryan.' It was the end of an era – for Wales and Ryan Giggs: loyal Welshman and patriotic as they come, a true hero in the valleys, that day and always.

CHAPTER 18

THE GOAL-DEN BOY

'Of all the people I've seen dealing with superstar status, Ryan has handled it best.'

Gary Pallister, former Manchester United defender

'Ryan's a real character – streetwise and wickedly funny.'

Roy Keane

Ryan Giggs is arguably the greatest player ever to grace the Premiership – discuss. I would contend that you could make a fair argument for that being the case. Of course, you would also throw in the likes of Thierry Henry, Eric Cantona, Cristiano Ronaldo and Gianfranco Zola. But have any of them done so much for the English game – contributed as much and done so in such style and, considering Ryan's achievements, so humbly, graciously and in such a civilised, gentlemanly way?

I think not. Ryan Giggs was the first 'celebrity' footballer of the Premiership – a modern version of George Best when the new top-flight was formed in 1992 (but obviously without the destructive tendencies and addictions). In his first full season at United, he received more than 6,000 Valentine's Day cards and once brought the M4 around Cardiff to a halt because he was doing a book signing in the city. Giggs was a new face after football's dark days of the mid to late 1980s – a welcome relief from the trauma of Hillsborough, Heysel and hooliganism.

He was a breath of fresh air to accompany the new world of football that welcomed in the Nineties – new stadia, improved facilities, the arrival of more foreign stars and the glam era of the newly formed Premiership; a period of wealth and fun was ushered in after the generation of greyness and austerity. Football had moved on, thank God!

And Giggs was the first star of the new era. Publishers clamoured to produce books on his life and football career, and he was even given his own television show in 1994 – *Ryan Giggs' Soccer Skills*. His face featured on magazine covers and he became an idol for young boys and a pin-up for girls. More than anyone, he took the new age of football into a more mainstream audience: he was a marketing man's dream and became a household name.

The Premier League had found the star it needed to launch football into the stratosphere, with big money and big opportunities. Players like Ryan were finally afforded the acclaim and stardom their talent deserved.

Giggs was the first player since George Best to truly capture the public's admiration and interest. He was Best without the baggage and, ironically enough, George would be one of the first to see the pressures the young protégé would face. But he knew Ryan had a chance, with the protective shield that Sir Alex and United threw around him. He believed Giggs might succeed off the pitch in keeping his life together, whereas he himself had failed so sadly in the full public glare. Best admired Giggs: as a player of the highest level and a level headed young man. Indeed, he once famously quipped after watching him perform dazzling skills at United's training ground, 'One day they might even say that I was another Ryan Giggs.'

The protective shield thrown around Giggsy was evident from the start. He was kept away from the press microphones and encouraged to put his football first rather than promotional work. Of course, United accepted they couldn't ask him to live like a hermit and that some outside work was inevitable. Hence the acquiescence to his requests to front a TV show and do a couple of books.

And eventually he would be allowed to take part in more promotional work. He cashed in with adverts for Reebok, Citizen watches, Fuji and even Quorn burgers. Giggs was the poster boy and the marketing man's dream while David Beckham was still trying to get into United's first team. As BBC Sport observed: 'Giggs had the million-pound boot deal [Reebok], the lucrative sponsorship deals in the Far East [Fuji] and the celebrity girlfriends [Dani Behr, Davinia Taylor] at a time when Beckham was being sent on loan to Preston North End.'

Giggs himself commented on his introduction to the celebrity life in a 2005 interview with the *Independent*: 'When I was 19, 20 I was going out with Dani Behr and it sort of doubled the exposure [he got from the media]. I was down in London, photographers were chasing us in cars and I just didn't like it. The relationship ended anyway. It was nothing to do with that, but I didn't like it full stop. I probably made a conscious effort not to do it. And I am lucky in the respect that I lived in the area that I grew up and I have the same friends.'

United held him back as long as they could – protecting their interests and his. Ryan's first company car at United was a Ford Escort Mexico – provided on the advice of a certain Mr Ferguson who didn't want money and fame going to his wonderboy's head. In a rare bout of rebelliousness and ostentation, Giggs would ditch the company motor and splash out close to £30k on a new BMW 325. Paid for in cash... at the tender age of eighteen!

But that was a singular diversion from the script. For all his riches, big motors, £3 million home in Worsley, near Manchester, and £1 million penthouse flat in Deansgate, central Manchester, Ryan Giggs remains surprisingly grounded; down-to-earth, endearingly earnest, intelligent and approachable. He always has time to sign autographs for those who pay his wages. Despite all this, some pundits believe he is too earnest and too bland because he does not make earth-shattering or controversial comments in the few interviews that he gives.

It is undeniable that when he does appear on TV, being interviewed after a match, that he can seem overly concerned with sticking to the script rather than indulging in any amusing off-the-cuff comments or observations but that is the nature of the man and the upbringing he has had at Manchester United. Let's not forget he has been at United since he was a boy and has been groomed and educated by the club's senior figures like his boss, Sir Alex. There comes a certain responsibility with being a senior United star and Ryan ticks all the boxes. He does not speak out of turn or rock the boat, and his aim when being interviewed is to give a professional analysis of the game and a straight answer to every question. In many ways, he is an ambassador in the same way as Sir Bobby Charlton – the man whose club appearances record Giggs broke in May 2008.

Team-mates, past and current, do not recognise the Ryan Giggs who is often portrayed as being a bit dull. Roy Keane says Ryan has a 'wicked' sense of humour and is far from bland or dour. Wayne Rooney loves chatting to him and the younger players at United find him interesting and place great value in his comments and advice. Rafael, in particular, enjoys talking to Giggs on the training field and learning from the master.

The simple fact is that, like Paul Scholes, Ryan does not see the need to constantly throw himself into the limelight. Indeed, he much prefers to let his feet do the talking on the pitch rather than try to hog back-page headlines with contentious comments.

Steve Bruce once summed up Giggs's attitude to the press and his own fame in this way to BBC Sport: 'He doesn't like publicity; that's Ryan. He wants to keep a certain amount of privacy, and he doesn't flaunt the press or the publicity, because he doesn't have to. People write about him because of his ability.'

Ryan Giggs is no big star on a big ego trip. No, he is a sensible, civilised man who enjoys spending time with his wife Stacey and his two children, Liberty (known as Libby) and Zach. He says of family life and how it has stabilised him: 'It's important to have the right balance in your life as a footballer, especially the older you get. When you are young you can go out and do things that eighteen- and nineteen-year-old lads can do and in the next day's training, or at the next match, you will be able to recover in time. As you get older, you realise your body doesn't recover as quickly, so you need to adjust your lifestyle. For me personally having a young family with two kids now, I have a great balance in my life and I think it has helped my footballing career.'

Not that he hasn't always been a major star in terms of world football and celebrity in the eyes of his adoring public and he even made it onto an episode of TV's *The Simpsons* in November 2003. Giggsy was mentioned in 'The Regina Monologues', which saw the Simpson family in England. Marge is seen berating Homer for punching three men in the street, to which Homer replies, 'That was over soccer results. Can you believe they gave Giggs a yellow card in the box?'

Ryan was delighted with the mention, saying it was one of his greatest achievements! He told uefa.com: 'I didn't actually see it, but my mate who watches it all the time rang me up and said, "You've finally made it – you're on *The Simpsons*!" I was chuffed! I watch it, but I don't watch it all the time or anything like that. But so many really famous people have been on *The Simpsons*, so it was brilliant to be mentioned on it.'

But as the years rolled by, Giggs has inevitably matured to the point where he is no longer interested in being a celebrity for celebrity's sake. In many ways, he is a younger version of the man with whom he has spent his whole career – his mentor and father-figure, the one and only Sir Alex. It's hardly surprising that some of the old man's characteristics – determination, a certain stubbornness and mental toughness plus a strong desire to win – should rub off. After all, Ryan has worked for no other club boss in his 20-year professional career and the two are known to be very close.

'There is a mutual respect between us,' Ryan admits. 'But over the years I must admit that we have fallen out from time to time. We are both fighting for the same cause – to win games for Manchester United – and if we do fall out, it's soon forgotten about the next day. We are both hungry for success at Manchester United, so sometimes you do lose your temper, but we always get over it.'

And the boss has gone on record as saying he believes Ryan deserves even more recognition for his services to football and the tremendous way in which he has graced the sport. In January 2009, Sir Alex was asked a series of questions by celebrity fans of Manchester United. One was whether he thought Giggs should be knighted, like himself. His answer was revealing: 'Good question. Especially when you consider how the English rugby team, when they won three or four matches to win the World Cup, were given knighthoods and MBEs. Ryan Giggs has performed like a star for 20 years in the Premier League, going up and down that touchline. He's won 10 Premier League medals, I hope it's 11 this year, and two European Cups and what has he got, an MBE? It doesn't seem right. Longevity must surely surpass short-term success.'

Longevity, that's the word, plus success, glory and durability... and breaking records galore. In his 20 years at United, Giggs has gone into the history books for a whole list of achievements. He is the only Manchester United player to have appeared in all 11 Premier League-winning teams and the only player to win 11 league titles. He is the only Manchester United player to have played in all three League

Cup-winning teams; the only Manchester United player to have played in both UEFA Champions League-winning teams; the only player to have scored in 11 consecutive Champions League tournaments; the only player to have scored in 13 different Champions League tournaments; the only player to have scored in every Premier League campaign since its inception and, finally, of course, he has notched up the most appearances by a Manchester United player. Not bad for a lad from a working-class family in Wales!

What people also admire about Ryan Giggs is the way he has conducted himself over the years, his discipline both on and off the pitch and his willingness to help younger players by patiently spending time with them and encouraging them.

It was appropriate that he would take the most-appearances record from Sir Bobby Charlton. Like the great man of former years, Ryan has had an almost unblemished disciplinary record. He has rarely been in trouble with referees or the authorities; he has shown respect and been granted it in return.

Giggs has never been sent off for Manchester United and his only club indiscretion came in the autumn of 2003 when he was fined £7,500 for his part in the fallout from United's game with Arsenal at Old Trafford in September 2003. The punishment arose from the unsavoury incidents at the end of the 0-0 draw. Patrick Vieira had clashed with Ruud van Nistelrooy and was sent off for a second yellow card offence, with Arsenal claiming the Dutchman had feigned injury as Vieira lashed out. Moments later, United were awarded a penalty and when van Nistelrooy missed the spot kick, he was confronted by Arsenal's Martin Keown, Lauren and Ray Parlour.

Giggs was charged for running into Arsenal's Lauren during

the mêlée surrounding van Nistelrooy at the end of the game. He was fined and warned about his future conduct at an FA disciplinary hearing.

And he was also punished for two indiscretions at international level. He was sent off for the only time in his career in 2001 when the Welsh lost 3-2 to Norway in Olso. The dismissal followed two bookable offences, for dissent and a foul. It was a night he must have wanted to forget as he captained his country for the third time. He added insult to injury by throwing his skipper's armband to the ground in disgust as he headed for an 85th-minute early bath in the World Cup qualifier. It was also Wales's 12th game without a win, equalling their worst sequence, set in 1970.

His other international indiscretion, as noted earlier, came in November 2003 during the fiery Euro 2004 play-off against Russia. He would receive a two-match ban for deliberately elbowing Vadim Evseev in the face after the big defender gave him a rough ride.

Ryan Giggs's career will be better remembered, though, for the plethora of trophies, the breaking of numerous records – and the golden goals the boy had a habit of scoring, often when United needed them most.

Of course, *the* goal that Giggs will always be remembered for is the one he scored against Arsenal back in the 1999 FA Cup semi-final replay – the one that propelled the Red Devils to Wembley and to another stage of the treasured Treble. United fans still remember the extra-time goal as if it had happened yesterday. A stray pass from Patrick Vieira was intercepted by Giggs and he ran all of 60 yards, dribbling past Vieira, Lee Dixon, Martin Keown and Tony Adams before unleashing an unstoppable shot that soared over David Seaman into the roof of the net. Absolutely unbelievable! Even when he had seen off all those Arsenal defenders, he still had to get the ball home from an acute angle.

United fans leapt to their feet as one, paying homage to their hero. They belted out the words, 'Giggs, Giggs will tear you apart again' – their wondrous version of the Joy Division song 'Love Will Tear Us Apart'.

Ryan would be slightly embarrassed when he saw the TV replays of the goal and his shirt-waving celebration – it was not his way to bare his chest in public, he was usually far more unassuming. But in April 2009, almost exactly 10 years later, he said that he might consider a repeat strip show if he scored a similar goal against Arsenal in the Champions League semi-final ties! 'Of course I remember it, and know I will be remembered for it. It was a great moment at Villa Park for me, personally, and for the team a massive turning point in the season that ended in the Treble, a massive night,' he observed.

'I don't know if I like it – because people remember the celebration more than the goal. I used to say I would never do it again, but you never know. When you score a goal, especially an important one like that, the feelings rise up and you've no control over yourself, you just haven't. That's what football is all about. You never know what's going to happen next. If I score an important winning goal again in the last minute, I might just do it.'

David Beckham had put United ahead after 17 minutes at Villa Park that memorable night in '99, but Dennis Bergkamp equalised after 51 minutes. Then Nicolas Anelka had a goal disallowed and Roy Keane was sent off. Peter Schmeichel saved a 90th-minute penalty from Bergkamp but then, in the 19th minute of extra-time, Ryan Giggs wriggled in to grab the most famous goal of his career.

At the time he admitted that it was 'one of my greatest ever goals and one of the most important', while Sir Alex heaped on the praise, saying nothing his protégé did would surprise him – but even he was stunned by the sheer wonder of the strike and the skill that Ryan had shown in pulling it off.

'It was a cracker, brilliant!' the boss declared. 'I think we deserved the win. We had no complaints about the sending-off of Roy Keane; the players have played in agony to get the victory – and Ryan's gone and got us it!'

Some compared the wondergoal to John Barnes's sizzler for England against Brazil in June 1984 – but I rate it as better than that because he had more distance to cover and more work to do in getting the strike on target. That is not disrespecting Barnes's goal – he did brilliantly at the Maracaña stadium, dribbling through Brazil's backline and around the keeper before tapping home. Afterwards Barnes said, 'The Brazilians were just shocked and I suppose that's why they didn't tackle me, because they thought there's no way an Englishman is going to do this so... we'll let him try and do whatever he wants.'

But there was no such complacency among the hardman back line of the Gunners at Villa Park that humid April night in 1999. Adams and Keown were well aware of Giggs's capabilities and did their best to stop him at any cost, but they could not get close enough. The goal was all the more important as it sealed a 2-1 win for United after killing off the Gunners when they had been in control. They were running the show after the sending-off of Keane, but Ryan's goal totally deflated them, taking the sting out of their game.

That was the brilliance of Giggs: a true big match player. He could turn it on at any time, but he never shirked or hid away during the games that could have a crucial bearing on United's season. A match winner and a trophy winner, he was United's big game hunter for many seasons.

Even deflated Gunners boss Arsène Wenger took time out to praise Giggs for his winner that night: 'It is not easy to take a defeat, but what you can demand of a team is they give everything. I am very sad today because it was not our night and we were unlucky. That's football. The two teams are very close to each other and in the end the luckiest won. There's no reproach. I would just like to congratulate Manchester United. They were fantastic – and it was a fantastic goal by Giggs to decide the outcome of the game. I am very sad, but they have shown again they are a great team – and Giggs has shown what a great player he is.'

Dazed Gunners keeper David Seaman was also generous in his praise, saying, 'I expected Ryan to lay it off, but he just kept on coming – and it was a real shock when he beat the lot and was right in on goal. His finish was exceptional, too. Ryan just smashed his shot past me from a narrow angle.'

Ferguson, inevitably, was delighted and fulsome in his praise: 'Given the context [United being down to 10 men], this has to be one of the best goals ever scored in major football.'

Other great goals by the maestro include a Premier League gem against Queens Park Rangers at Loftus Road in February 1994. Once again, he darted past a befuddled back four before beating the keeper from a tight angle.

There were also two memorable strikes in Europe: both against Juventus, the first coming on 1 October 1997, the second on 23 February 2003. I have picked them out too because both had great significance attached to them.

In 1997, United dominated Premier League matches but still failed to do so in Europe. But Ryan's goal – the third l in a 3-2 triumph at Old Trafford – gave them belief that they could finally crack Europe as well as England.

Alessandro del Piero put Juve ahead in the first minute and it looked like being a tough old night for an already jittery United (who were without their injured inspirational skipper Roy Keane). But Teddy Sheringham headed them level and Paul Scholes made it 2-1 to United. But it was Ryan's goal, with just a minute to go, that steadied nerves. Zinedine Zidane pulled another back for the visitors, but Giggs had killed them off after he steamed in from the left and gave keeper Angelo Peruzzi no chance with a rasping shot.

United would go on to qualify from the group stages and only fell in the last eight to Monaco. They were starting to believe – and, of course, just two years after that meeting with Juve, they would turn belief into joy as they won the Champions League in Barcelona.

While Giggs's goal against the Turin giants gave United hope in 1997, the next time he scored against them in 2003 had great personal significance. As already mentioned in an earlier chapter, for the first time in his career Ryan had been having a rough time of it with some fans at Old Trafford. They questioned if his heart was still with United (after constant hints that Inter Milan were keen on buying him) and whether he was washed up, but he showed his worth with two goals in a brilliant 3-0 win in Turin.

It was the second of the brace that stood out. In a similar style to the Arsenal goal (but not quite that good!), he picked up a stray pass in midfield and powered forwards, leaving defenders in his wake and eventually stroking the ball home. He then pointed to the back of his shirt – as if to tell those who moaned and groaned about his displays that, yes, he was still the great Ryan Giggs and yes, he still gave his all for the club he loved, Manchester United.

The wondershow in Turin meant that United had yet again booked their place in the last eight of the Champions League – no bad achievement for a player some cynics at Old Trafford reckoned was past his sell-by date or had become distracted by thoughts of a transfer to the San Siro. Ryan's opener in Turin marked the first time Juventus had conceded a Champions League goal at home in 722 minutes – and it was a great boost for the Welsh winger, who had been booed by United fans after poor displays against Blackburn and Arsenal.

Of course, Giggs would score many other great goals for United and the fans would rally round the player who was an authentic Red legend. He would always have a special place in the hearts of true fans, whatever the doubters might say about his contributions over the years.

The depth of love and affection most fans felt for him was highlighted when a crowd of 67,500 turned up for his testimonial at Old Trafford in August 2001. The tribute after 10 years of loyal service left him £1 million richer – but also shone a light on the remarkable bond between himself and United fans. The match against Celtic ended in a 4-3 win for the visitors, but he was visibly moved by the appreciation and respect shown towards him by an adoring crowd. Afterwards he admitted: 'Tonight I was nervous, the most nervous I've ever been, but I thoroughly enjoyed it.'

He thanked the fans for turning out in their thousands – and also thanked his hero for coming out of retirement for the first time since quitting United four years previously. Yes, the great Eric Cantona turned up and turned out – a sign of the respect top professionals also had for the winger. Ryan said: 'I asked Eric to come over and play whatever part he wanted in the game. He came over and it was great to see Eric play here again.'

In an emotional address on the pitch after the game, Giggs added, 'I'd like to thank the gaffer [Sir Alex Ferguson], all the staff here and the players. We've had a hard trip to the Far East and for them to perform like that is brilliant. I'd also like to thank my family, who have stood by me through everything.'

Then he showed his appreciation to the fans for their support, telling them that he owed them and that he would try to repay them for years to come: 'Thanks for all your support over the last 10 years and I'll try and play my best for you over the rest of my career.'

And for the next nine years, he would do just that. In December 2009, fans showed yet again just how much they respect Ryan Giggs and value his incredible contribution to Manchester United and to football as a whole when they voted him BBC Sports Personality of the Year. Giggs was considered an outsider when the nominations were announced – he was up against the likes of Formula 1 World Champion Jenson Button, heavyweight champ David Haye and heptathlete Jessica Ennis. But he stormed the public vote, knocking Button into second place by over 50,000 votes to claim the prestigious award. As he collected the trophy, a visibly emotional, yet typically self-effacing Giggs remarked: 'This is a shock… this is a shock, as you can tell by the speech I've prepared! I grew up watching this programme. To see the people that have won it and to be here is unbelievable.'

A man of the people, loved by his people… and who loved his people just as much in return; a true great – and a gentleman too. Surely, it can't be too long before Giggsy gets the call from the Palace – and the Queen says, 'Arise, Sir Ryan.'

BIBLIOGRAPHY

Daily Mirror
Daily Mail
Sir Alex Ferguson, *Managing My Life: My Autobiography*
Steve Bruce, BBC Sport
Paul Parker, BBC Sport
Gary Pallister
Roy Keane
Wayne Rooney
David Jones
Ryan Giggs, *Giggs: The Autobiography*
Joe Lovejoy
Ryan Giggs (with Colin Cameron), *Chasing Perfection*
Ryan Giggs, *Ryan Giggs: My Story*

The *Guardian*

James Lawton, the *Independent*

Jonathan Northcroft, the *Sunday Times*

Lee Clayton, the *Daily Mail*

Neil Custis, the *Sun*

Alex Butler, the *Sunday Times*

Steven Hayes

www.manutd.com

Hugh McIlvanney, the *Sunday Times*

Sam Wallace, the *Independent*

Henry Winter, the *Daily Telegraph*

Steven Gerrard

Steve McMahon

Gordon Taylor

Ole Gunnar Solskjaer

Eric Harrison

Marc Bennetts, *Football Dynamo: Modern Russia and the People's Game*

www.uefa.com